RUSSIAN

in 10 minutes a day®

by Kristine Kershul, M.A., University of California, Santa Barbara

Consultants: Kamal Bouranov
Marianna Ilyina
Alla A. Smyslova

Bilingual Books, Inc.
1719 West Nickerson Street, Seattle, WA 98119
Tel: (206) 284-4211 Fax: (206) 284-3660
www.bilingualbooks.org • www.10minutesaday.com

Third printing, May 2000

 ISBN 0-944502-47-4

Can you say this?

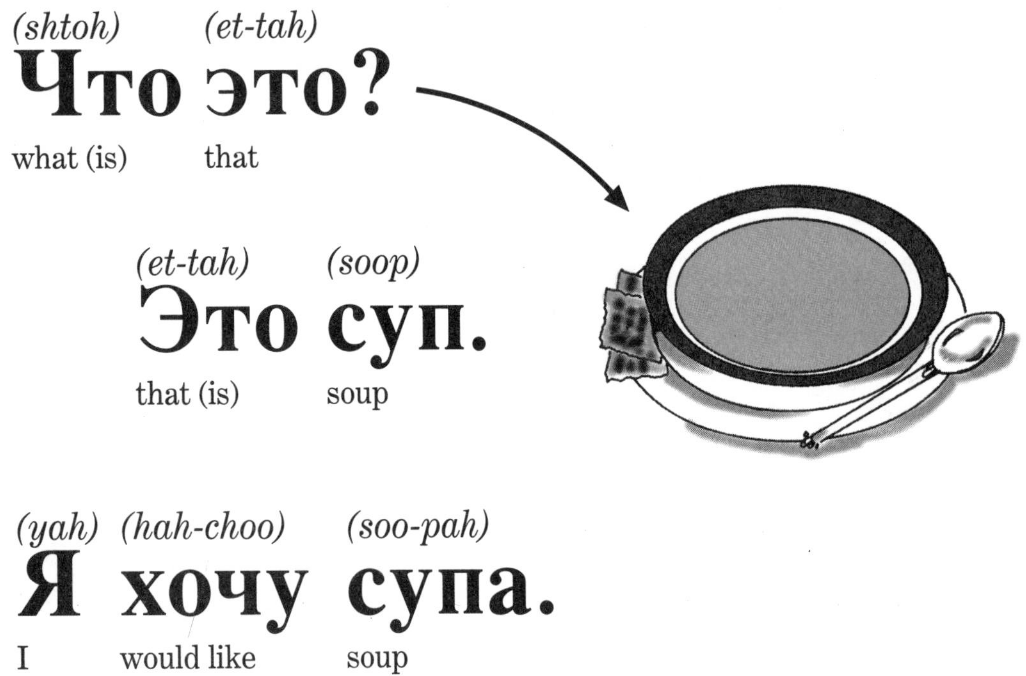

(shtoh) (et-tah)
Что это?
what (is) that
(et-tah) (soop)
Это суп.
that (is) soup
(yah) (hah-choo) (soo-pah)
Я хочу супа.
I would like soup

If you can say this, you can learn to speak Russian. You will be able to easily order Russian tea, vodka, ballet tickets, caviar, pastry, or anything else you wish. You simply ask **"Что это?"** *(shtoh)(et-tah)* and, upon learning what it is, you can order it with **"Я хочу этого"** *(yah) (hah-choo) (et-tah-vah)*. Sounds easy, doesn't it?

The purpose of this book is to give you an **immediate** speaking ability in Russian. When you first see Russian words, they can appear to be forbidding. However, they are not when you know how to decode and pronounce these new letters. This book offers above each word a unique and easy system of pronunciation which walks you through learning Russian.

If you are planning a trip or moving to where Russian is spoken, you will be leaps ahead of everyone if you take just a few minutes a day to learn the easy key words that this book offers. Start with Step 1 and don't skip around. Each day work as far as you can comfortably go in those 10 minutes. Don't overdo it. Some days you might want to just review. If you forget a word, you can always look it up in the glossary. Spend your first 10 minutes studying the map on the previous page. And yes, have fun learning your new language.

As you work through the Steps, always use the special features which only this series offers. You have sticky labels and flash cards, free words, puzzles, and quizzes. When you have completed the book, cut out the menu guide and take it along on your trip. Do not forget your "Pocket Pal™" which is designed to be carried with you everywhere on your travels and to provide essential backup in case you forget an important word now and then.

1 *(ahl-fah-veet)* Алфавит
alphabet

Above all new words is an easy pronunciation guide. Refer to this Step whenever you need help, but remember, spend no longer than 10 minutes a day. Here are five Russian letters which look and sound like English.

(ah)	*(k)*	*(m)*	*(oh or ah)*	*(t)*
а	**к**	**м**	**о**	**т**

Russian has seven letters which look like English, but be careful; they are not pronounced like English.

(v)	*(eh or yeh)*	*(n)*	*(r)*	*(s)*	*(oo)*	*(h or hk)*
в	**е**	**н**	**р**	**с**	**у**	**х**

The following Russian letters look quite different from English. They are easy to pronounce once you decode them. Practice writing out the individual letters to the best of your ability. Are you ready?

(b)	*(g)*	*(d)*	*(yoh)*	*(zh)*	*(z)*	*(ee)*	*(varies, see list)*	*(l)*	*(p)*
б	**г**	**д**	**ё**	**ж**	**з**	**и**	**й**	**л**	**п**

Г, Г

(f)	*(ts)*	*(ch or sh)*	*(sh)*	*(shch)*	*(ih or ee)*	*(eh)*	*(yoo)*	*(yah)*
ф	**ц**	**ч**	**ш**	**щ**	**ы**	**э**	**ю**	**я**

Я, Я

Here is the entire Russian alphabet in ***Russian*** alphabetical order for quick reference. Practice these new letters and sounds with the examples given which are mostly Russian first names. A black underline indicates a man's name and a blue underline is for a woman's.

Russian letter	English sound	Example	*Write it here*
а	ah	**Анна** *(ahn-nah)*	
б	b	**Борис** *(bahr-ees)*	
в	v	**Вадим** *(vah-deem)*	
г	g (or v)	**Глеб** *(gleb)*	Глеб, Глеб
д	d	**Дмитрий** *(dmee-tree)*	
е	eh *(as in let)* yeh *(as in yet)*	**Елена** *(eh-lyen-ah)*	
ё	yoh	**Фёдор** *(fyoh-dor)*	

ж	zh	**Жанна** *(zhahn-nah)*	____________
з	z	**Зина** *(zee-nah)*	____________
и	ee	**Никита** *(nee-kee-tah)*	____________
й *(varies)*	oy/ay/i/ee	**Майя** *(my-yah)*	____________
к	k	**Катя** *(kaht-yah)*	____________
л	l	**Лариса** *(lah-ree-sah)*	____________
м	m	**Максим** *(mahk-seem)*	____________
н	n	**Николай** *(nee-kah-lie)*	____________
о *(varies)*	oh	**Ольга** *(ohl-gah)*	____________
	ah	**Полина** *(pah-lee-nah)*	____________
п	p	**Паша** *(pah-shah)*	____________
р	r	**Рина** *(ree-nah)*	____________
с	s	**Сергей** *(syair-gay)*	____________
т	t	**Татьяна** *(taht-yah-nah)*	____________
у	oo	**Эдуард** *(ed-oo-ard)*	____________
ф	f	**Софья** *(sohf-yah)*	____________
х	h (or hk)	**Михаил** *(mee-hah-eel)*	____________
ц	ts *(as in cats)*	**Царёв** *(tsar-yohv)*	____________
ч	ch (or sh)	**Вячеслав** *(vyah-cheh-slahv)*	____________
ш	sh	**Саша** *(sah-shah)*	____________
щ *(varies)*	shch/sh	**Щукин** *(shchoo-keen)*	____________
ъ	no sound, called a hard sign, a word divider		
ы *(varies)*	ih/ee	**Рыбаков** *(rih-bah-kohv)*	____________
ь	no sound, called a soft sign, a word divider		
э *(varies)*	eh	**Элла** *(el-lah)*	____________
ю	yoo	**Юрий** *(yoor-ee)*	____________
я	yah	**Юлия** *(yool-ee-yah)*	____________

By now you should have a reasonable grasp on the Russian alphabet. Letters can change their pronunciation depending upon whether they are stressed or unstressed. Take the letter **о.** It is pronounced "*oh*" when stressed and "*ah*" otherwise. Do not worry about it, you'll learn!

Sometimes the phonetics may seem to contradict your pronunciation guide. Don't panic! The easiest and best-possible phonetics have been chosen for each individual word. Pronounce the phonetics just as you see them. Don't over-analyze them. Speak with a Russian accent and, above all, enjoy yourself!

2 Key Question Words

When you arrive in *(rahs-see-yoo)* **Россию,** (Russia) the very first thing you will need to do is ask questions — "Where is the bus stop?" "Where can I exchange money?" "Where *(gdyeh)* **(где)** is the lavatory?" "*(gdyeh)* **Где** (where) is a restaurant?" "*(gdyeh)* **Где** (where) do I catch a taxi?" "*(gdyeh)* **Где** (where) is a good hotel?" "*(gdyeh)* **Где** is my luggage?" — and the list will go on and on for the entire length of your visit. In Russian, there are SEVEN KEY QUESTION WORDS to learn. For example, the seven key question words will help you find out exactly what you are ordering in a restaurant before you order it — and not after the surprise (or shock!) arrives. Notice that "what" and "who" are differentiated by only one letter, so be sure not to confuse them. Take a few minutes to study and practice saying the seven basic question words listed below. Then cover the *(roos-skee)* **русский** (Russian) with your hand and fill in each of the blanks with the matching *(roos-skeem)* **русским** (Russian) *(slah-vahm)* **словом.** (word)

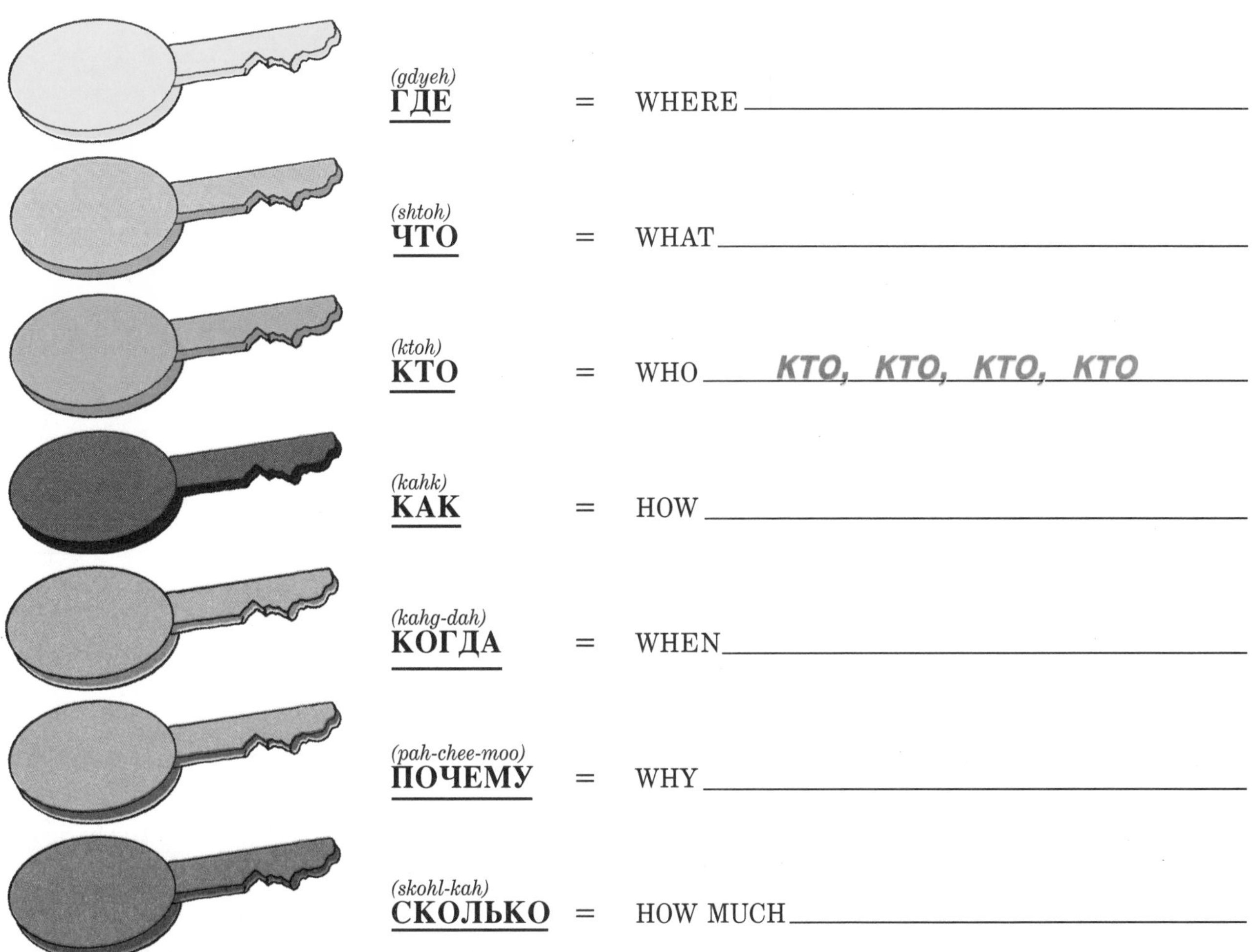

(gdyeh) **ГДЕ** = WHERE ______________________

(shtoh) **ЧТО** = WHAT ______________________

(ktoh) **КТО** = WHO ___КТО, КТО, КТО, КТО___

(kahk) **КАК** = HOW ______________________

(kahg-dah) **КОГДА** = WHEN ______________________

(pah-chee-moo) **ПОЧЕМУ** = WHY ______________________

(skohl-kah) **СКОЛЬКО** = HOW MUCH ______________________

Now test yourself to see if you really can keep these *(slah-vah)* **слова** (words) straight in your mind. Draw lines between the *(roos-skee-mee)* **русскими** (Russian) *(ee)* **и** (and) English equivalents below.

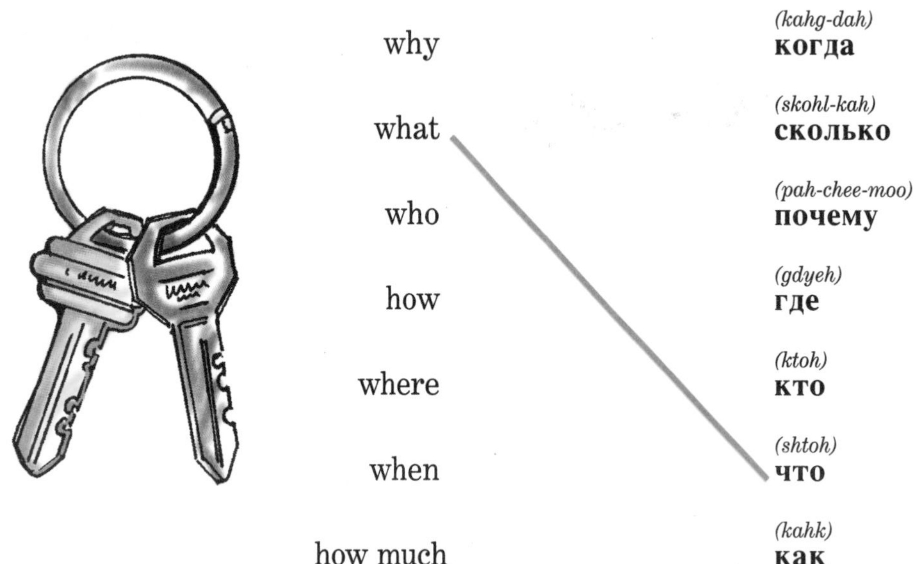

why	*(kahg-dah)* **когда**
what	*(skohl-kah)* **сколько**
who	*(pah-chee-moo)* **почему**
how	*(gdyeh)* **где**
where	*(ktoh)* **кто**
when	*(shtoh)* **что**
how much	*(kahk)* **как**

Examine the following questions containing these words. Practice the sentences out loud *(ee)* **и** (and) then practice by copying the Russian in the blanks underneath each question.

(shtoh) (et-tah)
Что это?
what (is) that?

____

(gdyeh) (sah-laht)
Где салат?
where (is) the salad

____

(ktoh) (et-tah)
Кто это?
who (is) that?

____

(kahg-dah) (bahl-yet)
Когда балет?
when (is) the ballet

Когда балет?

(skohl-kah) (et-tah) (stoy-eet)
Сколько это стоит?
how much (does) that cost

____

(kahk) (dee-lah)
Как дела?
how are things, how are you

____

(gdyeh) **"Где"** (where) will be your most used question *(sloh-vah)* **слово.** (word) Say each of the following *(roos-skee-yeh)* **русские** (Russian) sentences aloud. Then write out each sentence without looking at the example. If you don't succeed on the first try, don't give up. Just practice each sentence until you are able to do it easily.

Remember "**c**" is pronounced like an "s" *(ee)* **и** "**р**" is pronounced like an "r."

(gdyeh) (too-ahl-yet)
Где туалет?
where (is) a toilet

(gdyeh) (tahk-see)
Где такси?
where (is) a taxi

(gdyeh) (ahv-toh-boos)
Где автобус?
where (is) a bus

Где туалет? ____________ ____________

(gdyeh) (res-tah-rahn)
Где ресторан?
a restaurant

(bahnk)
Где банк?
a bank

(gah-stee-neet-sah)
Где гостиница?
a hotel, an inn

____________ ____________ ____________

Да (dah) [yes], you can see similarities between **русским** (roos-skeem) [Russian] **и** (ee) **английским** (ahn-glee-skeem) [English], if you look closely. **Русский** (roos-skee) **и** [and] **английский** are not related languages, but some words are surprisingly similar. Of course, they do not always sound the same when spoken by a Russian, but the similarities will certainly surprise you and make your work here easier. Listed below are five "free" **слов** (slohv) [words] beginning with **"а"** (ah) to help you get started. Be sure to say each **слово** (sloh-vah) aloud **и** (ee) then write out the **русское** (roos-skah-yeh) [Russian] **слово** (sloh-vah) [word] in the blank to the right.

☑ **абрикос** *(ah-bree-kohs)*..................	apricot		____________
☐ **август** *(ahv-goost)*......................	August		____________
☐ **авиация** *(ah-vee-aht-see-yah)*............	aviation	**а**	____________
☐ **Австралия** *(ahv-strah-lee-yah)*...........	Australia		____________
☐ **Австрия** *(ahv-stree-yah)*.................	Austria		____________

Free **слова** (slah-vah) [words] like these will appear at the bottom of the following pages in a yellow color band. They are easy — enjoy them! Don't forget to pronounce **"и"** as "ee."

3 Odds 'n Ends

(roos-skee) **Русский** [Russian] *(yah-zik)* **язык** [language] does not have *(slohv)* **слов** [words] for "the" and "a," which makes things easier for you. Russian *(slah-vah)* **слова** [words] also change their endings depending upon how they are used, so don't be surprised! Learn *(slah-vah)* **слова** [the words] and be prepared to see their endings change. Here are some examples.

word	book	chair
(sloh-vah) **слово**	*(kuh-nee-gah)* **книга**	*(stool)* **стул**
(slah-vah) **слова**	*(kuh-nee-gee)* **книги**	*(stool-ah)* **стула**
(sloh-voo) **слову**	*(kuh-nee-geh)* **книге**	*(stool-oo)* **стулу**
(sloh-vahm) **словом**	*(kuh-nee-goo)* **книгу**	*(stool-ohm)* **стулом**
(slohv) **слов**	*(kuh-nee-goy)* **книгой**	*(stool-yeh)* **стуле**
(slah-vah-mee) **словами**	*(kuh-neeg)* **книг**	*(stool-yah)* **стулья**

This only appears difficult because it is different from *(ahn-glee-skah-vah)* **английского** [English] *(yah-zih-kah)* **языка.** [language] Just remember the core of *(sloh-vah)* **слова** [the word] doesn't change, so you should always be able to recognize it. For instance, you will be understood whether you say *(kuh-nee-gah)* **книга** [book] or *(kuh-nee-goo)* **книгу.** Learn to look and listen for the core of the word, and don't worry about the different endings.

In Step 2 you were introduced to the Seven Key QuestionWords. These seven words are the basics, the most essential building blocks for learning Russian. Throughout this book you will come across keys asking you to fill in the missing question word. Use this opportunity not only to fill in the blank on that key, but to review all your question words. Play with the new sounds, speak slowly and have fun.

a

- ☐ **автобиография** *(ahv-tah-bee-ah-grah-fee-yah)*.. autobiography ______
- ☐ **автограф** *(ahv-toh-grahf)* .... autograph ______
- ☐ **автомат** *(ahv-tah-maht)* .... automat ______
- ☐ **автомобиль** *(ahv-tah-mah-beel)*............. automobile ______
- ☐ **автор** *(ahv-tar)*.............................. author ______

4 Look Around You

Before you proceed with this Step, situate yourself comfortably in your living room. Now look around you. Can you name the things that you see in this (kohm-nah-tyeh) **комнате** (room) in Russian? You can probably guess (lahm-pah) **лампа** (lamp) and maybe even (dee-vahn) **диван.** (divan, sofa) But let's learn the rest of them. After practicing these (slah-vah) **слова** (words) out loud, write them in the blanks below.

(lahm-pah) **лампа** lamp, light ______

(dee-vahn) **диван** sofa ______

(stool) **стул** chair ______

(kahv-yor) **ковёр** carpet ~~ковёр, ковёр~~

(stohl) **стол** table ______

(dvyair) **дверь** door ______

(chah-sih) **часы** clock ______

(zah-nahv-yes) **занавес** curtain ______

(teh-leh-fohn) **телефон** telephone ______

(ahk-noh) **окно** window ______

(kar-tee-nah) **картина** picture ______

In Step 3, you learned that (roos-skee-yeh) **русские** (Russian) (slah-vah) **слова** (words) vary. The correct form of each (sloh-vah) **слова** (word) will always be given to familiarize you with the variations. Now open your (kuh-nee-goo) **книгу** (book) to the sticky labels on page 17 and later on page 35. Peel off the first 11 labels (ee) **и** (and) proceed around your (kohm-nah-tih) **комнаты** (room) labeling these items in your home. This will help to increase your (roos-skah-yeh) **русское** (Russian) (sloh-vah) **слово** (word) power easily. Don't forget to say each (sloh-vah) **слово** (word) as you attach each label.

Now ask yourself, (gdyeh) (lahm-pah) **"Где лампа?"** (the lamp) and point at it while you answer, (tahm) (lahm-pah) **"Там лампа."** (there is the lamp)

Continue on down the list above until you feel comfortable with these new (slah-vah-mee) **словами.** (words)

- ☐ **агент** *(ah-gyent)*.......... agent ______
- ☐ **адвокат** *(ahd-vah-kaht)*.......... advocate, lawyer ______
- ☐ **адрес** *(ah-dres)*.......... address ______
- ☐ **Азия** *(ah-zee-yah)*.......... Asia ______
- ☐ **академия** *(ah-kah-dyeh-mee-yah)*.......... academy ______

а

(dohm)
дом = house

(voht) (dohm)
Вот дом.
here (is) the house

(kah-bee-nyet)
кабинет
study

(vahn-nah-yah)
ванная
bathroom

(koohk-nyah)
кухня
kitchen

(spahl-nyah)
спальня
bedroom

(stah-loh-vah-yah)
столовая
dining room

(gah-stee-nah-yah)
гостиная
living room

(gah-rahzh)
гараж
garage

(pahd-vahl)
подвал
basement

While learning these new **слова** *(slah-vah)* (words), let's not forget:

(ahv-tah-mah-beel) (mah-shee-nah)
автомобиль/ машина
automobile, car

(mah-tah-tsee-kul)
мотоцикл
motorcycle

(vyeh-lah-see-pyed)
велосипед
bicycle

☐ **аккуратный** *(ahk-koo-raht-nee)*	fastidious, neat, accurate	______
☐ **акробат** *(ah-krah-baht)*	acrobat	______
☐ **акт** *(ahkt)*	act	**а** ______
☐ **актёр** *(ahk-tyor)*	actor	______
☐ **акцент** *(ahkt-syent)*	accent	______

(kohsh-kah)
кошка
cat

(sahd)
сад
garden

сад, сад, сад

(tsvet-ih)
цветы
flowers

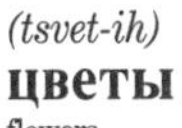

(sah-bah-kah)
собака
dog

(pahch-toh-vee) (yahsh-chik)
почтовый ящик
mailbox

(poach-tah)
почта
mail

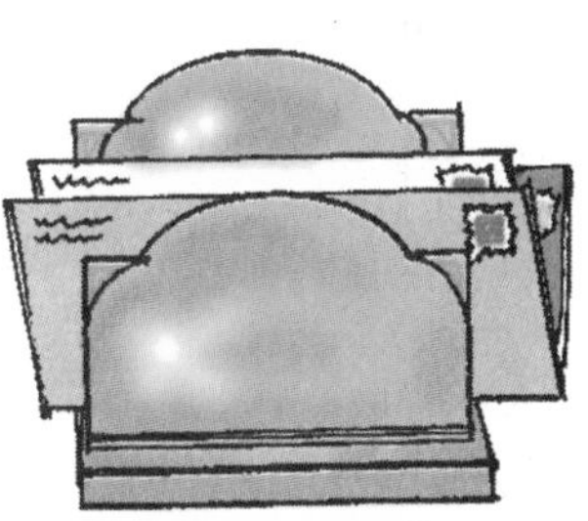

Peel off the next set of labels **и** (ee) wander through your **дом** (dohm) learning these new **слова** (slah-vah) [words]. It will be somewhat difficult to label your **кошку** (kohsh-koo) [cat], **цветы** (tsvet-ih) [flowers] or **собаку** (sah-bah-koo) [dog], but be creative. Practice by asking yourself, **"Где машина?"** (gdyeh) (mah-shee-nah) [the car] and reply, **"Вот машина."** (voht) (mah-shee-nah) [here (is)] **"Где дом?"** (gdyeh)

☐ **алгебра** *(ahl-gyeh-brah)*	algebra	________________
☐ **алкоголь** *(ahl-kah-gohl)*	alcohol, alcoholic drinks	________________
☐ **Америка** *(ah-myeh-ree-kah)*	America **а**	________________
☐ **— американец** *(ah-myeh-ree-kah-nyets)* . . .	American male	________________
☐ **— американка** *(ah-myeh-ree-kahn-kah)*	American female	________________

5 *(ah-deen)* Один, *(dvah)* два, *(tree)* три
one, two, three

Consider for a minute how important numbers are. How could you tell someone your phone number, your address *(ee-lee)* **или** (or) your hotel room if you had no numbers? And think of how difficult if would be if you could not understand the time, the price of an apple *(ee-lee)* **или** (or) the correct bus to take. When practicing *(chee-slah)* **числа** (numbers) below, notice the similarities which have been underlined for you between *(ah-deen)* **один** (one) and *(ah-deen-nud-tset)* **одиннадцать** (eleven), *(tree)* **три** (three) and *(tree-nahd-tset)* **тринадцать** (thirteen), and so on.

0	*(nohl)* **ноль**	______	10	*(dyes-yet)* **десять**	______
1	*(ah-deen)* **один**	______	11	*(ah-deen-nud-tset)* **одиннадцать**	______
2	*(dvah) (dveh)* **два/ две**	______	12	*(dveh-nahd-tset)* **двенадцать**	______
3	*(tree)* **три**	______	13	*(tree-nahd-tset)* **тринадцать**	______
4	*(cheh-tir-ee)* **четыре**	______	14	*(cheh-tir-nud-tset)* **четырнадцать**	______
5	*(pyaht)* **пять**	______	15	*(pyaht-nahd-tset)* **пятнадцать**	______
6	*(shest)* **шесть**	______	16	*(shest-nahd-tset)* **шестнадцать**	______
7	*(syem)* **семь**	семь, семь, семь	17	*(sim-nahd-tset)* **семнадцать**	______
8	*(voh-syem)* **восемь**	______	18	*(vah-sim-nahd-tset)* **восемнадцать**	______
9	*(dyev-yet)* **девять**	______	19	*(div-yet-nahd-tset)* **девятнадцать**	______
10	*(dyes-yet)* **десять**	______	20	*(dvahd-tset)* **двадцать**	______

☑ **алло!** *(ahl-loh)* . . . . hello! — *алло! алло! алло! алло! алло!*
☐ **Англия** *(ahn-glee-yah)* . . . . England
☐ — where they speak **по-английски** *(pah-ahn-glee-skee)*
☐ **— англичанин** *(ahn-glee-chah-neen)* . . . . . . Englishman
☐ **— англичанка** *(ahn-glee-chahn-kah)* . . . . Englishwoman

а

Use these **числа** *(chee-slah)* numbers on a daily basis. Count to yourself **по-русски** *(pah-roos-skee)* in Russian when you brush your teeth, exercise **или** *(ee-lee)* or commute to work. Fill in the blanks below according to **числам** *(chee-slahm)* numbers given in parentheses. Now is also a good time to learn these two **очень** *(oh-chen)* very important phrases.

(yah) (hah-choo) (koo-peet)
я хочу купить ____________________
I would like to buy

(mwee)(hah-teem) (koo-peet)
мы хотим купить ____________________
we would like to buy

(yah) (hah-choo) (koo-peet) **Я хочу купить** ________ (1) I would like to buy	*(aht-krit-koo)* **открытку.** postcard	*(skohl-kah)* **Сколько?** ________ (1) how many, how much
(hah-choo) (koo-peet) **Я хочу купить** ________ (7) I would like	*(mar-ahk)* **марок.** stamps	*(skohl-kah)* **Сколько?** ________ (7)
(hah-choo) (koo-peet) **Я хочу купить** ________ (8)	*(mar-ahk)* **марок.** stamps	*(skohl-kah)* **Сколько?** ________ (8)
(hah-choo) (koo-peet) **Я хочу купить** ________ (5)	**марок.**	*(skohl-kah)* **Сколько?** ________ (5) how many
(mwee) (hah-teem) (koo-peet) **Мы хотим купить** ________ (9) we would like to buy	*(aht-krih-tahk)* **открыток.** postcards	*(skohl-kah)* **Сколько?** ________ (9)
(mwee) (hah-teem) **Мы хотим купить** ________ (10) we would like	*(aht-krih-tahk)* **открыток.** postcards	*(skohl-kah)* **Сколько?** ________ (10)
(yah) (hah-choo) **Я хочу** ________ (to buy) ________ (1) I would like	*(beel-yet)* **билет.** ticket	*(skohl-kah)* **Сколько?** ________ (1)
(mwee) (hah-teem) **Мы хотим купить** ________ (4) we would like	*(beel-yet-ah)* **билета.** tickets	*(skohl-kah)* **Сколько?** ________ (4)
____ (we) *(hah-teem)* **хотим купить** ________ (11) would like	*(beel-yet-ahv)* **билетов.**	**Сколько?** ________ (11)
(yah) (hah-choo) **Я хочу** ________ (to buy) ________ (3) would like	*(chahsh-kee) (chah-yah)* **чашки чая.** cups of tea	**Сколько?** ________ (3)
(hah-teem) **Мы хотим купить** ________ (4) would like to buy	*(chahsh-kee) (koh-fyeh)* **чашки кофе.** cups of coffee	________ (how much) ________ (4)

a

- ☐ **анекдот** *(ah-nyek-doht)* . . . . anecdote, joke ________
- ☐ **антенна** *(ahn-tyen-nah)* . . . . antenna ________
- ☐ **антибиотики** *(ahn-tee-bee-oh-tee-kee)* . . . . . . antibiotics ________
- ☐ **аппетит** *(ah-peh-teet)* . . . . appetite ________
- ☐ **апрель** *(ahp-ryel)* . . . . April ________

Now see if you can translate the following thoughts **на** (nah) [nto] **русский** (roos-skee) [Russian]. **Ответы** (aht-vyet-ih) [the answers] are provided upside down at the bottom of the page.

1. I would like to buy seven postcards.

____

2. I would like to buy nine stamps.

____

3. We would like to buy four cups of tea.

____

4. We would like to buy three tickets.

____

Review **числа** (chee-slah) [numbers] 1 through 20. Write out your telephone number, fax number, and cellular number. Then write out a friend's telephone number and then a relative's telephone number.

(2 0 6) 3 4 0 — 4 4 2 2

два ноль шесть ______________________________________

(__ __ __) __ __ __ — __ __ __ __

____

(__ __ __) __ __ __ — __ __ __ __

____

ОТВЕТЫ

1. Я хочу купить семь открыток.
2. Я хочу купить девять марок.
3. Мы хотим купить четыре чашки чая.
4. Мы хотим купить три билета.

6 (tsvet-ah) Цвета
colors

(tsvet-ah) **Цвета** (colors) are the same (pah-roos-skee) **по-русски** (in Russian) as they are (pah-ahn-glee-skee) **по-английски** (in English) — they just have different (ee-myen-ah) **имена.** (names)

Red used to be the national (tsvet) **цвет** (color) in (sah-vyet-skahm) **Советском** (Soviet) (sah-yoo-zeh) **Союзе.** (Union) (tsvet-ah) **Цвета** (colors) of the new (rahs-see-skah-vah) **российского** (Russian) flag are — (byeh-lee) **белый,** (white) (gah-loo-boy) **голубой** (light blue) **и** (krahs-nee) **красный.** (red) Let's learn the basic (tsvet-ah) **цвета.** (colors) Once you've learned (tsvet-ah) **цвета,** (the colors) quiz yourself. What color are your shoes? Your eyes? Your hair? Your house?

(roh-zah-vwee)
розовый
pink

____

(krahs-nee)
красный
red

____

(ah-rahn-zheh-vwee)
оранжевый
orange

____

(byeh-lee)
белый
white

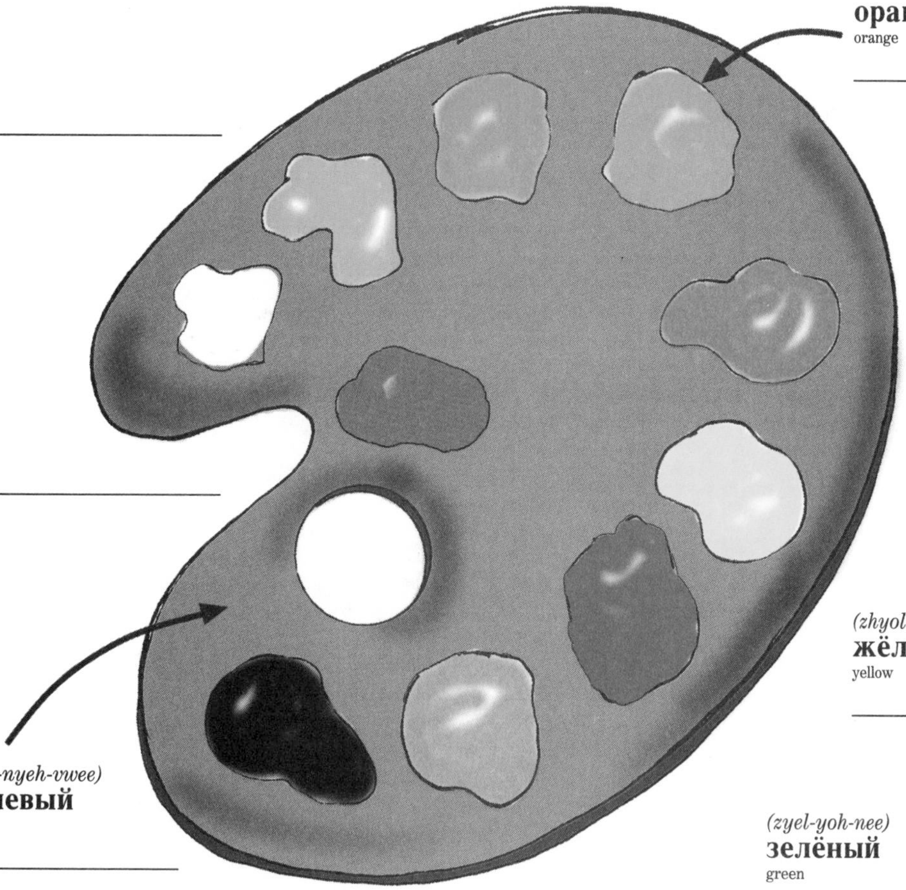

____

(see-nee)
синий
blue

____

(syeh-ree)
серый
gray

____

(zhyol-tee)
жёлтый
yellow

____

(kah-reech-nyeh-vwee)
коричневый
brown

____

(zyel-yoh-nee)
зелёный
green

____

(chyor-nee)
чёрный
black

____

(gah-loo-boy)
голубой
light blue

____

☐ **арена** *(ar-yen-ah)*	arena		______________
☐ **арест** *(ar-yest)*	arrest		______________
☐ **армия** *(ar-mee-yah)*........................	army	**а**	______________
☐ **аспирин** *(ah-spee-reen)*....................	aspirin		______________
☐ **астронавт** *(ah-strah-nahvt)*................	astronaut		______________

Peel off the next group of labels **и** *(ee)* proceed to label these **цвета** *(tsvet-ah)* colors **в** *(vuh)* in your **доме.** *(doh-myeh)* house Identify the two or three dominant colors in the flags below.

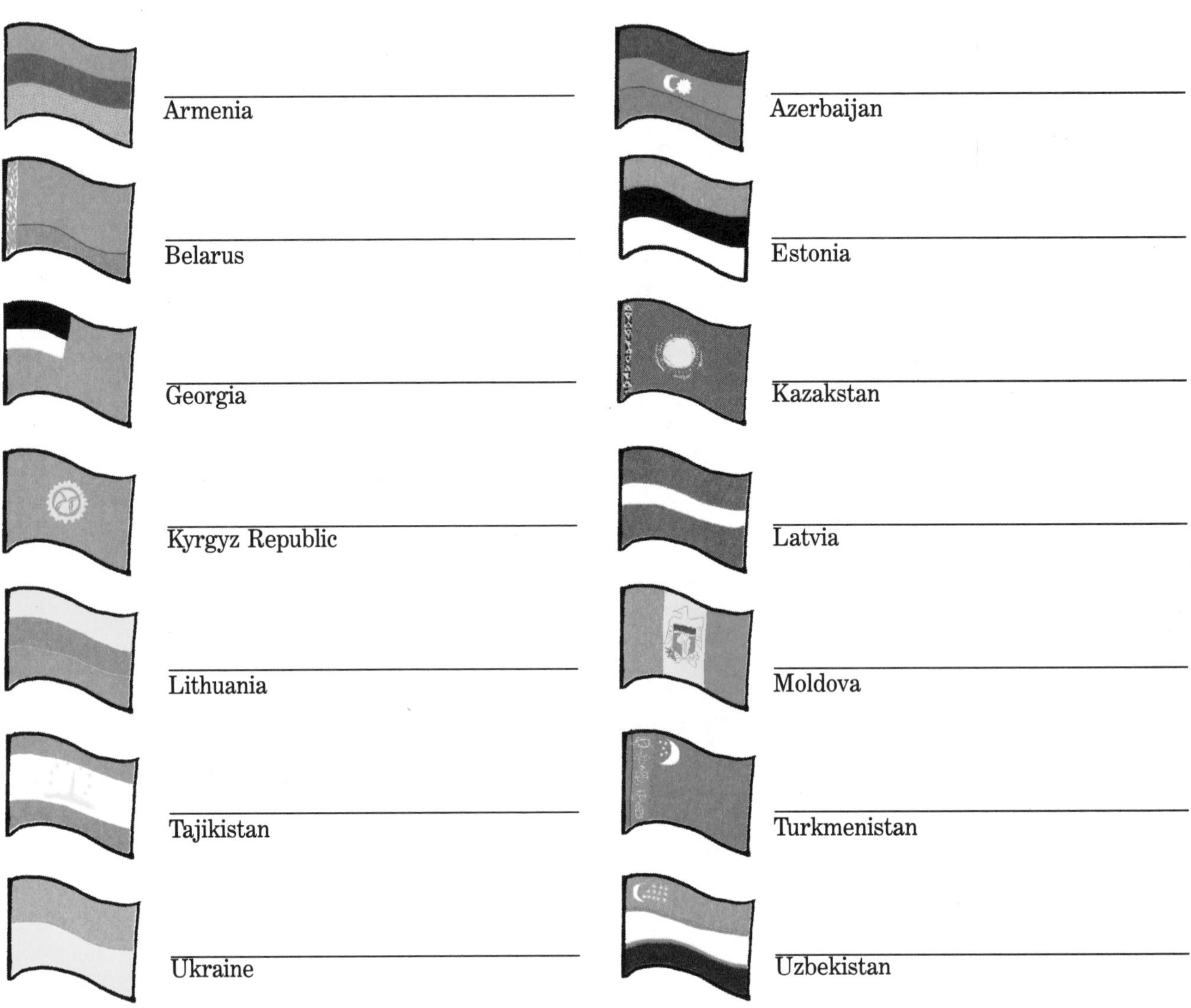

You should be able to use your **русский** language skills in any of the above countries. Kyrgyz may be the official language of the Kyrgyz Republic, but **русский** may be more commonly used **и** understood.

______ (where) ____________ (where is) **такси?** *(tahk-see)*

______ (what) ____________ (what is) **это?**

☐ **атлет** *(aht-lyet)*	athlete	**а**
☐ **Африка** *(ah-free-kah)*	Africa	
☐ **аэродром** *(ah-air-ah-drohm)*	aerodrome, airport	
☐ **багаж** *(bah-gahzh)*	baggage	**б**
☐ **базар** *(bah-zar)*	bazaar	

(lahm-pah)
лампа

(dee-vahn)
диван

(stool)
стул

(kahv-yor)
ковёр

(stohl)
стол

(dvyair)
дверь

(chah-sih)
часы

(zah-nahv-yes)
занавес

(teh-leh-fohn)
телефон

(ahk-noh)
окно

(kar-tee-nah)
картина

(dohm)
дом

(kah-bee-nyet)
кабинет

(vahn-nah-yah)
ванная

(koohk-nyah)
кухня

(spahl-nyah)
спальня

(stah-loh-vah-yah)
столовая

(gah-stee-nah-yah)
гостиная

(gah-rahzh)
гараж

(pahd-vahl)
подвал

(ahv-tah-mah-beel)
автомобиль

(mah-tah-tsee-kul)
мотоцикл

(vyeh-lah-see-pyed)
велосипед

(kohsh-kah)
кошка

(sahd)
сад

(tsvet-ih)
цветы

(sah-bah-kah)
собака

(pahch-toh-vee) (yahsh-chik)
почтовый ящик

(poach-tah)
почта

(nohl)
0 ноль

(ah-deen)
1 один

(dvah)
2 два

(tree)
3 три

(cheh-tir-ee)
4 четыре

(pyaht)
5 пять

(shest)
6 шесть

(syem)
7 семь

(voh-syem)
8 восемь

(dyev-yet)
9 девять

(dyes-yet)
10 десять

(kah-reech-nyeh-vwee)
коричневый

(krahs-nee)
красный

(roh-zah-vwee)
розовый

(ah-rahn-zheh-vwee)
оранжевый

(byeh-lee)
белый

(zhyol-tee)
жёлтый

(syeh-ree)
серый

(chyor-nee)
чёрный

(see-nee)
синий

(zyel-yoh-nee)
зелёный

(gah-loo-boy)
голубой

(doh-brah-yeh) (oo-trah)
доброе утро

(doh-brih) (dyen)
добрый день

(doh-brih) (vyeh-cher)
добрый вечер

(spah-koy-nay) (noh-chee)
спокойной ночи

(kahk) (dee-lah)
Как дела?

(hah-lah-deel-neek)
холодильник

(plee-tah)
плита

(vee-noh)
вино

(pee-vah)
пиво

(mah-lah-koh)
молоко

(mah-slah)
масло

(sole)
соль

(pyeh-rets)
перец

(bah-kahl)
бокал

(stah-kahn)
стакан

(gah-zyeh-tah)
газета

(chahsh-kah)
чашка

(veel-kah)
вилка

(nohzh)
нож

(sahl-fyet-kah)
салфетка

(tar-yel-kah)
тарелка

(lohzh-kah)
ложка

(shkahf)
шкаф

(chy)
чай

(koh-fyeh)
кофе

(hlyeb)
хлеб

(pah-zhahl-oos-tah)
пожалуйста

(spah-see-bah)
спасибо

(eez-vee-neet-yeh)
извините

STICKY LABELS

This book has over 150 special sticky labels for you to use as you learn new words. When you are introduced to one of these words, remove the corresponding label from these pages. Be sure to use each of these unique self-adhesive labels by adhering them to a picture, window, lamp, or whatever object it refers to. And yes, they are removable! The sticky labels make learning to speak Russian much more fun and a lot easier than you ever expected. For example, when you look in the mirror and see the label, say

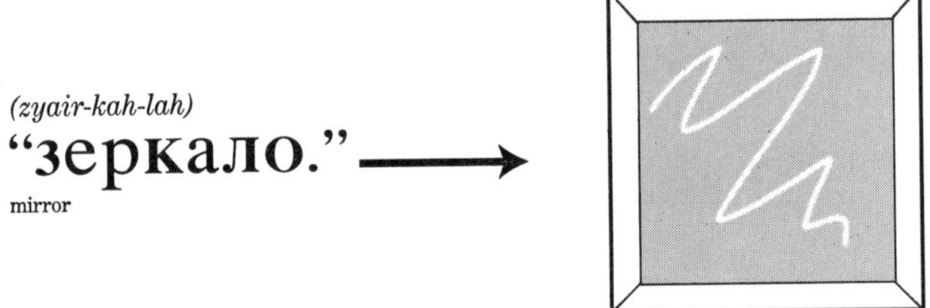

Don’t just say it once, say it again and again. And once you label the refrigerator, you should never again open that door without saying

(hah-lah-deel-neek)
“холодильник.”
refrigerator

By using the sticky labels, you not only learn new words, but friends and family learn along with you! The sooner you start, the sooner you can use these labels at home

7 

(dyen-gee)
Деньги
money

Before starting this Step, go back and review Step 5. It is important that you can count to *(dvahd-tset)* **двадцать** (twenty) without looking *(vuh)* **в** (at) *(kuh-nee-goo)* **книгу.** (the book) Let's learn the larger *(chee-slah)* **числа** (numbers) now. After practicing aloud *(roos-skee-yeh)* **русские** (Russian) numbers 10 through 11,000 below, write these *(chee-slah)* **числа** in the blanks provided. Again, notice the similarities (underlined) between *(chee-slah-mee)* **числами** (numbers) such as *(tree)* **три** (3), *(tree-nahd-tset)* **тринадцать** (13), *(treed-tset)* **тридцать** (30), *(tree-stah)* **триста** (300), and **три** *(tih-syah-chee)* **тысячи** (3000).

10	*(dyes-yet)* **десять** ________	1000	*(tih-syah-chah)* **тысяча** ________
20	*(dvahd-tset)* **двадцать** ________	2000	**две** *(tih-syah-chee)* **тысячи** ________
30	*(treed-tset)* **тридцать** ________	3000	**три** *(tih-syah-chee)* **тысячи** ________
40	*(so-rahk)* **сорок** сорок, сорок	4000	**четыре тысячи** ________
50	*(peed-dyes-yaht)* **пятьдесят** ________	5000	*(pyaht)* **пять** *(tih-syahch)* **тысяч** ________
60	*(shest-dyes-yaht)* **шестьдесят** ________	6000	**шесть тысяч** ________
70	*(syem-dyes-yet)* **семьдесят** ________	7000	**семь тысяч** ________
80	*(voh-syem-dyes-yet)* **восемьдесят** ________	8000	**восемь тысяч** ________
90	*(dyev-yah-noh-stah)* **девяносто** ________	9000	**девять тысяч** ________
100	*(stoh) (soht) (stah)* **сто/сот/ста** ________	10,000	**десять тысяч** ________
500	*(pyet-soht)* **пятьсот** ________	10,500	**десять тысяч** *(pyet-soht)* **пятьсот** ________
1000	*(tih-syah-chah)* **тысяча** ________	11,000	*(ah-deen-nud-tset)* **одиннадцать тысяч** ________

Вот две important phrases to go with all these **числа.** Say them out loud over and over and then write them out twice as many times.

(oo) (men-yah) (yest)
у меня есть ________________
I have

(oo) (nahs) (yest)
у нас есть ________________
we have

☐ **бал** *(bahl)*	ball (dance)		________
☐ **балалайка** *(bah-lah-lie-kah)*	balalaika		________
☐ **балерина** *(bah-leh-ree-nah)*	ballerina	**б**	________
☐ **балет** *(bahl-yet)*	ballet		________
☐ **балкон** *(bahl-kohn)*	balcony		________

The unit of currency **в** *(vuh)* [in] **России** *(rahs-see-ee)* [Russia] is the **рубль** *(roo-bil)*, abbreviated **руб.** or **р.** Let's learn the various kinds of **рублей** *(roo-blay)*. Always be sure to practice each **слово** *(sloh-vah)* out loud. You will not be able to exchange money before your arrival **в** *(vuh)* [in] **Россию** *(rahs-see-yoo)* so take a few minutes now to familiarize yourself with Russian and Central Asian currency.

в России

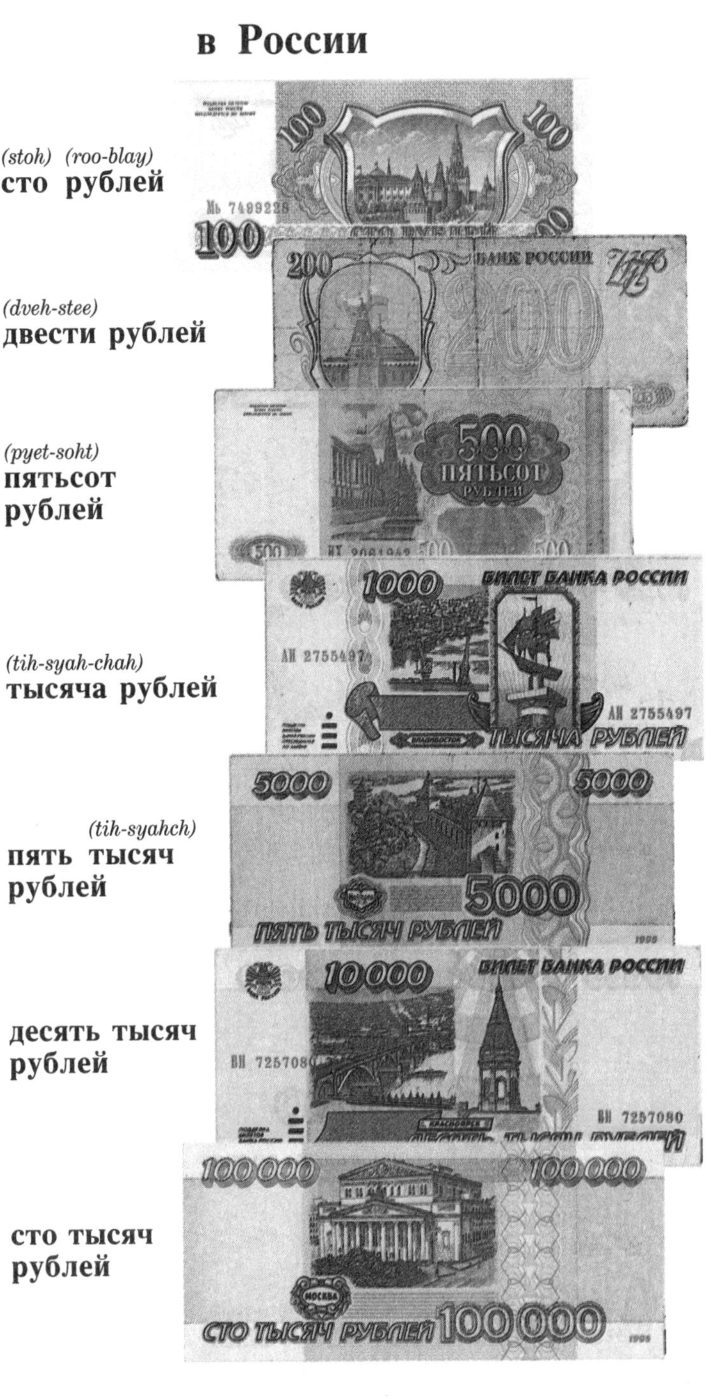

(stoh) (roo-blay)
сто рублей

(dveh-stee)
двести рублей

(pyet-soht)
пятьсот рублей

(tih-syah-chah)
тысяча рублей

(tih-syahch)
пять тысяч рублей

десять тысяч рублей

сто тысяч рублей

в Кыргызской республике

(kir-geez-skoy) (rehs-poo-bleek-yeh)

в Казахстане

(kah-zahk-stahn-yeh)

в Узбекистане

(ooz-bek-ee-stahn-yeh)

- ☐ **банан** *(bah-nahn)* .... banana
- ☐ **бандит** *(bahn-deet)* .... bandit, robber
- ☐ **бар** *(bar)* .... bar (restaurant)
- ☐ **баржа** *(bar-zhah)* .... barge
- ☐ **барьер** *(bar-yair)* .... barrier

б

Review *(chee-slah)* **числа** [the numbers] *(dyes-yet)* **десять** [ten] through **десять** *(tih-syahch)* **тысяч** again. *(tyep-yair)* **Теперь,** [now] *(kahk)* **как** [how] do you say "twenty-two" *(ee-lee)* **или** [or] "fifty-three" *(pah-roos-skee)* **по-русски?** Put the numbers together in a logical sequence just as you do in English. See if you can say *(ee)* **и** [and] write out *(chee-slah)* **числа** [the numbers] on this *(strah-neet-seh)* **странице.** [page] *(aht-vyet-ih)* **Ответы** [answers] are at the bottom of *(strah-neet-sih)* **страницы.** [page]

1. ______________________________ (2500 = 2000 + 500)

2. ______________________________ (8350 = 8000 + 300 + 50)

3. ______________________________ (4770 = 4000 + 700 + 70)

4. ______________________________ (9610 = 9000 + 600 + 10)

Now, **как** would you say the following **по-русски?**

5. ______________________________ (I have 4000 rubles.)

6. ______________________________ (We have 1050 rubles.)

To ask how much something costs *(pah-roos-skee)* **по-русски,** one asks — *(skohl-kah)* **Сколько** *(et-tah)* **это** *(stoy-eet)* **стоит?**

Now you try it. ______________________________ (How much does that cost?)

Answer the following questions based on the numbers in parentheses.

7. *(skohl-kah)* **Сколько** [how much] *(et-tah)* **это** [this] *(stoy-eet)* **стоит?** [costs] *(et-tah)* **Это** [this] *(stoy-eet)* **стоит** [costs] ______________ (1000) *(roo-blay)* **рублей.** [rubles]

8. **Сколько это стоит? Это стоит** ______________ (5000) *(roo-blay)* **рублей.**

9. **Сколько** *(stoy-eet)* **стоит** [costs] *(kuh-nee-gah)* **книга?** [the book] *(kuh-nee-gah)* **Книга стоит** ______________ (6000) *(roo-blay)* **рублей.**

10. **Сколько стоит** *(kar-tah)* **карта?** [the map] **Карта стоит** ______________ (17,000) **рублей.**

ОТВЕТЫ

1. две тысячи пятьсот
2. восемь тысяч триста пятьдесят
3. четыре тысячи семьсот семьдесят
4. девять тысяч шестьсот десять
5. У меня есть четыре тысячи рублей.
6. У нас есть тысяча пятьдесят рублей.
7. тысяча
8. пять тысяч
9. шесть тысяч
10. семнадцать тысяч

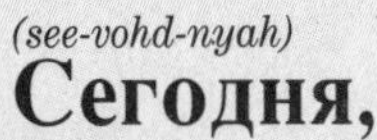

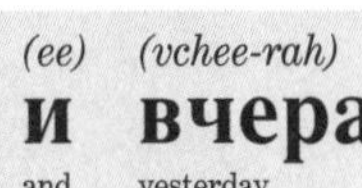

8 Сегодня, завтра и вчера

(see-vohd-nyah) **Сегодня,** today — *(zahv-trah)* **завтра** tomorrow — *(ee)* **и** and — *(vchee-rah)* **вчера** yesterday

(kah-lyen-dar)
Календарь
calendar

____

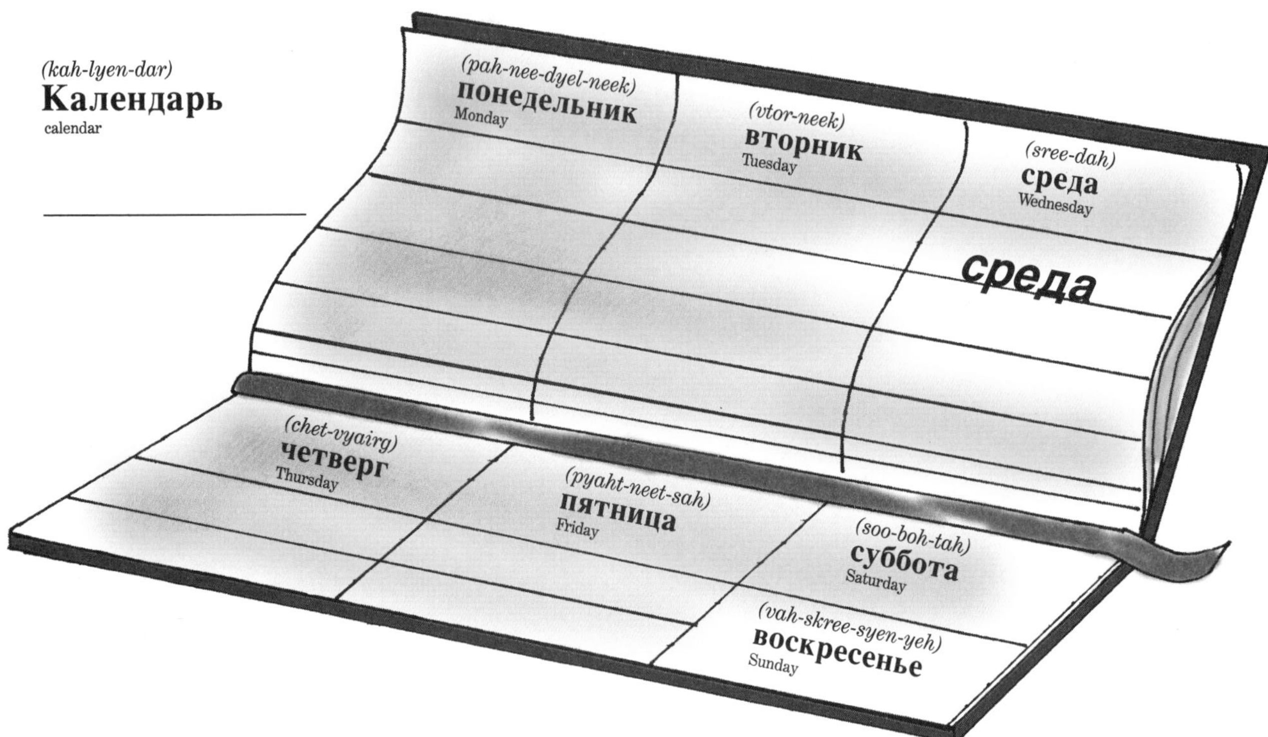

Learn the days of the week by writing them in the *(kah-lyen-dar-eh)* **календаре** above and then move on to the *(cheh-tir-ee)* **четыре** (four) parts to each *(den-yah)* **дня.** (day)

(oo-trah)
утро
morning

(dyen)
день
day, afternoon

(vyeh-cher)
вечер
evening

(nohch)
ночь
night

______________________ ______________________ ______________________ ______________________

☐ **бас** *(bahs)*	bass (voice)		______________________
☐ **баскетбол** *(bah-sket-bohl)*	basketball		______________________
☐ **батальон** *(bah-tahl-yohn)*	battalion	**б**	______________________
☐ **батарея** *(bah-tar-yeh-yah)*	battery		______________________
☐ **Бельгия** *(byel-gee-yah)*	Belgium		______________________

It is (oh-chen) **очень** (very) (vahzh-nah) **важно** (important) to know the days of the week (ee) **и** the various parts of the day as well as these **три слова**.

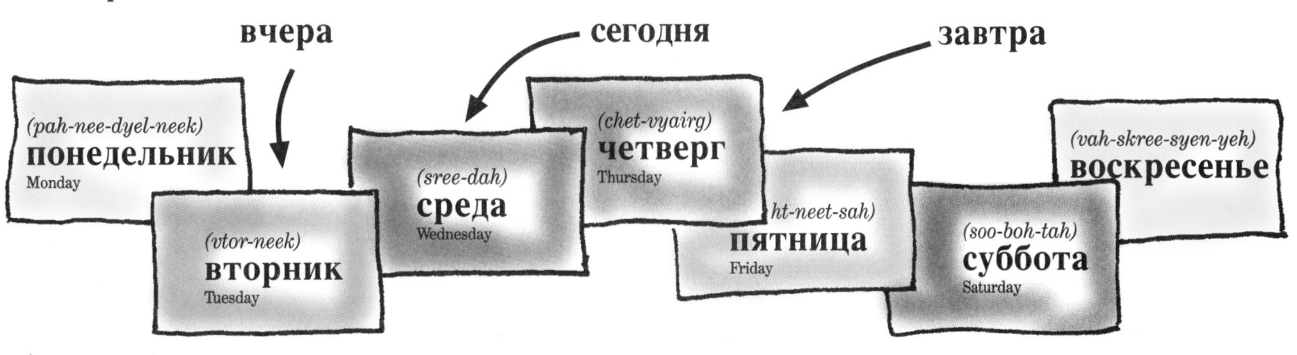

(shtoh) **Что** (what (is)) (see-vohd-nyah) **сегодня?** ____________________ (zahv-trah) **Что завтра?** ____________________

Что (bih-lah) **было** (was) (vchee-rah) **вчера?** ____________________ (sree-dah) **Сегодня среда,** (dah) **да?** (yes) So ____________ (tomorrow)

(chet-vyairg) **четверг и** ____________ (yesterday) (vtor-neek) **вторник.** (vuh) **"В"** can mean "on," so **"в** (vah-skree-syen-yeh) **воскресенье** (oo-trahm) **утром"** means "on Sunday morning." Fill in the following blanks **и** then check your answers at the bottom of (strah-neet-sih) **страницы.**

a.	on Sunday morning	=	____________
b.	on Friday morning	=	____________
c.	on Saturday evening	=	____________
d.	on Thursday afternoon	=	____________
e.	on Thursday evening	=	____________
f.	yesterday evening	=	____________
g.	yesterday morning	=	____________
h.	tomorrow morning	=	____________

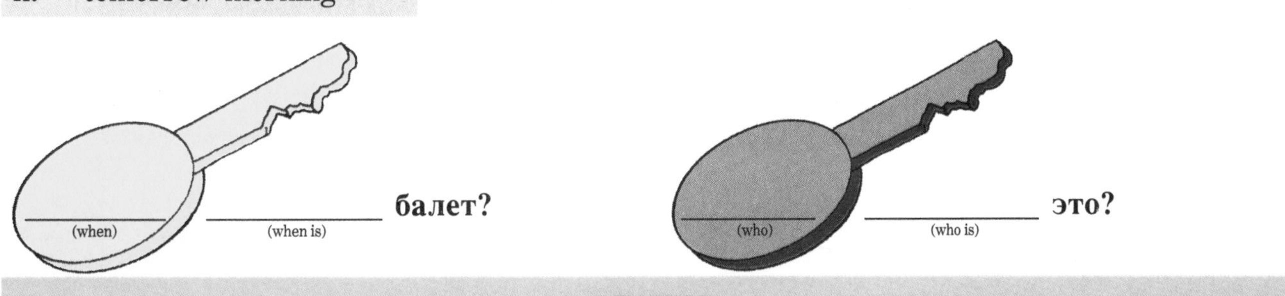

ОТВЕТЫ

a.	в воскресенье утром	d.	в четверг днём	g.	вчера утром
b.	в пятницу утром	e.	в четверг вечером	h.	завтра утром
c.	в субботу вечером	f.	вчера вечером		

Knowing the parts of *(den-yah)* **дня** (day) will help you to learn the various *(roos-skee-yeh)* **русские** (Russian) greetings below. Practice these every day until your trip.

(doh-brah-yeh) (oo-trah)
доброе утро ____________________
good morning

(doh-brih) (dyen)
добрый день ____________________
good day, hello

(doh-brih) (vyeh-cher)
добрый вечер ____________________
good evening

(spah-koy-nay) (noh-chee)
спокойной ночи ____________________
good night

Take the next *(cheh-tir-ee)* **четыре** (four) labels **и** stick them on the appropriate things in your *(doh-myeh)* **доме** (house). Make sure you attach them to the correct items, as they are only **по-русски.** How about the bathroom mirror for *(doh-brah-yeh oo-trah)* "**доброе утро**"? *(ee-lee)* **Или** (or) your alarm clock for *(spah-koy-nay) (noh-chee)* "**спокойной ночи**"? Let's not forget,

(kahk) (dee-lah)
Как дела? ____________________
how are you, how are things

Now for some *(dah)* "**да**" (yes) or *(nyet)* "**нет**" (no) questions –

Are your eyes **синие?** ____________ Are your shoes **коричевые?** ____________

Is your favorite color **красный?** ____________ Is today **суббота?** ____________

Do you own a **собака?** ____________ Do you own a **кошка?** ____________

You are about one-fourth of your way through *(et-toy) (kuh-nee-gee)* **этой книги** (this book) **и** it is a good time to quickly review **слова** you have learned before doing the crossword puzzle on the next *(strah-neet-seh)* **странице** (page).

(oo-dah-chee) **Удачи!** (good luck) Or, as one says *(pah-ahn-glee-skee)* **по-английски,** (in English) "good luck to you!"

ОТВЕТЫ TO THE CROSSWORD PUZZLE

ACROSS

1. банк
2. гостиница
3. купить
4. да
5. страница
6. кухня
7. столовая
8. зелёный
9. два or две
10. нет
11. русский
12. кабинет
13. где
14. оранжевый
15. пятьсот
16. стоит
17. почему
18. открытка
19. четырнадцать
20. лампа
21. кофе
22. картина
23. утро
24. слова
25. салат
26. стол
27. это

DOWN

1. когда
2. такси
3. коричневый
4. туалет
5. телефон
6. кто
7. сорок
8. или
9. сегодня
10. шестнадцать
11. пятьдесят
12. дверь
13. синий
14. балет
15. автомобиль
16. сколько
17. суп
18. как
19. почта
20. один
21. красный
22. пять
23. хочу
24. ноль
25. цвет
26. окно

CROSSWORD PUZZLE

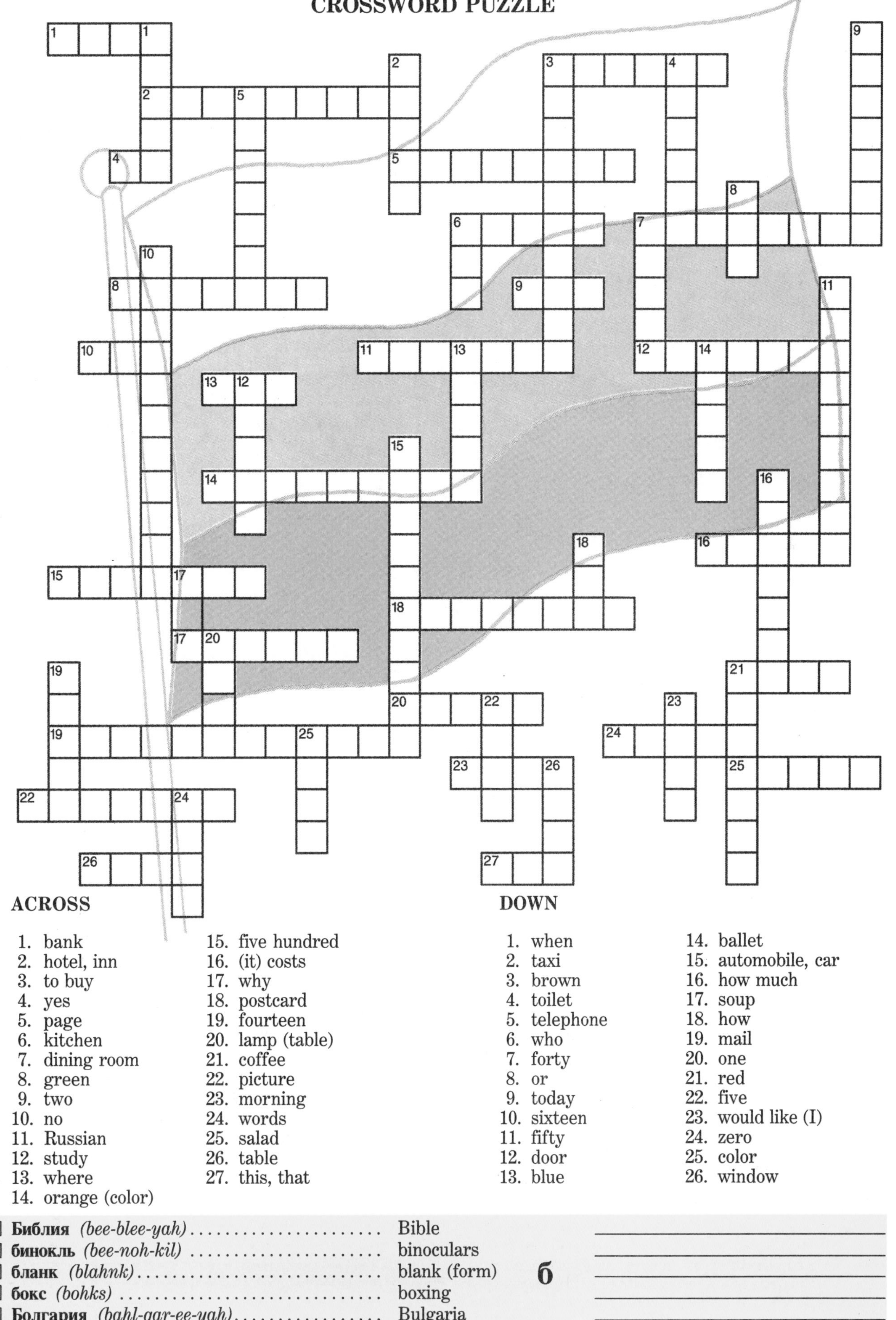

ACROSS

1. bank
2. hotel, inn
3. to buy
4. yes
5. page
6. kitchen
7. dining room
8. green
9. two
10. no
11. Russian
12. study
13. where
14. orange (color)
15. five hundred
16. (it) costs
17. why
18. postcard
19. fourteen
20. lamp (table)
21. coffee
22. picture
23. morning
24. words
25. salad
26. table
27. this, that

DOWN

1. when
2. taxi
3. brown
4. toilet
5. telephone
6. who
7. forty
8. or
9. today
10. sixteen
11. fifty
12. door
13. blue
14. ballet
15. automobile, car
16. how much
17. soup
18. how
19. mail
20. one
21. red
22. five
23. would like (I)
24. zero
25. color
26. window

☐ **Библия** *(bee-blee-yah)*	Bible	
☐ **бинокль** *(bee-noh-kil)*	binoculars	
☐ **бланк** *(blahnk)*	blank (form)	**б**
☐ **бокс** *(bohks)*	boxing	
☐ **Болгария** *(bahl-gar-ee-yah)*	Bulgaria	

9 В, на, под . . .

(vuh) (nah) (pohd)
in on under

Русские *(roos-skee-yeh)* Russian prepositions (words like "in," "on," "through" and "next to") are easy to learn, **и** *(ee)* they allow you to be precise **с** *(suh)* with a minimum of effort. Instead of having to point **шесть** *(shest)* six times at a piece of yummy pastry you would like, you can explain precisely which one you want by saying it is behind, in front of, next to **или** *(ee-lee)* under the piece of pastry that the salesperson is starting to pick up. Let's learn some of these **маленькие** *(mah-lyen-kee-ee)* little **слова.** words

(pohd) **под** ______ under	*(nah)* **на** ______ on, into
(nahd) **над** ______ over	*(pyeh-red)* **перед** ______ in front of
(myezh-doo) **между** ______ between	*(zah)* **за** ______ behind
(ryah-dahm) (suh) **рядом с** ______ next to	*(eez)* **из** ______ out of, from
(vuh) **в** ______ into, in	*(pee-rohg)* **пирог** ______ cake, pie, pastry!

Fill in the blanks on the next **странице** *(strah-neet-seh)* page with the correct prepositions according to those you just learned.

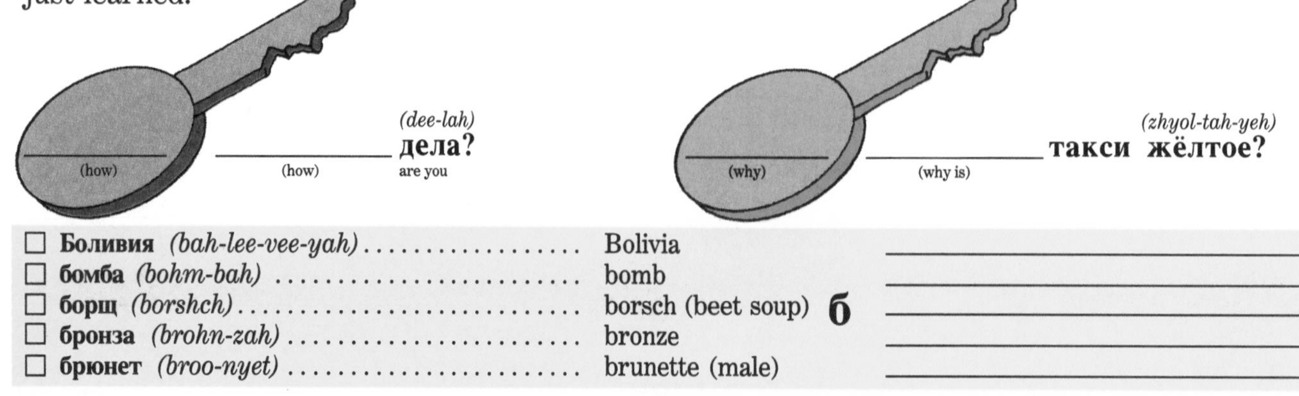

- ☐ **Боливия** *(bah-lee-vee-yah)* .... Bolivia
- ☐ **бомба** *(bohm-bah)* .... bomb
- ☐ **борщ** *(borshch)* .... borsch (beet soup) **б**
- ☐ **бронза** *(brohn-zah)* .... bronze
- ☐ **брюнет** *(broo-nyet)* .... brunette (male)

(pee-rohg) **Пирог** ________ *(stah-lyeh)* **столе.**
(on) table

(sah-bah-kah) **Собака** ________ *(stah-lohm)* **столом.**
dog (under) table

(vrahch) **Врач** ________ *(gah-stee-neet-seh)* **гостинице.**
doctor (in)

(gdyeh) **Где** *(vrahch)* **врач?** ________
doctor

(moozh-chee-nah) **Мужчина** ________ *(gah-stee-neet-say)* **гостиницей.**
man (in front of) hotel

Где *(moozh-chee-nah)* **мужчина?** ________
man

(teh-leh-fohn) **Телефон** ________ *(kar-tee-noy)* **картиной.**
telephone (next to) picture

Где *(teh-leh-fohn)* **телефон?** ________
telephone

(tyep-yair) **Теперь** (now) fill in each blank on the picture below with the best possible one of these *(mah-lyen-kee-ee)* **маленькие** (little) **слова.** (words) Do you recognize the towers of *(sah-boh-rah)* **Собора** *(vah-see-lee-yah)* **Василия** *(blah-zhen-nah-vah)* **Блаженного?**

________ (over)

________ (on)

________ (behind)

________ (next to)

________ (between)

________ (in)

________ (in front of)

________ (under)

- ☐ **бульвар** *(bool-var)* . . . . boulevard
- ☐ **бюрократ** *(byoo-rah-kraht)* . . . . bureaucrat
- ☐ **ваза** *(vah-zah)* . . . . vase
- ☐ **вальс** *(vahls)* . . . . waltz
- ☐ **Ватикан** *(vah-tee-kahn)* . . . . Vatican

б ________
____
____

в ________
____

10 В январе, феврале, марте

(vuh) (yahn-var-yeh) (fyev-rahl-yeh) (mart-yeh)
В январе, феврале, марте
in January February March

You have learned **дни недели** *(dnee) (nee-dyel-ee)* days (of) week, so now it is time to learn **месяцы года** *(myes-yet-sih) (go-dah)* months (of) year **и** all the different kinds of **погоды** *(pah-go-dih)* weather.

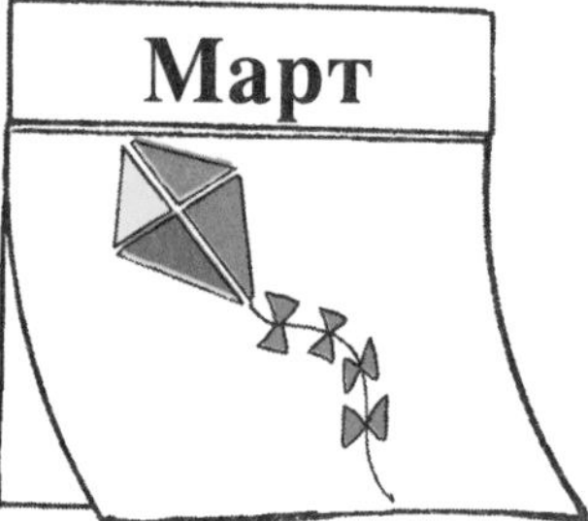

When someone asks, "**Какая сегодня погода?**" *(kah-kah-yah) (see-vohd-nyah) (pah-go-dah)* how is today weather, you have a variety of answers. Let's learn them but first, does this sound familiar?

(treed-tset) (dnay) (syen-tyah-bryeh) (ahp-ryel-yeh) (ee-yoon-yeh) (nah-yah-bryeh)
Тридцать дней в сентябре, апреле, июне и ноябре.
thirty days September April June November

- ☐ **веранда** *(vee-rahn-dah)* .... veranda
- ☐ **витамин** *(vee-tah-meen)* .... vitamin
- ☐ **водка** *(vohd-kah)* .... vodka
- ☐ **Волга** *(vohl-gah)* .... Volga River
- ☐ **волейбол** *(vah-lay-bohl)* .... volleyball

В

(kah-kah-yah) (see-vohd-nyah) (pah-go-dah)
Какая сегодня погода? ____________________

(vuh) (yahn-var-yeh) (ee-dyoht) (snyeg)
В январе идёт снег. ____________________
in January it snows

(fyev-rahl-yeh)
В феврале идёт снег. ____________________
February it snows

(mart-yeh) (dohzhd)
В марте идёт дождь. ____________________
it rains

(ahp-ryel-yeh) (dohzhd)
В апреле идёт дождь. ____________________

(mah-yeh) (vyet-ren-ah)
В мае ветрено. ____________________
windy

(ee-yoon-yeh) (vyet-ren-ah)
В июне ветрено. ____________________
June

(ee-yool-yeh) (zhar-kah)
В июле жарко. ____________________
hot

(ahv-goost-yeh)
В августе жарко. ____________________
hot

(syen-tyah-bryeh) (hah-roh-shah-yah) (pah-go-dah)
В сентябре хорошая погода. ____________________
September good weather

(ahk-tyah-bryeh) (hoh-lahd-nah)
В октябре холодно. ____________________
cold

(nah-yah-bryeh) (hoh-lahd-nah)
В ноябре холодно. ____________________
cold

(dee-kah-bryeh) (plah-hah-yah)
В декабре плохая погода. ____________________
bad

(kah-kah-yah) (pah-go-dah) (vuh) (fyev-rahl-yeh)
Какая погода в феврале? ____________________
how is February

(ahp-ryel-yeh)
Какая погода в апреле? ____________________
April

(nah-yah-bryeh)
Какая погода в ноябре? ____________________
November

(ahv-goost-yeh)
Какая погода в августе? ____________________
August

Г

☐ **газ** *(gahz)*	natural gas	____________
☐ **газета** *(gah-zyeh-tah)*	gazette, newspaper	____________
☐ **— газетчик** *(gah-zyet-cheek)*	newspaper man	____________
☐ **галерея** *(gahl-yair-eh-yah)*	gallery	____________
☐ **генерал** *(gee-nee-rahl)*	general	____________

Теперь for the seasons of **года** . . .
year

(zee-moy) **зимой** in winter	(lyet-ahm) **летом** in summer	(oh-syen-yoo) **осенью** in autumn	(vees-noy) **весной** in spring

______________ ______________ ______________ ______________

(tsel-see) **Цельсий** Celsius (fah-ren-gate) **Фаренгейт** Fahrenheit

°C	°F
100	212
37	98.6
20	68
0	32
-17.8	0
-23.3	-10

градусы

At this point, it is (hah-roh-shah-yah) **хорошая** (good) idea to familiarize yourself (suh) **с** (roos-skee-mee) **русскими** (tem-pee-rah-too-rah-mee) **температурами** (temperatures).

Carefully study the thermometer because (tem-pee-rah-too-rih) **температуры в России** are calculated on the basis of Celsius (not Fahrenheit).

To convert °C to °F, multiply by 1.8 and add 32.

37 °C x 1.8 = 66.6 + 32 = 98.6 °F

To convert °F to °C, subtract 32 and multiply by 0.55.

98.6 °F - 32 = 66.6 x 0.55 = 37 °C

(kah-kah-yah) **Какая температура** (nar-mahl-nah-yah) **нормальная** (normal) **по** (tsel-see-yoo) **Цельсию** (Celsius)**?**

Какая температура (zah-myair-zah-nee-yah) **замерзания** (freezing point) **по Цельсию?**

☐ **Греция** *(gret-see-yah)* . . . . Greece
☐ — where they speak **по-гречески** *(pah-greh-chee-skee)*
☐ **география** *(gee-ah-grah-fee-yah)* . . . . geography
☐ **геология** *(gee-ah-loh-gee-yah)* . . . . geology
☐ **— геолог** *(gee-oh-lahg)* . . . . geologist

Г

11 Семья и дом

(syem-yah) (dohm)
family house

One of the charming aspects **в** (vuh) **России** concerns names. A father's first name becomes the middle name for both his sons **и** daughters. Daughters add **-овна,** (ohv-nah) **-евна,** (yev-nah) or **-ична** (eech-nah) to the father's first name **а** (ah) (and) sons add **-ович,** (ah-veech) **-евич,** (yev-eech) or **-ич.** (eech) Both the individual's first name **и** the father's name (patronymic) are constantly used **по-русски.** (pah-roos-skee) Study the family tree below **и** then practice these new words on the next **странице.**

Анна Петровна
бабушка
grandmother

Николай Борисович
дедушка
grandfather

Иван Николаевич
отец
father

Нина Алексеевна
мать
mother

Мария Николаевна
тётя
aunt

Глеб Владимирович
дядя
uncle

Олег Иванович
сын
son

Зинаида Ивановна
дочь
daughter

- ☐ **геометрия** *(gee-ah-myet-ree-yah)* .... geometry
- ☐ **Гибралтар** *(gee-brahl-tar)* .... Gibraltar
- ☐ **гид** *(geed)* .... guide
- ☐ **гимнастика** *(geem-nah-stee-kah)* .... gymnastics
- ☐ **гитара** *(gee-tah-rah)* .... guitar

Г

Let's learn how to identify "**семья**" (*syem-yah*, family) by name. Study the following examples carefully.

Как (how) **вас** (*vahs*, are you) **зовут?** (*zah-voot*, called) ______________________

Меня (*men-yah*, I) **зовут** (*zah-voot*, am called) ______________________ (your name)

родители (*rah-dee-tee-lee*) — parents

отец (*aht-yets*, father) ______________________

Как (*kahk*, how) **зовут** (*zah-voot*, is called) **отца?** (*aht-tsah*, father) **Отца** (*aht-tsah*, father) **зовут** (*zah-voot*, is called) Иван

мать (*maht*, mother) ______________________

Как (*kahk*, how) **зовут** (*zah-voot*, is called) **мать?** (*maht*, mother) **Мать** (*maht*, mother) **зовут** (*zah-voot*, is called) ______________________

дети (*dyeh-tee*) — children

Сын (*sin*) **и дочь** (*dohch*) = **брат** (*braht*, brother) **и сестра!** (*see-strah*, sister)

сын (*sin*, son) ______________________

Как (*kahk*, how) **зовут** (*zah-voot*, is called) **сына?** (*sin-ah*, son) **Сына зовут** ______________________

дочь (*dohch*, daughter) ______________________

Как (*kahk*, how) **зовут** (*zah-voot*, is called) **дочь?** (*dohch*, daughter) **Дочь зовут** ______________________

родственники (*rohd-stveen-nee-kee*) — relatives

дедушка (*dyeh-doosh-kah*, grandfather) ______________________

Как (how) **зовут** (*zah-voot*, is called) **дедушку?** (*dyeh-doosh-koo*, grandfather) ______________________

бабушка (*bah-boosh-kah*, grandmother) ______________________

Как зовут бабушку? (*bah-boosh-koo*, grandmother) ______________________

Now you ask —

______________________ (how are you called, what's your name?)

And answer —

______________________ (my name is . . .)

Г

- ☐ **грамм** (*grahm*) . . . . gram ______________
- ☐ **гранит** (*grah-neet*) . . . . granite ______________
- ☐ **группа** (*groop-pah*) . . . . group ______________
- ☐ **ГУМ** (*goom*) . . . . department store in Moscow ______________
- ☐ **гусь** (*goose*) . . . . goose ______________

(koohk-nyah)
Кухня
kitchen

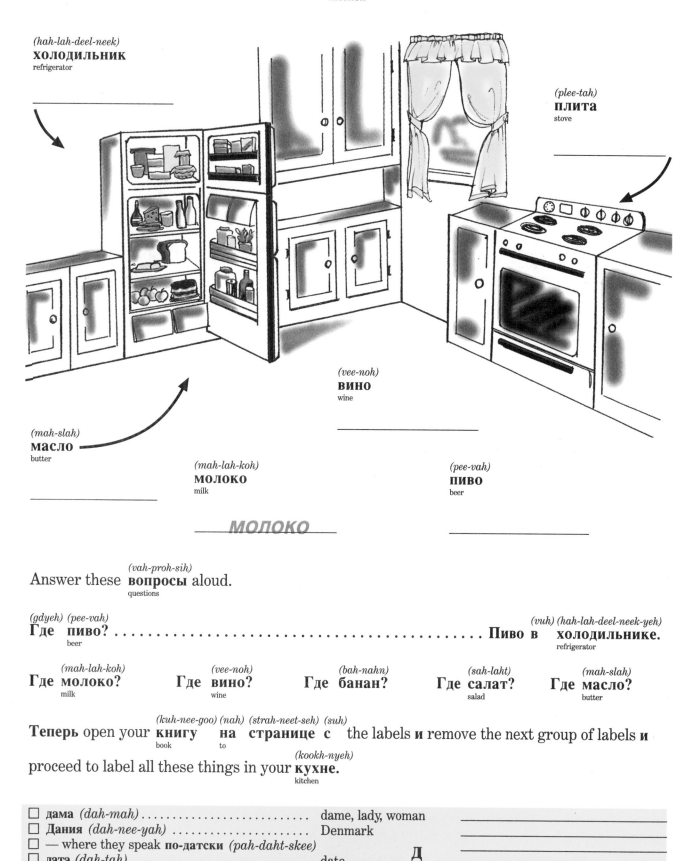

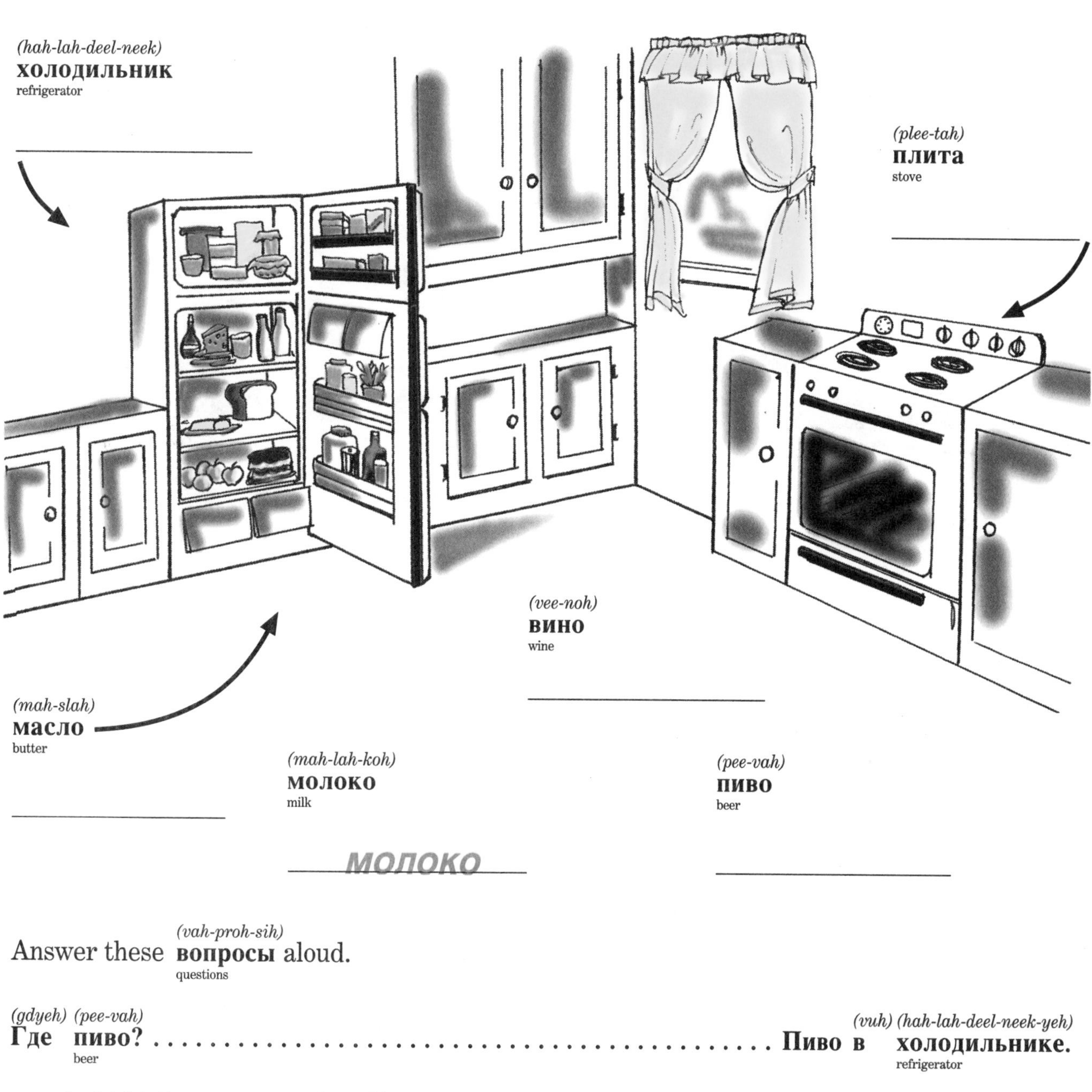

Answer these **вопросы** *(vah-proh-sih)* (questions) aloud.

Где *(gdyeh)* **пиво?** *(pee-vah)* (beer) . . . . **Пиво в** *(vuh)* **холодильнике.** *(hah-lah-deel-neek-yeh)* (refrigerator)

Где молоко? *(mah-lah-koh)* (milk) **Где вино?** *(vee-noh)* (wine) **Где банан?** *(bah-nahn)* **Где салат?** *(sah-laht)* (salad) **Где масло?** *(mah-slah)* (butter)

Теперь open your **книгу** *(kuh-nee-goo)* (book) **на** *(nah)* (to) **странице с** *(strah-neet-seh) (suh)* the labels **и** remove the next group of labels **и** proceed to label all these things in your **кухне.** *(kookh-nyeh)* (kitchen)

☐ **дама** *(dah-mah)*	dame, lady, woman		____________________
☐ **Дания** *(dah-nee-yah)*	Denmark		____________________
☐ — where they speak **по-датски** *(pah-daht-skee)*		**Д**	____________________
☐ **дата** *(dah-tah)*	date		____________________
☐ **делегат** *(dyeh-leh-gaht)*	delegate		____________________

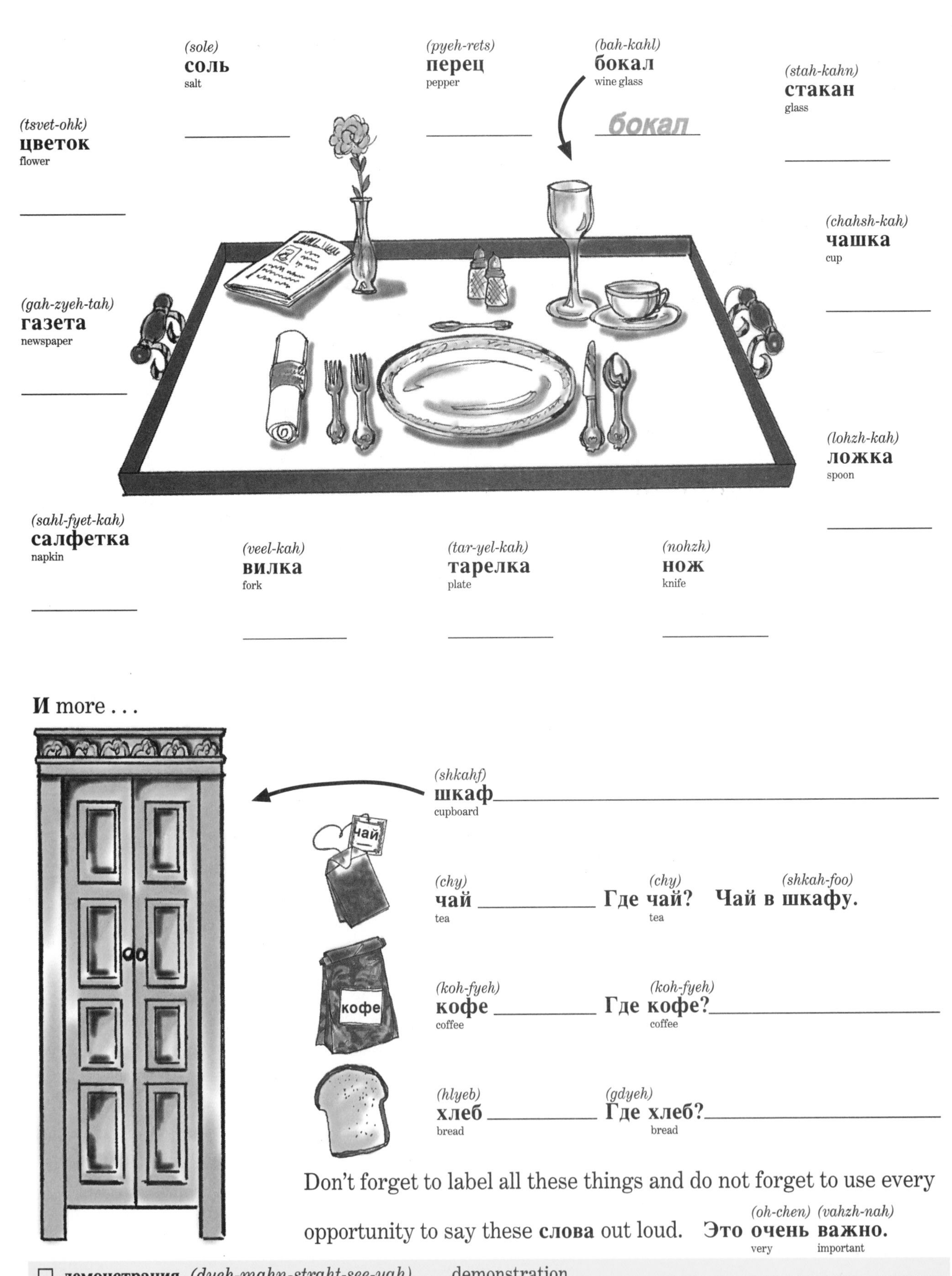

(sole) **соль** salt

(pyeh-rets) **перец** pepper

(bah-kahl) **бокал** wine glass

(stah-kahn) **стакан** glass

(tsvet-ohk) **цветок** flower

(chahsh-kah) **чашка** cup

(gah-zyeh-tah) **газета** newspaper

(lohzh-kah) **ложка** spoon

(sahl-fyet-kah) **салфетка** napkin

(veel-kah) **вилка** fork

(tar-yel-kah) **тарелка** plate

(nohzh) **нож** knife

И more . . .

(shkahf) **шкаф** ____________ cupboard

(chy) **чай** ____________ tea   **Где** *(chy)* **чай?** tea   **Чай в** *(shkah-foo)* **шкафу.**

(koh-fyeh) **кофе** ____________ coffee   **Где** *(koh-fyeh)* **кофе?** coffee ____________

(hlyeb) **хлеб** ____________ bread   *(gdyeh)* **Где** **хлеб?** bread ____________

Don't forget to label all these things and do not forget to use every opportunity to say these **слова** out loud. **Это** *(oh-chen)* **очень** very *(vahzh-nah)* **важно.** important

☐ **демонстрация** *(dyeh-mahn-straht-see-yah)* . .	demonstration	____________
☐ **джаз** *(dzhahz)*	jazz	____________
☐ **джин** *(dzheen)*	gin **Д**	____________
☐ **диагноз** *(dee-ahg-nahz)*	diagnosis	____________
☐ **диаграмма** *(dee-ah-grahm-mah)*	diagram, blueprint	____________

(krah-vaht)
кровать

(pah-doosh-kah)
подушка

(ah-dee-yah-lah)
одеяло

(boo-deel-neek)
будильник

(zyair-kah-lah)
зеркало

(oo-mih-vahl-neek)
умывальник

(pah-lah-tyent-sah)
полотенца

(too-ahl-yet)
туалет

(doosh)
душ

(kah-rahn-dahsh)
карандаш

(teh-leh-vee-zar)
телевизор

(rooch-kah)
ручка

(zhoor-nahl)
журнал

(kuh-nee-gah)
книга

(kahmp-yoo-tyer)
компьютер

(ahch-kee)
очки

(boo-mah-gah)
бумага

(kar-zee-nah)
корзина

(pees-moh)
письмо

(mar-kah)
марка

(aht-krit-kah)
открытка

(pahs-part)
паспорт

(beel-yet)
билет

(cheh-mah-dahn)
чемодан

(soom-kah)
сумка

(boo-mahzh-neek)
бумажник

(dyen-gee)
деньги

(kreh-deet-nah-yah) (kar-tahch-kah)
кредитная карточка

(dah-rohzh-nih-yeh) (cheh-kee)
дорожные чеки

(foh-tah-ahp-pah-raht)
фотоаппарат

(foh-tah-plyohn-kah)
фотоплёнка

(koo-pahl-nee) (kahst-yoom)
купальный костюм

(koo-pahl-nee) (kahst-yoom)
купальный костюм

(sahn-dahl-ee-ee)
сандалии

(tyohm-nih-yeh) (ahch-kee)
тёмные очки

(zoob-nah-yah) (shchoht-kah)
зубная щётка

(zoob-nah-yah) (pahs-tah)
зубная паста

(mwee-lah)
мыло

(breet-vah)
бритва

(dyeh-zah-dah-rahnt)
дезодорант

(rahs-chohs-kah)
расчёска

(pahl-toh)
пальто

(zohn-teek)
зонтик

(plahshch)
плащ

(pyair-chaht-kee)
перчатки

(shlyah-pah)
шляпа

(shlyah-pah)
шляпа

(sah-pah-gee)
сапоги

(too-flee)
туфли

(krahs-sohv-kee)
кроссовке

(kahst-yoom)
костюм

(gahl-stook)
галстук

(roo-bahsh-kah)
рубашка

(plah-tohk)
платок

(peed-zhahk)
пиджак

(bryoo-kee)
брюки

(dzheen-sih)
джинсы

(shohr-tih)
шорты

(my-kah)
майка

(troo-sih)
трусы

(my-kah)
майка

(plaht-yeh)
платье

(blooz-kah)
блузка

(yoob-kah)
юбка

(svee-tyair)
свитер

(kahm-bee-naht-see-yah)
комбинация

(leef-cheek)
лифчик

(troo-sih)
трусы

(nah-skee)
носки

(kahl-goht-kee)
колготки

(pee-zhah-mah)
пижама

(nahch-nah-yah) (roo-bahsh-kah)
ночная рубашка

(bahn-nee) (hah-laht)
банный халат

(tah-poach-kee)
тапочки

(yah) (ah-myeh-ree-kah-nyets)
Я американец

(yah) (hah-choo) (ee-zoo-chaht) (roos-skee)
Я хочу изучать русский

(men-yah) (zah-voot)
Меня зовут____________ .

PLUS . . .

This book includes a number of other innovative features unique to the ***"10 minutes a day®"*** series. At the back of this book, you will find twelve pages of flash cards. Cut them out and flip through them at least once a day.

On pages 118, 119 and 120 you will find a beverage guide and a menu guide. Don't wait until your trip to use them. Clip out the menu guide and use it tonight at the dinner table. Take them both with you the next time you dine at your favorite Russian restaurant.

When you are ready to leave, cut out your Pocket Pal™ and keep it with you at all times! By using the special features in this book, you will be speaking Russian before you know it.

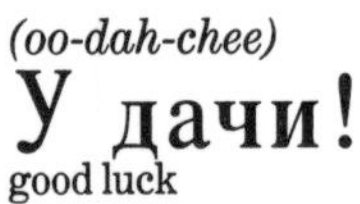

(ree-lee-gee-ee)
Религии
religions

(vuh) (ree-lee-gee-ee)
В России there is a wide variety of **религий.**
religions

(ree-lee-gee-yah)
A person's **религия** is usually one of the following.
religion

1. (prah-vah-slahv-nah-yah)
православная ____________
Orthodox woman

(prah-vah-slahv-nee)
православный ____________
Orthodox man

2. (yev-ray-kah)
еврейка ____________
Jewish woman

(yev-ray)
еврей еврей, еврей, еврей
Jewish man

3. (kah-tah-leech-kah)
католичка ____________
Catholic woman

(kah-toh-leek)
католик ____________
Catholic man

4. (moo-sool-mahn-kah)
мусульманка ____________
Moslem woman

(moo-sool-mah-neen)
мусульманин ____________
Moslem man

(mnoh-gah) (krah-see-vik) (tsair-kvay) (vuh)
You will see **много** (many) **красивых** (pretty) **церквей** (churches) like this during your holiday **в России. Теперь** let's learn how to say "I am" **по-русски** (pah-roos-skee): **я** (yah) (I am) я, я, я ____________

Test yourself - write each sentence on the next page for more practice. Add your own personal variations as well.

____________ (how much) ____________ (how much) **это?**

Д

☐ **диван** *(dee-vahn)*	divan, sofa	____________
☐ **дизель** *(dee-zyel)*	diesel	____________
☐ **диплом** *(dee-plohm)*	diploma	____________
☐ **дипломат** *(dee-plah-maht)*	diplomat	____________
☐ **директор** *(dee-rek-tar)*	director	____________

(kah-tah-leech-kah)
Я **католичка.** ____________
I (am)

(prah-vah-slahv-nah-yah)
Я **православная.** ____________

(yev-ray)
Я **еврей.** ____________

(ah-myeh-ree-kah-nyets)
Я **американец.** ____________
American

(vuh) (rahs-see-ee)
Я **в** **России.** ____________

(kah-nah-dyets)
Я **канадец.** ____________
Canadian

(yah) (vuh) (tsair-kvee)
Я **в** **церкви.** ____________
I (am) in church

(yah) (koohk-nyeh)
Я **в кухне.** ____________

(moo-sool-mah-neen)
Я **мусульманин.** ____________

(yev-ray-kah)
Я **еврейка.** ____________

(gah-stee-neet-seh)
Я **в** **гостинице.** ____________
hotel

(res-tah-rahn-yeh)
Я **в** **ресторане.** ____________
restaurant

(hah-choo) (yest)
Я **хочу** **есть.** ____________
want to eat, I'm hungry

(hah-choo) (peet)
Я **хочу** **пить.** ____________
want to drink, I'm thirsty

To negate any of these statements, simply add "**не**" (nyeh) (not) after "**Я.**"

(kah-tah-leech-kah)
Я **не** **католичка.** ____________
I (am) not

(yev-ray)
Я **не** **еврей.** ____________

Go through and drill these sentences again but with "**не.**" (nyeh)

Теперь take a piece of paper. Our **семья** (syem-yah) from earlier had a reunion. Identify everyone below by writing **правильное** (prah-veel-nah-yeh) (correct) **русское** (roos-skah-yeh) **слово** for each person — **мать,** (maht) **дочь** (dohch) and so on. Don't forget the **собака!** (sah-bah-kah)

☐ **дискуссия** *(dee-skoos-see-yah)*	discussion		____________
☐ **доктор** *(dohk-tar)*	doctor		____________
☐ **документ** *(dah-koo-myent)*	document	**Д**	____________
☐ **доллар** *(dohl-lar)*	dollar		____________
☐ **драма** *(drah-mah)*	drama		____________

12 Изучайте! (ee-zoo-chay-tee) learn

You have already used **два** very important verbs: **я** (yah) I **хочу** (hah-choo) would like and **у меня есть** (oo) (men-yah) (yest) I have. Although you might be able to get by with only these verbs, let's assume you want to do better. First a quick review.

How do you say **"I"** **по-русски?** (pah-roos-skee) ________________

How do you say **"we"** **по-русски?** ________________

Compare these **два** (dvah) two charts **очень** (oh-chen) very carefully **и** learn these **шесть** (shest) six **слов** (slohv) now.

I = **я** (yah)	________________	we = **мы** (mwee)	________________
he = **он** (ohn)	________________	you = **вы** (vwee)	________________
she = **она** (ah-nah)	________________	they = **они** (ah-nee)	________________

Not too hard, is it? Draw lines between the matching English **и русские** (roos-skee-yeh) **слова** (slah-vah) below to see if you can keep these **слова** straight in your mind.

(mwee) **мы**	I
(ohn) **он**	you
(ah-nee) **они**	he
(yah) **я**	we
(vwee) **вы**	she
(ah-nah) **она**	they

Ж

- ☐ **жакет** *(zhah-kyet)* . . . . jacket ________________
- ☐ **жасмин** *(zhahs-meen)* . . . . jasmine ________________
- ☐ **желе** *(zhel-yeh)* . . . . jelly ________________
- ☐ **журнал** *(zhoor-nahl)* . . . . journal, magazine ________________
- ☐ **— журналист** *(zhoor-nah-leest)* . . . . journalist ________________

(tyep-yair) **Теперь** close **книгу** *(ee)* **и** write out both columns of this practice on *(boo-mahg-yeh)* **бумаге** (paper). How did *(vwee)* **вы** do?

(hah-rah-shoh) **Хорошо** (good) *(ploh-hah)* **или** (or) **плохо?** (bad) *(hah-rah-shoh)* **Хорошо** (good) **или** *(nyet)* **нет?** (not) **Теперь** that *(vwee)* **вы** (you) know these **слова,** *(vwee)* **вы** (you) can say almost anything **по-русски** with one basic formula: the "plug-in" formula.

To demonstrate, let's take *(shest)* **шесть** (six) basic **и** practical verbs **и** see how the "plug-in" formula works. Write the verbs in the blanks after **вы** have practiced saying them out loud many times.

(zah-kah-zih-vaht) **заказывать** to order, to reserve	______	*(pahv-tar-yaht)* **повторять** to repeat	______
(pah-koo-paht) **покупать** to buy	покупать, покупать	*(pah-nee-maht)* **понимать** to understand	______
(ee-zoo-chaht) **изучать** to learn	______	*(gah-vah-reet)* **говорить** to speak	______

Besides the familiar words already circled, can *(vwee)* **вы** find *(cheh-tir-ee)* **четыре** of the above verbs in the puzzle below? When **вы** find them, write them in the blanks to the right.

Ю	К	О	Г	Д	А	С	Э	Ц	Ч	П
Ф	О	П	О	К	У	П	А	Т	Ь	Я
Э	Ш	Э	В	Ы	Ж	И	Г	Д	Е	Т
Ч	К	П	О	В	Т	О	Р	Я	Т	Ь
Й	А	Я	Р	К	Д	Ш	Ю	С	Р	Щ
П	О	Н	И	М	А	Т	Ь	Ё	И	Ф
О	Н	И	Т	Ц	Ы	К	Т	О	Й	Х
Х	А	З	Ь	Ж	В	Б	А	Л	Е	Т

1. ______
2. ______
3. ______
4. ______

☐ **зона** *(zoh-nah)*	zone		______
☐ **зоопарк** *(zah-ah-park)*	zoo	**З**	______
☐ **импортный** *(eem-part-nee)*	imported		______
☐ **Индия** *(een-dee-yah)*	India	**И**	______
☐ **индустриальный** *(een-doo-stree-ahl-nee)*	industrial		______

Study the following patterns carefully.

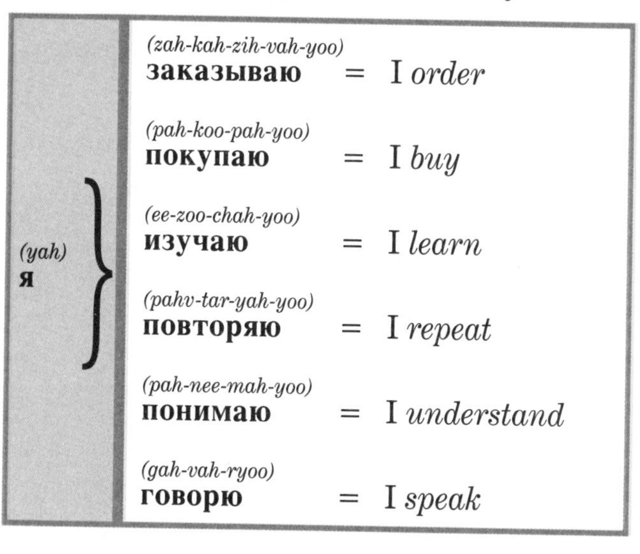

(yah) я	(zah-kah-zih-vah-yoo) **заказываю**	=	I *order*
	(pah-koo-pah-yoo) **покупаю**	=	I *buy*
	(ee-zoo-chah-yoo) **изучаю**	=	I *learn*
	(pahv-tar-yah-yoo) **повторяю**	=	I *repeat*
	(pah-nee-mah-yoo) **понимаю**	=	I *understand*
	(gah-vah-ryoo) **говорю**	=	I *speak*

(ohn) **он** / (ah-nah) **она**	(zah-kah-zih-vah-yet) **заказывает**	=	he/she *orders*
	(pah-koo-pah-yet) **покупает**	=	he/she *buys*
	(ee-zoo-chah-yet) **изучает**	=	he/she *learns*
	(pahv-tar-yah-yet) **повторяет**	=	he/she *repeats*
	(pah-nee-mah-yet) **понимает**	=	he/she *understands*
	(gah-vah-reet) **говорит**	=	he/she *speaks*

Note:
- With all these verbs, the first thing you do is drop the final "**ть**" from the basic verb form.
- With **я**, you add **-ю** *(yoo)* or **-у** *(oo)* to the basic verb form. This is basically the sound "*oo*."
- With **он** or **она**, you add the sound "*yet*" (**-ет**) to the basic verb form or the sound "*eet*" (**-ит**).

Some verbs just will not conform to the pattern! But don't worry. Speak slowly **и** clearly, **и** you will be perfectly understood whether you say *(ee-zoo-chah-yoo)* **изучаю** or *(ee-zoo-chah-yet)* **изучает**. **Русские** (Russians) will be delighted that you have taken the time to learn their language.

Here's your pattern for *(mwee)* **мы** (we). Add the sound "*yem*" (**-ем**) or "*eem*" (**-им**).

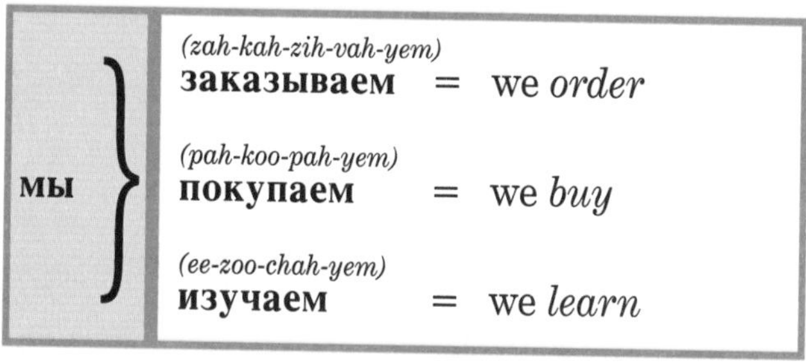

мы	(zah-kah-zih-vah-yem) **заказываем**	=	we *order*
	(pah-koo-pah-yem) **покупаем**	=	we *buy*
	(ee-zoo-chah-yem) **изучаем**	=	we *learn*

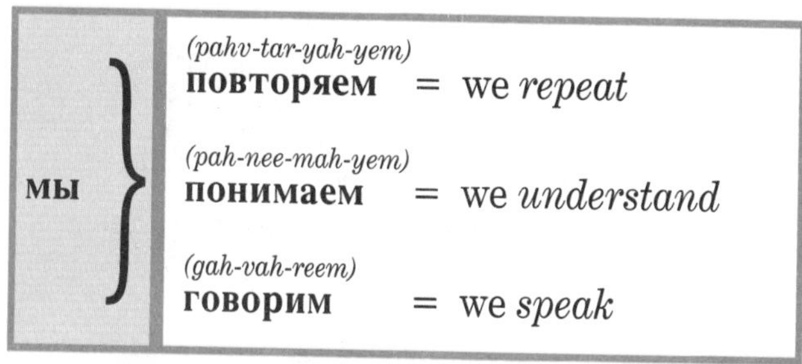

мы	(pahv-tar-yah-yem) **повторяем**	=	we *repeat*
	(pah-nee-mah-yem) **понимаем**	=	we *understand*
	(gah-vah-reem) **говорим**	=	we *speak*

И

- ☐ **инженер** *(een-zhyen-yair)* . . . . engineer
- ☐ **инспектор** *(een-spyek-tar)* . . . . inspector
- ☐ **институт** *(een-stee-toot)* . . . . institute
- ☐ **инструктор** *(een-strook-tar)* . . . . instructor
- ☐ **инструмент** *(een-stroo-myent)* . . . . instrument

Here's your pattern for *(vwee)* **вы.** Add the sound "*yet-yeh*" (**-ете**) or "*eet-yeh*" (**-ите**).

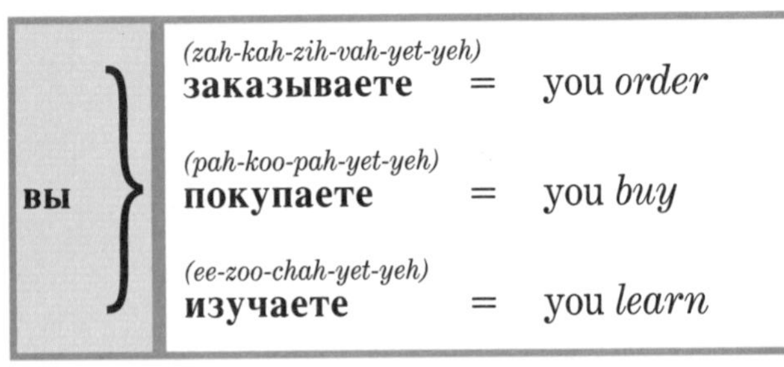

вы	*(zah-kah-zih-vah-yet-yeh)* **заказываете**	=	you *order*
	(pah-koo-pah-yet-yeh) **покупаете**	=	you *buy*
	(ee-zoo-chah-yet-yeh) **изучаете**	=	you *learn*

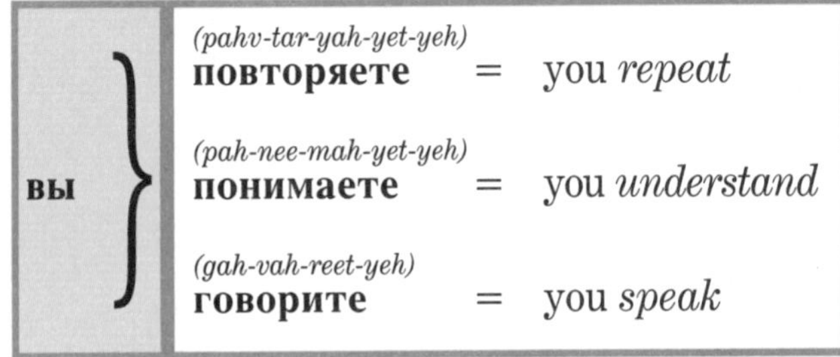

вы	*(pahv-tar-yah-yet-yeh)* **повторяете**	=	you *repeat*
	(pah-nee-mah-yet-yeh) **понимаете**	=	you *understand*
	(gah-vah-reet-yeh) **говорите**	=	you *speak*

Here's your pattern for *(ah-nee)* **они,** (they) which calls for the sound "*yoot*" (**-ют**) or sometimes "*yaht*" (**-ят**).

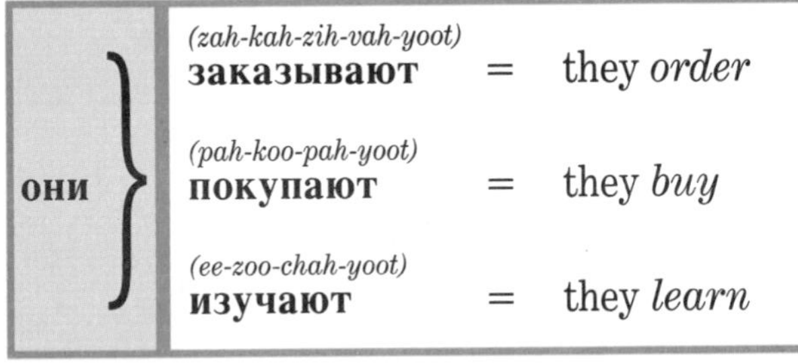

они	*(zah-kah-zih-vah-yoot)* **заказывают**	=	they *order*
	(pah-koo-pah-yoot) **покупают**	=	they *buy*
	(ee-zoo-chah-yoot) **изучают**	=	they *learn*

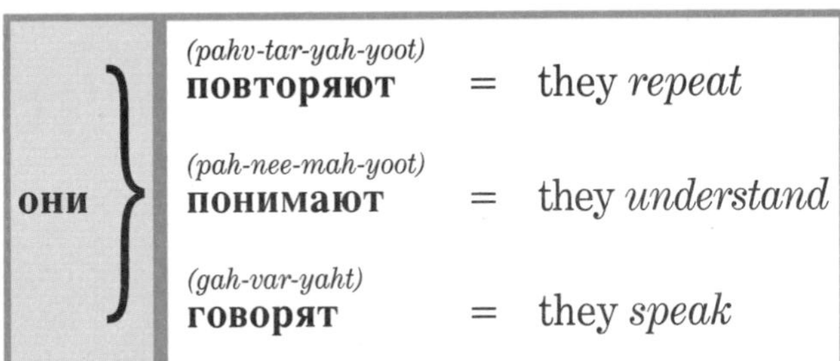

они	*(pahv-tar-yah-yoot)* **повторяют**	=	they *repeat*
	(pah-nee-mah-yoot) **понимают**	=	they *understand*
	(gah-var-yaht) **говорят**	=	they *speak*

(voht) **Вот** (here are) *(shest)* **шесть** (six) more verbs.

(yek-haht) **ехать** to go (by vehicle), to ride	______________
(pree-yez-zhaht) **приезжать** to arrive	______________
(vee-dyet) **видеть** to see	______________
(zheet) **жить** to live, to reside	______________
(zhdaht) **ждать** to wait for	______________
(ees-kaht) **искать** to look for	______________

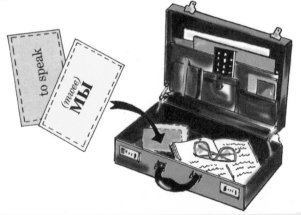

At the back of *(kuh-nee-gee)* **книги, вы** will find twelve *(strah-neets)* **страниц** (pages) of flash cards to help you learn *(noh-vih-yeh)* **новые** (new) **слова.** Cut them out; carry them in your briefcase, purse, pocket **или** knapsack; **и** review them whenever *(vwee)* **вы** have a free moment.

☐ **интеллигент** *(een-tyel-lee-gyent)*	intellectual	______________
☐ **интервью** *(een-tyair-view)*	interview	______________
☐ **интерес** *(een-tyair-yes)*	interest	**и** ______________
☐ **интернациональный** *(een-tyair-naht-see-ah-nahl-nee)*	international	______________
☐ **информация** *(een-far-maht-see-yah)*	information	______________

Теперь it is your turn to practice, **что** (shtoh) (what) **вы** (vwee) have learned. Fill in the following blanks with the correct form of the verb. Each time **вы** write out the sentence, be sure to say it aloud.

(zah-kah-zih-vaht)
заказывать
to order, to reserve

(yah) **Я** ______________________ **стакан** *(stah-kahn)* glass **воды.** *(vah-dih)* water

Он / Она ______________________ **бокал** *(bah-kahl)* **вина.** *(vee-nah)*

(mwee) **Мы** ______________________ **стакан молока.** *(mah-lah-kah)*

(vwee) **Вы** ______________________ **две чашки** *(chahsh-kee)* cups (of) **чая.** *(chah-yah)* tea

(ah-nee) **Они** ______________________ **три чашки кофе.** *(koh-fyeh)*

(pah-koo-paht)
покупать
to buy

Я ______________________ **книгу.** book

Он / Она покупает/______________________ **салат.**

Мы ______________________ **лампу.** *(lahm-poo)*

Вы ______________________ **часы.** *(chah-sih)* clock

Они ______________________ **билет.** *(beel-yet)* ticket

(ee-zoo-chaht)
изучать
to learn

Я ______________________ **русский.** *(roos-skee)* Russian

Он / Она ______________________ **русский.**

Мы ______________________ **английский.** *(ahn-glee-skee)* English

Вы изучаете/______________________ **английский.**

Они ______________________ **немецкий.** *(nee-myet-skee)* German

(pahv-tar-yaht)
повторять
to repeat

что? что? что?

(yah) **Я** ______________________ **слово.** *(sloh-vah)*

Он / Она ______________________ **ответы.** *(aht-vyet-ih)* answers

Мы ______________________ **ответы.**

Вы ______________________ **число.** *(chee-sloh)* numbers

Они ______________________ **вопросы.** *(vah-proh-sih)*

(pah-nee-maht)
понимать
to understand

Я ______________________ **по-английски.** *(pah-ahn-glee-skee)*

Он / Она ______________________ **по-русски.**

Мы ______________________ **по-немецки.** *(pah-nee-myet-skee)* German

Вы ______________________ **по-французски.** *(pah-frahn-tsoo-skee)* French

Они ______________________ **по-испански.** *(pah-ee-spahn-skee)* Spanish

(gah-vah-reet)
говорить
to speak, to say

Как дела?

Я ______________________ **по-русски.** *(pah-roos-skee)* Russian

Он / Она ______________________ **по-английски.**

Мы ______________________ **по-итальянски.** *(pah-ee-tahl-yahn-skee)* Italian

Вы ______________________ **по-русски.**

Они ______________________ **по-английски.**

☐	**Исландия** *(ees-lahn-dee-yah)*	Iceland		______________
☐	**история** *(ees-toh-ree-yah)*	history	**И**	______________
☐	**Италия** *(ee-tah-lee-yah)*	Italy		______________
☐	— where they speak **по-итальянски** *(pah-ee-tahl-yahn-skee)*		**К**	______________
☐	**кабина** *(kah-bee-nah)*	cabin, booth		______________

Now take a break, walk around the room, take a deep breath and do the next six verbs.

(yek-haht)
ехать
to go, to ride

Я ______________ *(vuh)* в (to) *(rahs-see-yoo)* **Россию.**

Он едет/ ______________ в *(mahsk-voo)* **Москву.**
Она

Мы едем/ ______________ в *(pyeh-tyair-boorg)* **Петербург.**

Вы ______________ в *(gah-stee-neet-soo)* **гостиницу.** (hotel)

Они ______________ в *(neezh-nee)* **Нижний** (Nizhny) *(nohv-gah-rohd)* **Новгород.** (Novgorod)

(pree-yez-zhaht)
приезжать
to arrive

Я ______________ *(eez)* **из** (from) *(mahsk-vih)* **Москвы.**

Он ______________ *(eez)* **из** *(kah-nah-dih)* **Канады.** (Canada)
Она

Мы ______________ **из** *(rahs-see-ee)* **России.**

Вы ______________ **из** *(pyeh-tyair-boor-gah)* **Петербурга.**

Они ______________ **из** *(ahv-strah-lee-ee)* **Австралии.** (Australia)

(vee-dyet)
видеть
to see

Я ______________ *(gah-stee-neet-soo)* **гостиницу.** (hotel)

Он ______________ *(tahk-see)* **такси.** (taxi)
Она

Мы видим/ ______________ *(res-tah-rahn)* **ресторан.** (restaurant)

Вы ______________ *(bahnk)* **банк.** (bank)

Они ______________ *(mahsk-voo)* **Москву.**

(zheet)
жить
to live, to reside

Я ______________ *(vuh)* **в** *(rahs-see-ee)* **России.**

Он живёт/ ______________ **в** *(ah-myeh-ree-kyeh)* **Америке.** (America)
Она

Мы живём/ ______________ **в** *(kah-nah-dyeh)* **Канаде.** (Canada)

Вы ______________ **в** *(ahn-glee-ee)* **Англии.** (England)

Они ______________ **в** *(ahv-strah-lee-ee)* **Австралии.** (Australia)

(zhdaht)
ждать
to wait for

Я ______________ *(tahk-see)* **такси.**

Он ______________ *(ahv-toh-boo-sah)* **автобуса.** (bus)
Она

Мы ждём/ ______________ *(ee-vah-nah)* **Ивана.** (Ivan)

Вы ждёте/ ______________ *(ahn-noo)* **Анну.** (Anna)

Они ______________ *(men-yoo)* **меню.** (menu)

(ess-kaht)
искать
to look for

Я ______________ *(mar-koo)* **марку.** (stamp)

Он ищет/ ______________ *(tsvet-ih)* **цветы.** (flowers)
Она

Мы ищем/ ______________ *(too-ahl-yet)* **туалет.**

Вы ______________ *(dohm)* **дом.** (house)

Они ______________ *(kuh-nee-goo)* **книгу.** (book)

- ☐ **камера** *(kah-myair-ah)* . . . . chamber, cell
- ☐ **Канада** *(kah-nah-dah)* . . . . Canada
- ☐ **канал** *(kah-nahl)* . . . . canal
- ☐ **канарейка** *(kah-nah-ray-kah)* . . . . canary
- ☐ **кандидат** *(kahn-dee-daht)* . . . . candidate

К

Да *(dah)* yes, it is hard to get used to all those **новым** *(noh-vim)* new **словам.** But just keep practicing **и** *(ee)*, before **вы** *(vwee)* know it, **вы** will be using them naturally. **Теперь** is a perfect time to turn to the back of this **книги** *(kuh-nee-gee)*, clip out your verb flash cards **и** start flashing. Don't skip over your free **слова** either. Check them off in the box provided as **вы изучаете** *(ee-zoo-chah-yet-yeh)* learn each one. See if **вы** *(vwee)* can fill in the blanks below. The correct **ответы** are at the bottom of **этой** *(et-toy)* this **страницы.**

1. ______________________________
(I speak Russian.)

2. ______________________________
(We learn Russian.)

3. ______________________________
(She understands English.)

4. ______________________________
(He arrives from America.)

5. ______________________________
(They live in Canada.)

6. ______________________________
(You buy a book.)

In the following Steps, **вы** *(vwee)* will be introduced to more verbs **и вы** should drill them in exactly the same way as **вы** *(vwee)* did in this section. Look up **новые** *(noh-vih-yeh)* new **слова** in your **словаре** *(slah-var-yeh)* dictionary **и** make up your own sentences. Try out your **новые** *(noh-vih-yeh)* new **слова** for that's how you make them yours to use on your holiday. Remember, the more **вы** *(vwee)* practice **теперь** *(tyep-yair)*, the more enjoyable your trip will be. **Удачи!** *(oo-dah-chee)* good luck

ОТВЕТЫ

1. **Я говорю по-русски.**
2. **Мы изучаем русский.**
3. **Она понимает по-английски.**
4. **Он приезжает из Америку.**
5. **Они живут в Канаде.**
6. **Вы покупаете книгу.**

13 Сколько времени?

(skohl-kah) (vreh-mee-nee)
Сколько времени?
what time is it

(vwee) **Вы** know, (kahk) **как** to tell (dnee) **дни** days (of) (nee-dyel-ee) **недели** week **и** (myeh-syet-sih) **месяцы** months (of) (go-dah) **года,** year so now let's learn to tell time. As a traveler (vuh) **в России, вы** need to be able to tell time in order to make (zah-kahz) **заказ** reservations **и** to catch (poh-yez-dah) **поезда** trains **и автобусы.** buses (voht) **Вот** here are the "basics."

What time is it?	=	(vreh-mee-nee) **Сколько времени?** ____
	=	(kah-toh-ree) (chahs) **Который час?** ____
o'clock, hour	=	(chahs) **час** ____
minutes	=	(mee-noot) **минут** ____
half	=	(pah-lah-vee-nah) **половина** ____
minus	=	(byez) **без** ____
a quarter toward	=	(chet-virt) **четверть** ____
a quarter from	=	(byez) (chet-virt-ee) **без четверти** ____

Теперь quiz yourself. Fill in the missing letters below.

hour = | ч | а | _ | minus = | б | _ | з | o'clock = | ч | а | _ |

quarter toward = | ч | е | т | _ | _ | _ | т | ь |

half = | п | о | _ | о | в | _ | _ | а | and finally

What time is it? | к | _ | т | _ | р | ы | _ | × | ч | _ | с | ? |

- ☐ **капитал** *(kah-pee-tahl)* . . . . capital (money) ____
- ☐ **— капиталист** *(kah-pee-tah-leest)* . . . . . capitalist ____
- ☐ **карамель** *(kah-rah-myel)* . . . . caramel **К** ____
- ☐ **класс** *(klahs)* . . . . class ____
- ☐ **классик** *(klahs-seek)* . . . . classic ____

Теперь, как are these **слова** used? Study **примеры** *(pree-myair-ih)* examples **внизу.** *(vnee-zoo)* below When **вы** think it through, it really is **не** *(nyeh)* not too difficult. Just notice that the pattern changes after the halfway mark. Through the halfway mark **вы** use the special endings **-ого** *(oh-vah/ah-vah)* and **-его.** *(yeh-vah)*

Пять **часов.** *(chah-sohv)* o'clock	5.00	Пять часов.
Десять *(dyes-yet)* ten **минут** *(mee-noot)* minutes (toward) **шестого.** *(shest-oh-vah)* sixth hour	5.10	
Четверть *(chet-virt)* **шестого.**	5.15	
Двадцать *(dvahd-tset)* twenty **минут** *(mee-noot)* minutes (toward) **шестого.** *(shest-oh-vah)* sixth hour	5.20	
Половина *(pah-lah-vee-nah)* half (of) **шестого.** sixth hour	5.30	
Без *(byez)* minus **двадцати** *(dvahd-tset-ee)* twenty (from) **шесть.** *(shest)* six	5.40	
Без четверти шесть.	5.45	
Без **десяти** *(dyes-yet-ee)* ten (from) **шесть.**	5.50	
Шесть **часов.** *(chah-shov)*	6.00	

See how **важно** important learning **числа** *(chee-slah)* numbers is? **Теперь** answer the following **вопросы** *(vah-proh-sih)* questions based on **часах** *(chah-sahk)* clocks below. **Ответы** are at the bottom of **страницы. Сколько** *(skohl-kah)* **времени?** *(vreh-mee-nee)*

1. 8.00 ____________________
2. 7.15 ____________________
3. 4.30 ____________________
4. 9.20 ____________________

ОТВЕТЫ

1. Восемь часов.
2. Четверть восьмого.
3. Половина пятого.
4. Двадцать минут десятого.

When *(vwee)* **вы** answer a *(kahg-dah)* **"когда"** (when) question, say *(vuh)* **"в"** (at) before *(vwee)* **вы** give the time. *(aht-vyet-ih)* **Ответы** *(vnee-zoo)* **внизу.**

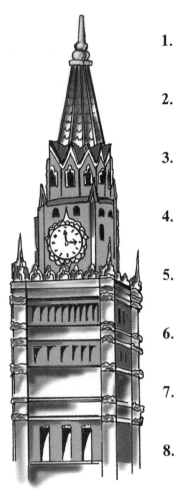

1. **Когда** *(pree-hoh-deet)* **приходит** (comes) *(poh-yezd)* **поезд?** (train) ______________________ (at 6:00)

2. *(kahg-dah)* **Когда** *(pree-hoh-deet)* **приходит** (comes) *(ahv-toh-boos)* **автобус?** (bus) ______________________ (at 7:30)

3. *(kahg-dah)* **Когда** *(nah-chee-nah-yet-syah)* **начинается** (begins) *(kahn-tsairt)* **концерт?** (concert) ______________________ (at 8:00)

4. *(kahg-dah)* **Когда** *(nah-chee-nah-yet-syah)* **начинается** (begins) *(feelm)* **фильм?** (film) ______________________ (at 9:00)

5. **Когда** *(aht-krih-vah-yet-syah)* **открывается** (opens) *(res-tah-rahn)* **ресторан?** (restaurant) ______________________ (at 11:30)

6. **Когда** *(aht-krih-vah-yet-syah)* **открывается** (opens) *(bahnk)* **банк?** (bank) ______________________ (at 8:30)

7. **Когда** *(zah-krih-vah-yet-syah)* **закрывается** (closes) **банк?** ______________________ (at 5:30)

8. **Когда** *(zah-krih-vah-yet-syah)* **закрывается** (closes) **ресторан?** ______________________ (at 10:30)

(voht) **Вот** a quick quiz. Fill in the blanks with the correct *(chee-slah-mee)* **числами** (numbers).

9. **В** *(vuh)* **минуте** *(mee-noot-yeh)* (minute (there are)) ______________ (?) **секунд.** *(see-koond)* (seconds)

10. **В часе** *(chahs-yeh)* (hour) ______________ (?) **минут.** (minutes)

11. **В неделе** *(nee-dyel-yeh)* ______________ (?) **дней.** *(dnay)* (days)

12. **В году** *(gah-doo)* ______________ (?) **месяцев.** *(myeh-syet-syev)* (months)

13. **В году** ______________ (?) **недели.** *(nee-dyel-ee)* (weeks)

14. **В году** ______________ (?) **дней.**

ОТВЕТЫ

1. в шесть часов
2. в половине восьмого
3. в восемь часов
4. в девять часов
5. в половине двенадцатого
6. в половине девятого
7. в половине шестого
8. в половине одиннадцатого
9. шестьдесят
10. шестьдесят
11. семь
12. двенадцать
13. пятьдесят две
14. триста шестьдесят пять

Do **вы** remember your greetings from earlier? It is a good time to review them as they will always be *(oh-chen)* **очень** (very) *(vahzh-nih-yeh)* **важные** (important).

(vuh) **В** (at) *(voh-syem)* **восемь часов** *(oo-trah)* **утра** (in morning) **мы** *(gah-vah-reem)* **говорим** (say) *(doh-brah-yeh)* **"Доброе** (good) *(oo-trah)* **утро** (morning), **Мария** *(nee-kah-lah-yev-nah)* **Николаевна."**

(shtoh) **Что** (what) *(mwee)* **мы говорим?** Доброе утро, Мария Николаевна.

В *(chahs)* **час** (one) *(den-yah)* **дня** (in afternoon) *(mwee)* **мы говорим "Добрый** *(dyen)* **день, Иван** *(nee-kah-lah-yev-eech)* **Николаевич."**

(shtoh) **Что** *(mwee)* **мы говорим?** ______________________________

В восемь *(chah-sohv)* **часов** *(vyeh-cheh-rah)* **вечера** (in evening) **мы говорим** *(doh-brih)* **"Добрый** *(vyeh-cher)* **вечер, Анна** *(pee-trohv-nah)* **Петровна."**

(shtoh) **Что** *(mwee)* **мы говорим?** ______________________________

В *(dyes-yet)* **десять** (ten) **часов вечера** (in evening) **мы говорим** *(spah-koy-nay)* **"Спокойной** (good) *(noh-chee)* **ночи** (night), *(zee-nah-ee-dah)* **Зинаида."**

(shtoh) **Что** *(mwee)* **мы говорим?** ______________________________

(pah-roos-skee) **По-русски** (in Russian), the letter **"е"** is often pronounced *"yeh"* (as in the English word "yes"). When a letter such as **с, н, б, д** or **п** precedes the *"yeh"* sound, they can combine to make one sound. For example, the *(roos-skah-yeh)* **русское слово** for "no" is **"нет"** pronounced like "net" with a "y": *"nyet."* As you practice each of the following words, combine the sound of *"yeh"* with the letter that precedes it, making one, smooth sound.

(gdyeh) **где** where	*(syem)* **семь** seven	*(kah-bee-nyet)* **кабинет** study
(zdyes) **здесь** here	*(dyev-yet)* **девять** nine	*(byeh-lee)* **белый** white
(dyeh-tee) **дети** children	*(dyes-yet)* **десять** ten	*(syeh-ree)* **серый** gray

К

- ☑ **клоун** *(kloh-oon)* .... clown — клоун, клоун, клоун, клоун, клоун
- ☐ **коллекция** *(kahl-yekt-see-yah)* .... collection
- ☐ **командир** *(kah-mahn-deer)* .... commander
- ☐ **комедия** *(kah-myeh-dee-yah)* .... comedy
- ☐ **комиссар** *(kah-mees-sar)* .... commissar

Вот *(noh-vih-yeh)* **новые** (new) verbs for Step 13.

(yest) **есть** to eat ______________________

(peet) **пить** to drink ______________________

(yest) **есть** to eat

(yah) **Я** ______________________ *(soop)* **суп.**

Он / **Она** ______________________ *(borshch)* **борщ.**

Мы ______________________ *(mnoh-gah)* **много.** a lot

Вы ______________________ *(hlyeb)* **хлеб.** bread

Они ______________________ *(rih-bo)* **рыбу.** fish

пить to drink

Я пью/ ______________________ **молоко.** milk

Он / **Она** ______________________ *(byeh-lah-yeh)* **белое** white *(vee-noh)* **вино.**

(mwee) **Мы** пьём/ ______________________ *(pee-vah)* **пиво.**

Вы ______________________ *(vah-doo)* **воду.**

Они ______________________ *(chy)* **чай.** tea

As **вы** have probably noticed, the sound of the Russian letter "**й**" varies greatly. Here are some examples.

(kar-teen-koy) **картинкой** picture	*(yev-ray-kah)* **еврейка** Jewish woman	*(moo-zay)* **музей** museum	*(chy)* **чай** tea	*(syeh-ree)* **серый** gray

К

- ☐ **коммунист** *(kahm-moo-neest)* . . . . communist ______________________
- ☐ **компас** *(kohm-pahs)* . . . . compass ______________________
- ☐ **композитор** *(kahm-pah-zee-tar)* . . . . composer ______________________
- ☐ **конференция** *(kahn-fyair-yent-see-yah)* . . . . . conference ______________________
- ☐ **концерт** *(kahn-tsairt)* . . . . concert ______________________

(vwee)
Вы have learned a lot of material in the last few steps **и** that means it is time to quiz yourself. Don't panic, this is just for you **и** no one else needs to know how **вы** did. Remember, this is a chance to review, find out, *(shtoh)* **что вы** remember **и что вы** need to spend more time on. After **вы** have finished, check your *(aht-vyet-ih)* **ответы** in the glossary at the back of this book. Circle the correct answers.

кофе -	tea	coffee
нет -	yes	no
дядя -	aunt	uncle
или -	and	or
изучать -	to drink	to learn
ночь -	morning	night
вторник -	Friday	Tuesday
видеть -	to see	to look for
жарко -	cold	hot
деньги -	money	page
десять -	nine	ten
много -	many	bread

семья -	seven	family
дети -	children	grandfather
молоко -	butter	milk
соль -	pepper	salt
под -	under	over
врач -	man	doctor
июнь -	June	July
религии -	kitchen	religions
у меня есть -	I want	I have
жить -	to wait for	to live/reside
завтра -	yesterday	tomorrow
хорошо -	good	yellow

Как дела? What time is it? How are you? Well, how are you after this quiz?

☐ **коньяк** *(kahn-yahk)* .... cognac
☐ **корт** *(kort)* .... court (tennis)
☐ **кот** *(koht)* .... cat (male)
☐ **краб** *(krahb)* .... crab
☐ **Куба** *(koo-bah)* .... Cuba

К

(syev-yair) Север (north) - *(yoog)* юг (south), *(vah-stohk)* восток (east) - *(zah-pahd)* запад (west)

If *(vwee)* **вы** are looking at *(kar-too)* **карту** (map) **и вы** see the following **слова**, it should *(nyeh)* **не** (not) be too difficult to figure out, *(shtoh)* **что** (what) *(ah-nee)* **они** (they) mean. Take an educated guess. **Ответы** *(vnee-zoo)* **внизу.** (below)

(syev-yair-nah-yah) **Северная** *(dah-koh-tah)* **Дакота**	*(yoozh-nah-yah)* **Южная Дакота**
Северная *(ah-myeh-ree-kah)* **Америка**	**Южная Америка**
Северная *(kah-rah-lee-nah)* **Каролина**	**Южная Каролина**
Северная *(kah-reh-yah)* **Корея**	**Южная** *(ah-free-kah)* **Африка**

Do **вы** recognize **русское** *(sloh-vah)* **слово** for east in *(vlah-dee-vah-stohk)* **"Владивосток"**? Here it means "eastern domain." *(vlah-dee-vah-stohk)* **Владивосток** is the easternmost seaport in **России.** It is also the terminus of the Trans-Siberian Railroad, 5700 miles east of *(mahsk-vih)* **Москвы.** (Moscow)

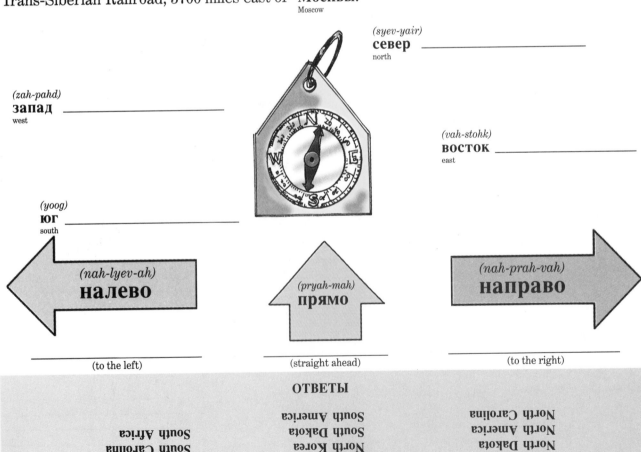

(syev-yair) **север** (north) ______________________

(zah-pahd) **запад** (west) ______________________

(vah-stohk) **восток** (east) ______________________

(yoog) **юг** (south) ______________________

(nah-lyev-ah) **налево** ______________________ (to the left)

(pryah-mah) **прямо** ______________________ (straight ahead)

(nah-prah-vah) **направо** ______________________ (to the right)

ОТВЕТЫ

North Dakota
North America
North Carolina
North Korea
South Dakota
South America
South Carolina
South Africa

These **слова** can go a long way. Say them aloud each time you write them in the blanks below.

(pah-zhahl-oos-tah)
пожалуйста ______________________________
please

(spah-see-bah)
спасибо ______________________________
thank you

(eez-vee-neet-yeh)
извините ______________________________
excuse me

(pah-zhahl-oos-tah)
пожалуйста ______________________________
you're welcome

(voht) **Вот** *(dvah)* **два** (two) typical *(dee-ah-loh-gah)* **диалога** (dialogues) *(dil-yah)* **для** (for) someone who is trying to find something. Write them out.

(bar-ees) **Борис:** *(eez-vee-neet-yeh)* **Извините.** (excuse me) **Где** *(gah-stee-neet-sah)* **гостиница** (hotel) *(oo-krah-ee-nah)* **Украина?** (Ukraina)

Извините. Где гостиница Украина?

(lyen-ah) **Лена:** *(prah-ee-dyoht-yeh)* **Пройдёте** (go) *(doh)* **до** (to) *(oo-leet-sih)* **улицы** (street) *(gairt-sen-ah)* **Герцена** **и** **там** (there) *(nah-prah-vah)* **направо.** (to the right)

____

(gah-stee-neet-sah) **Гостиница** *(oo-krah-ee-nah)* **Украина** *(nah)* **на** (on) *(oo-gloo)* **углу.** (corner)

____

(ahl-yeg) **Олег:** *(eez-vee-neet-yeh)* **Извините.** (excuse me) **Где** *(moo-zay)* **музей** (museum) *(tahl-stoh-vah)* **Толстого?** (Tolstoy)

____

(ohl-gah) **Ольга:** *(prah-ee-dyoht-yeh)* **Пройдёте** (go) *(nah-prah-vah)* **направо;** (to the right) *(pah-tohm)* **потом** (then) *(pryah-mah)* **прямо** (straight ahead) *(doh)* **до** (to) *(oo-leet-sih)* **улицы** (street)

____

(tahl-stoh-vah) **Толстого.** (Tolstoy) **Там** *(nah-lyev-ah)* **налево,** (to the left) **и** *(moo-zay)* **музей** *(nah)* **на** (on) *(oo-gloo)* **углу.** (corner)

____

Л

- ☐ **лаборатория** *(lah-bah-rah-toh-ree-yah)* ..... laboratory ______________
- ☐ **лимон** *(lee-mohn)* .... lemon ______________
- ☐ **— лимонад** *(lee-mah-nahd)* .... lemonade ______________
- ☐ **линия** *(lee-nee-yah)* .... line ______________
- ☐ **литература** *(lee-tyair-ah-too-rah)* .... literature ______________

Are **вы** *(vwee)* lost? There is no need to be lost if **вы** *(vwee)* have learned the basic direction **слова.** Do not try to memorize these **диалоги** *(dee-ah-loh-gee)* dialogues because **вы** will never be looking for precisely these places. One day, **вы** might need to ask **дорогу** *(dah-roh-goo)* directions to the **Большой** *(bahl-shoy)* Bolshoi **театр,** *(tee-ah-ter)* Theater **ГУМ** *(goom)* GUM Department Store or **Кремль.** *(kreml)* Kremlin Learn the key direction **слова и** be sure **вы** can find your destination. **Вы** may want to buy a guidebook to start planning which places **вы** would like to visit. Practice asking **дорогу** *(dah-roh-goo)* directions to these special places. What if the person responding to your **вопрос** *(vah-prohs)* answers too quickly for **вы** to understand the entire reply? Practice saying,

Извините. excuse me **Я** *(yah)* I **не** *(nyeh)* (do) not **понимаю.** *(pah-nee-mah-yoo)* understand **Пожалуйста,** *(pah-zhahl-oos-tah)* please **повторите!** *(pahv-tah-reet-yeh)* repeat **Спасибо.** *(spah-see-bah)*

Теперь say it again **и** then write it out below.

____
(Excuse me. I do not understand. Please repeat. Thank you.)

Да, *(dah)* yes, it is difficult at first but don't give up! **Когда** *(kahg-dah)* when the directions are repeated, **вы** will be able to understand if **вы** have learned the key **слова.** Let's review.

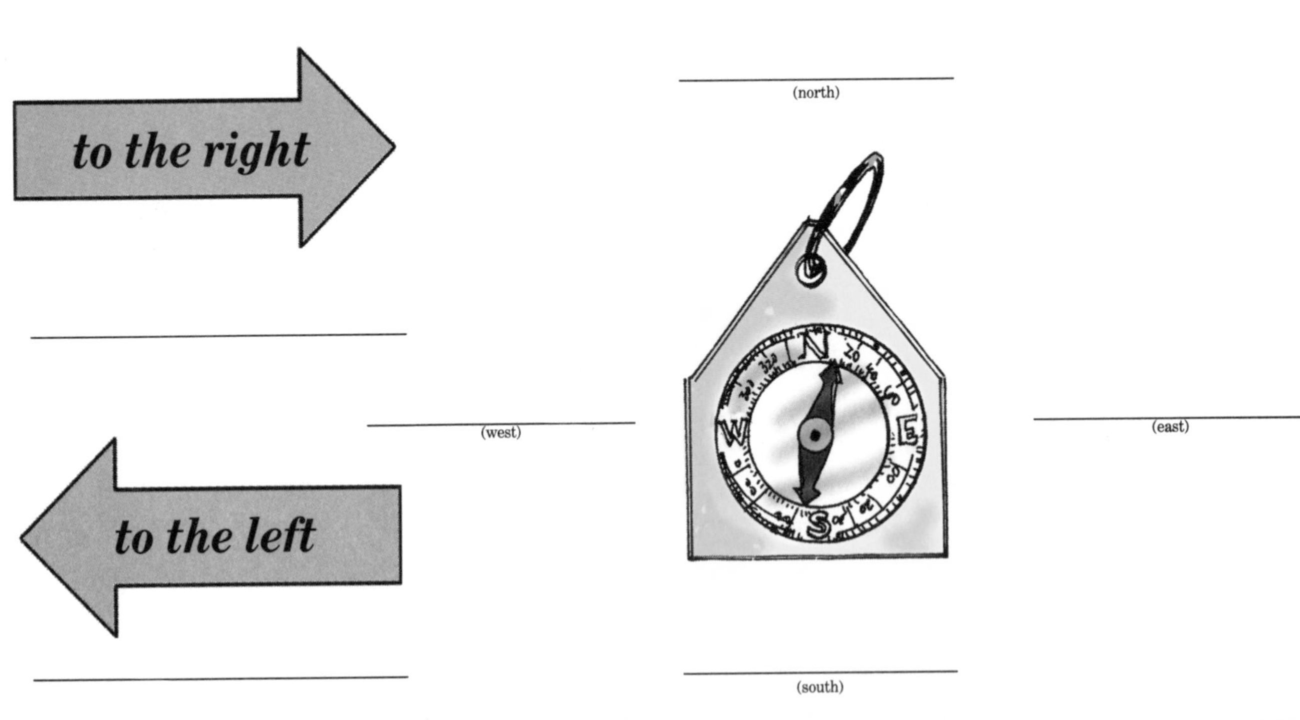

☐ **май** *(my)*	May		__________
☐ **март** *(mart)*	March		__________
☐ **масса** *(mahs-sah)*	mass	**M**	__________
☐ **мастер** *(mahs-tyair)*	master		__________
☐ **математика** *(mah-tyeh-mah-tee-kah)*	mathematics		__________

Вот (cheh-tir-ee) четыре (noh-vik) новых (new) verbs. (ah-nee) Они (they) are different from the patterns **вы** have learned, so pay close attention. **Вы** will probably use these verbs more than any others.

(yah) (hah-choo) **я хочу** — I would like ________	(men-yeh) (noozh-nah) **мне нужно** — I need ________
(men-yah) (zah-voot) **меня зовут** — my name is ________	(oo) (men-yah) (yest) **у меня есть** — I have ________

As always, say each sentence out loud. Say each **и** every **слово** carefully, pronouncing each **русский** sound as well as **вы** can.

(yah) (hah-choo)
я хочу
I would like

Я ________ (bah-kahl) **бокал** (glass of) (vee-nah) **вина.**

Он / **Она** ________ **стакан** (mah-lah-kah) **молока.**

(mwee) **Мы** хотим/ ________ **стакан** (vah-dih) **воды.**

Вы ________ **две** (chahsh-kee) **чашки** (cups (of)) (koh-fyeh) **кофе.**

Они (they) ________ **три чашки** (chah-yah) **чая.**

(men-yeh) (noozh-nah)
мне нужно
I need

(men-yeh) **Мне** ________ (stah-kahn) **стакан** (lee-mah-nah-dah) **лимонада.** (lemonade)

(ee-moo) **Ему** / (yay) **Ей** ________ **стакан молока.**

Нам ________ **три** (chahsh-kee) **чашки** (chah-yah) **чая.**

(vahm) **Вам** ________ **две чашки чая.**

(eem) **Им** ________ **три чашки** (kah-kah-oh) **какао.** (cocoa)

(men-yah) (zah-voot)
меня зовут . . .
my name is

(men-yah) **Меня** ________ (nah-tahl-yah) **Наталья.**

(yee-voh) **Его** / (yee-yoh) **Её** ________ **Олег/Ольга.**

(nahs) **Нас** (our names are) ________ (bar-ees) **Борис и** (lyen-ah) **Лена.**

(vahs) **Вас** (your name is) ________ (ahn-tohn) **Антон.**

(eehk) **Их** (their names are) ________ (ahn-nah) **Анна и** (pyoh-ter) **Пётр.**

(oo) (men-yah) (yest)
у меня есть
I have

(oo) **У** (men-yah) **меня** ________ (pyaht) **пять** (tih-syahch) **тысяч** (roo-blay) **рублей.**

У (nyeh-voh) **него** / **У** (nyeh-yoh) **неё** ________ (shest) **шесть тысяч рублей.**

У нас есть/ ________ (dveh) **две** (tih-syah-chee) **тысячи рублей.**

У (vahs) **вас** ________ (voh-syem) **восемь тысяч рублей.**

У (neehk) **них** ________ (dyev-yet) **девять тысяч рублей.**

М

- ☐ **материя** *(mah-tyair-ee-yah)* . . . . material ________
- ☐ **матч** *(mahtch)* . . . . match (game) ________
- ☐ **машина** *(mah-shee-nah)* . . . . machine (car) ________
- ☐ **медаль** *(myeh-dahl)* . . . . medal ________
- ☐ **медик** *(myeh-deek)* . . . . medic ________

15 Наверху (nah-vyair-hoo) upstairs - внизу (vnee-zoo) downstairs, below

Теперь (tyep-yair) let's learn **больше** (bohl-shee) more **слов. Дом в** (dohm)(vuh) **Киеве** (kee-yev-yeh) Kiev. Go to your **спальню** (spahl-nyoo) bedroom **и** look around the **комнаты** (kohm-nah-tih) room. Let's learn the names of the things **в спальне** (spahl-nyeh) bedroom, just like **мы** (mwee) learned the various parts of **дома** (do-mah).

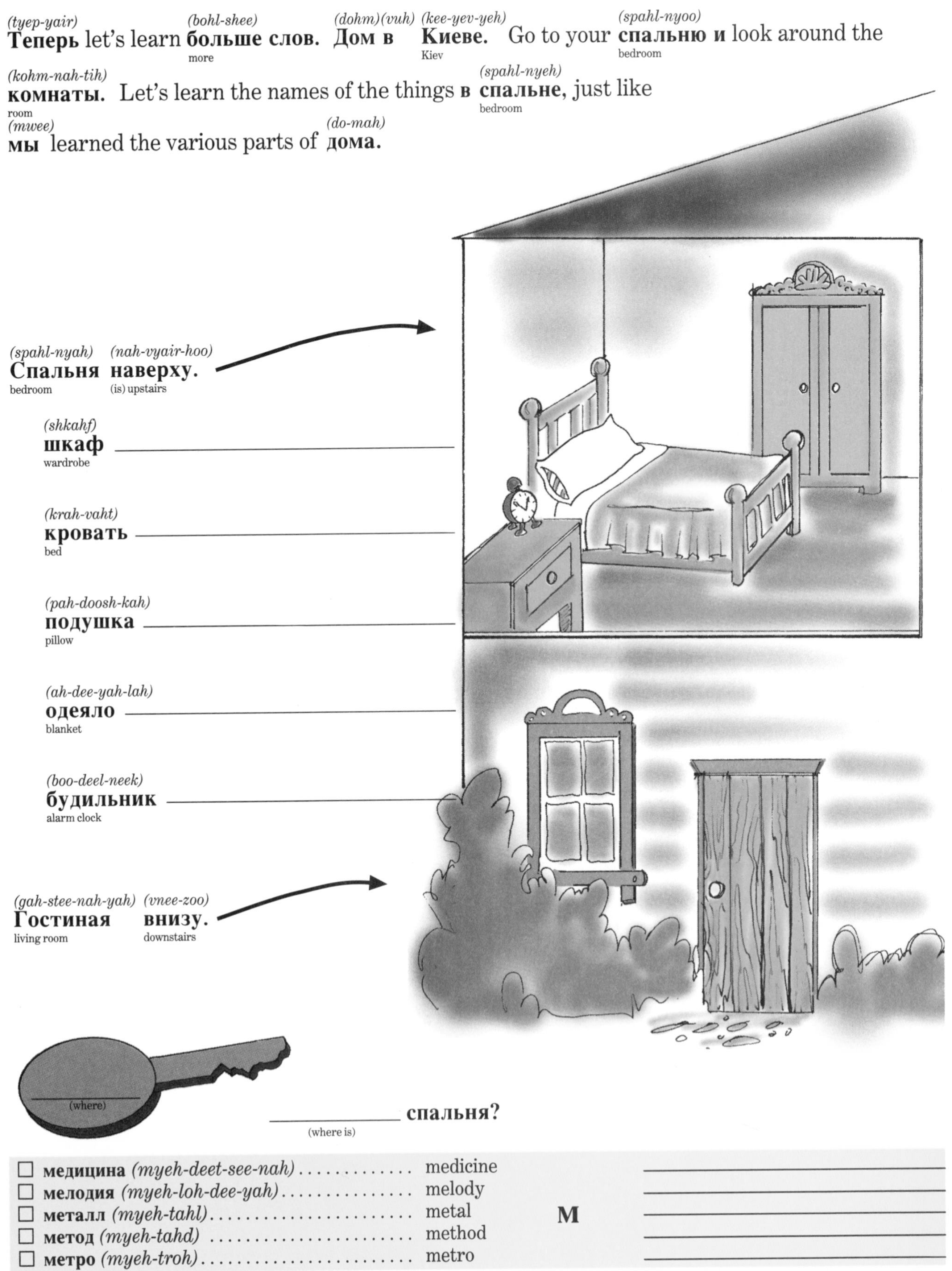

Спальня (spahl-nyah) bedroom **наверху** (nah-vyair-hoo) (is) upstairs.

шкаф (shkahf) wardrobe ______________________

кровать (krah-vaht) bed ______________________

подушка (pah-doosh-kah) pillow ______________________

одеяло (ah-dee-yah-lah) blanket ______________________

будильник (boo-deel-neek) alarm clock ______________________

Гостиная (gah-stee-nah-yah) living room **внизу** (vnee-zoo) downstairs.

______________ (where)

______________ (where is) **спальня?**

☐ **медицина** *(myeh-deet-see-nah)*	medicine		______________
☐ **мелодия** *(myeh-loh-dee-yah)*	melody		______________
☐ **металл** *(myeh-tahl)*	metal	**M**	______________
☐ **метод** *(myeh-tahd)*	method		______________
☐ **метро** *(myeh-troh)*	metro		______________

Теперь (*pyaht*), remove the next **пять** stickers **и** label these things **в** (*vuh*) your **спальне** (*spahl-nyeh*). Let's move **в** (*vwee*) (into) **ванную** (*vahn-noo-yoo*) (bathroom) **и** do the same thing. Remember, **ванная** (*vah-nah-yah*) means a **комната** (room) to bathe in. If **вы в ресторане, и вам** (you) **нужно** (need) to use the lavatory, **вы** want to ask for **туалет** (*too-ahl-yet*) not for **ванная** (*vahn-nah-yah*).

Restrooms are marked with the letters **Ж и М.** This should be easy to remember as **M** stands for men's just as it does in English.

Ж = **женский** (*zhen-skee*) — ladies' (restroom)

М = **мужской** (*moozh-skoy*) — men's (restroom)

Ванная (*vahn-nah-yah*) (bathroom) **тоже** (*toh-zheh*) (also) **наверху** (*nah-vyair-hoo*).

зеркало (*zyair-kah-lah*) — mirror ____________________

умывальник (*oo-mih-vahl-neek*) — washstand ____________________

полотенца (*pah-lah-tyent-sah*) — towels ____________________

туалет (*too-ahl-yet*) — toilet ____________________

душ (*doosh*) — shower ____________________

Кабинет (*kah-bee-nyet*) (study) **тоже** (*toh-zheh*) (also) **внизу** (*vnee-zoo*) (downstairs).

☐ **механик** (*myeh-hah-neek*)	mechanic	M	____________
☐ **микрофон** (*mee-krah-fohn*)	microphone		____________
☐ **миллион** (*meel-lee-ohn*)	million		____________
☐ **миниатюра** (*mee-nee-ah-tyoo-rah*)	miniature		____________
☐ **миссия** (*mees-see-yah*)	mission		____________

(nyeh)
Не forget to remove the next group of stickers **и** label these things in your **ванной** *(vahn-noy)* bathroom. Okay, it is time to review. Here's a quick quiz to see what you remember.

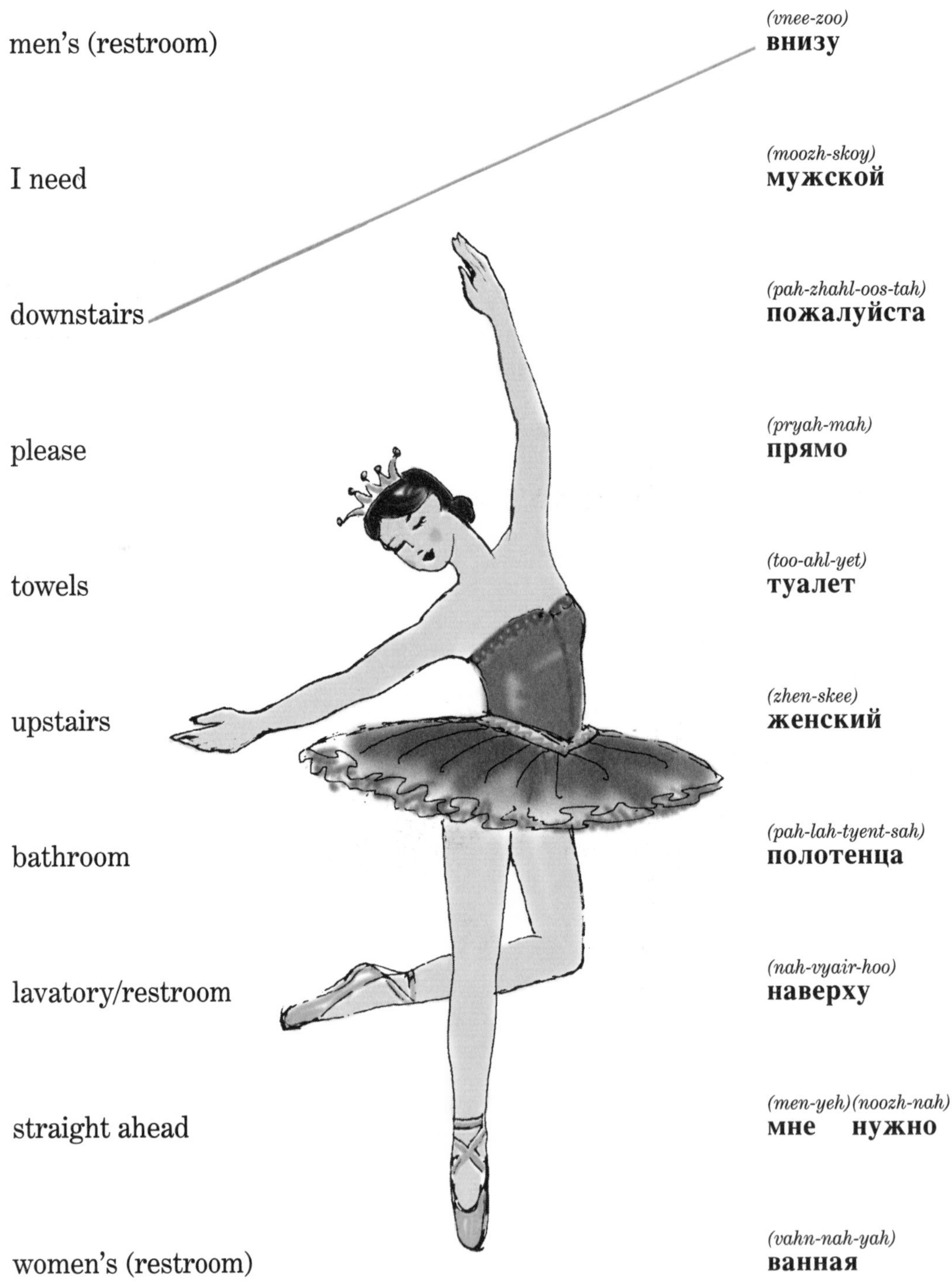

men's (restroom)	*(vnee-zoo)* **внизу**
I need	*(moozh-skoy)* **мужской**
downstairs	*(pah-zhahl-oos-tah)* **пожалуйста**
please	*(pryah-mah)* **прямо**
towels	*(too-ahl-yet)* **туалет**
upstairs	*(zhen-skee)* **женский**
bathroom	*(pah-lah-tyent-sah)* **полотенца**
lavatory/restroom	*(nah-vyair-hoo)* **наверху**
straight ahead	*(men-yeh)(noozh-nah)* **мне нужно**
women's (restroom)	*(vahn-nah-yah)* **ванная**

☐ **митинг** *(mee-teeng)*...................... meeting ________________
☐ **модель** *(mah-dyel)*....................... model ________________
☐ **момент** *(mah-myent)*..................... moment **М** ________________
☐ **мотор** *(mah-tor)*......................... motor ________________
☐ **муза** *(moo-zah)*.......................... muse ________________

Next stop — **кабинет** *(kah-bee-nyet)* study, specifically **стол в кабинете.** *(stohl)* desk, table *(kah-bee-nyet-yeh)* study **Что на столе?** *(shtoh)* what Let's identify things which one normally finds **на столе** or strewn about **дома.**

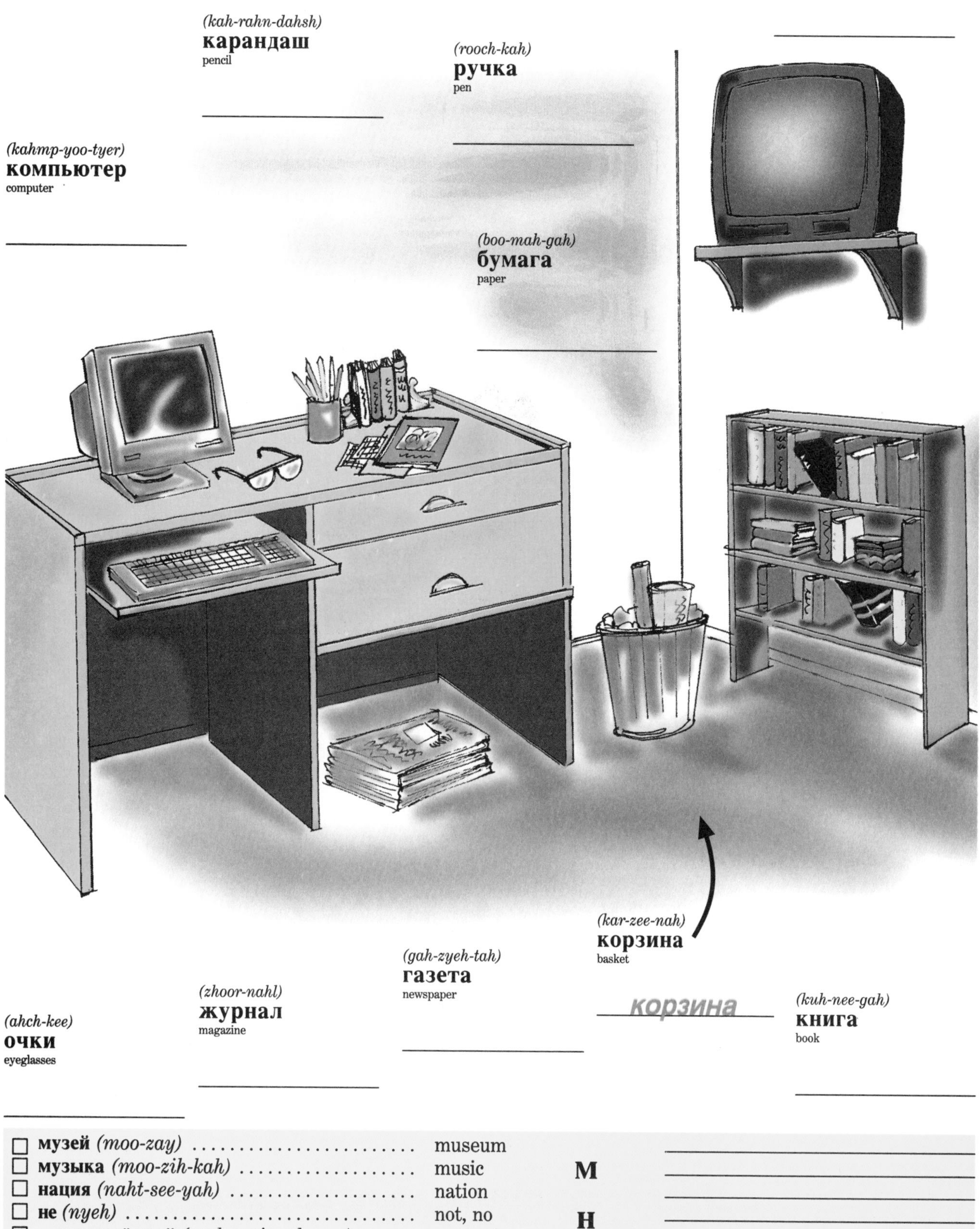

- ☐ **музей** *(moo-zay)* . . . . museum
- ☐ **музыка** *(moo-zih-kah)* . . . . music
- ☐ **нация** *(naht-see-yah)* . . . . nation
- ☐ **не** *(nyeh)* . . . . not, no
- ☐ — **несерьёзный** *(nyeh-syair-yohz-nee)* . . . . not serious

М

Н

Don't forget these essentials!

(pees-moh) **письмо** letter

(mar-kah) **марка** stamp

(aht-krit-kah) **открытка** postcard

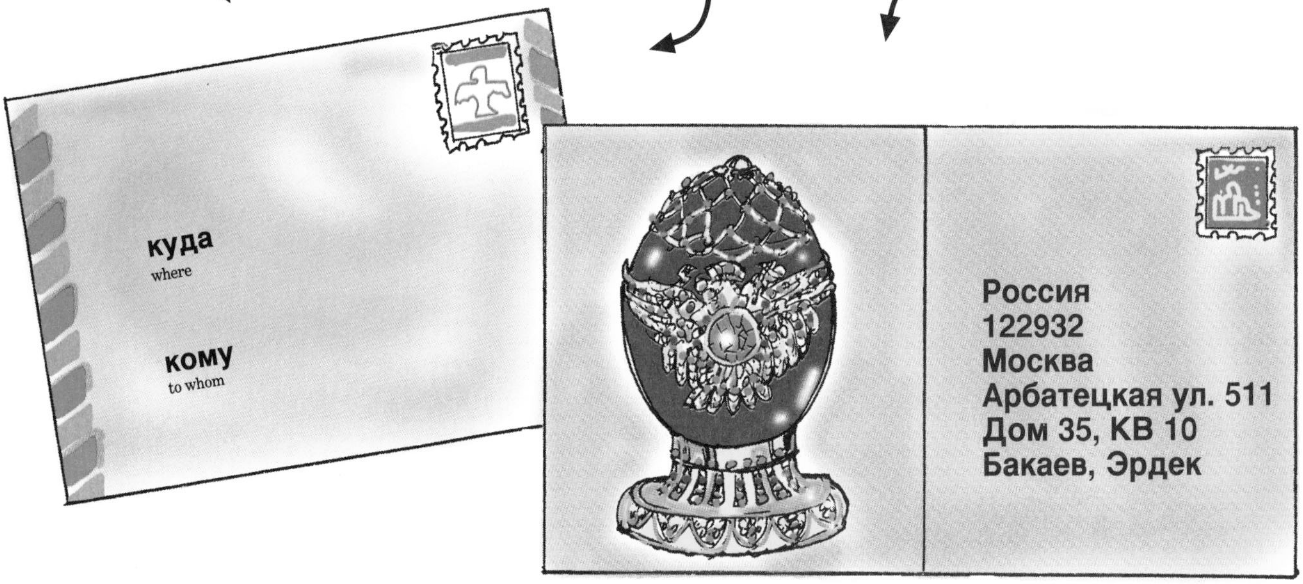

куда
where

кому
to whom

Россия
122932
Москва
Арбатецкая ул. 511
Дом 35, КВ 10
Бакаев, Эрдек

_______________ (letter) _______________ (stamp) _______________ (postcard)

You can purchase *(kahn-vyair-tih-ah-vee-ah)* **конверты-авиа** which are special airmail envelopes. *(ah-vee-ah)* **Авиа** is short for *(ah-vee-ah-poach-toy)* **"авиапочтой."** (by airmail) Did **вы** notice that Russian addresses are written in reverse order starting with the country, zip code, street, bulding and apartment numbers and ending with the name?

Теперь label these things **в кабинете** *(kah-bee-nyet-yeh)* with your stickers. Do not forget to say these **слова** out loud whenever **вы** write them, **вы** see them **или вы** apply the stickers.

Remember *(nyeh)* **<u>не</u>** (not) is extremely useful **по-русски.** Add **<u>не</u>** before a verb **и вы** negate the sentence.

Я	**хочу**	**бокал**	**вина.**
I	would like	a glass	wine

Я	**не хочу**	**бокал**	**вина.**
I	would not like	a glass	wine

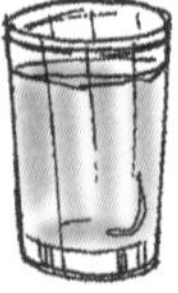

Simple, isn't it? **Теперь,** after you fill in the blanks on the next page, go back a second time

Н

- ☐ **нейлон** *(nay-lohn)* . . . . nylon _______________
- ☐ **нет!** *(nyet)* . . . . no! _______________
- ☐ **никель** *(neek-yehl)* . . . . nickel _______________
- ☐ **норма** *(nor-mah)* . . . . norm, standard _______________
- ☐ **нос** *(nohs)* . . . . nose _______________

and negate all these sentences by adding **"не"** before each verb. Practice saying these sentences out loud many times. Don't get discouraged! Just look at how much **вы** have already learned **и** think ahead to *(ee-krah)* **икра** (caviar), *(bahl-yet)* **балет и** adventure.

(prah-dah-vaht) **продавать** to sell ________________	*(pah-sih-laht)* **посылать** to send ________________
(spaht) **спать** to sleep ________________	*(zvah-neet)* **звонить** to phone ________________

(prah-dah-vaht)
продавать
to sell

Я ________________ *(tsvet-ih)* **цветы.** (flowers)

Он / Она ________________ *(frook-tih)* **фрукты.** (fruit)

Мы ________________ *(beel-yet-ih)* **билеты.**

Вы ________________ *(mnoh-gah)* **много** (many) *(beel-yet-ahv)* **билетов.**

Они ________________ *(aht-krit-kee)* **открытки.**

(pah-sih-laht)
посылать
to send

Я ________________ *(pees-moh)* **письмо.** (letter)

Он / Она ________________ *(aht-krit-koo)* **открытку.**

Мы посылаем/________________ *(kuh-nee-goo)* **книгу.**

Вы ________________ *(cheh-tir-ee)* **четыре** *(aht-krit-kee)* **открытки.**

Они ________________ **три** *(pees-mah)* **письма.**

(spaht)
спать
to sleep

Я ________________ *(vuh)* **в** *(spahl-nyeh)* **спальне.** (bedroom)

Он / Она ________________ **на** *(krah-vah-tee)* **кровати.**

Мы ________________ **в гостинице.**

Вы ________________ **в доме.**

Они ________________ **под** (under) *(ah-dee-yah-lahm)* **одеялом.** (blanket)

(zvah-neet)
звонить
to phone

Я ________________ **в** *(pyeh-tyair-boorg)* **Петербург.**

Он / Она ________________ **в** *(seh-sheh-ah)* **США.** (U.S.A.)

Мы ________________ **в** *(kah-nah-doo)* **Канаду.**

Вы ________________ **в** *(ahn-glee-yoo)* **Англию.** (England)

Они ________________ **во Владивосток.**

☐ **Норвегия** *(nar-vyeh-gee-yah)*	Norway		________________
☐ — where they speak **по-норвежски** *(pah-nar-vyezh-skee)*		**Н**	________________
☐ **ноябрь** *(nah-yah-bair)*	November		________________
☐ **октябрь** *(ahk-tyah-bair)*	October	**О**	________________
☐ **олимпиада** *(ah-leem-pee-ah-dah)*	Olympics		________________

Before **вы** proceed with the next step, *(pah-zhahl-oos-tah)* **пожалуйста** identify all the items *(vnee-zoo)* **внизу.**

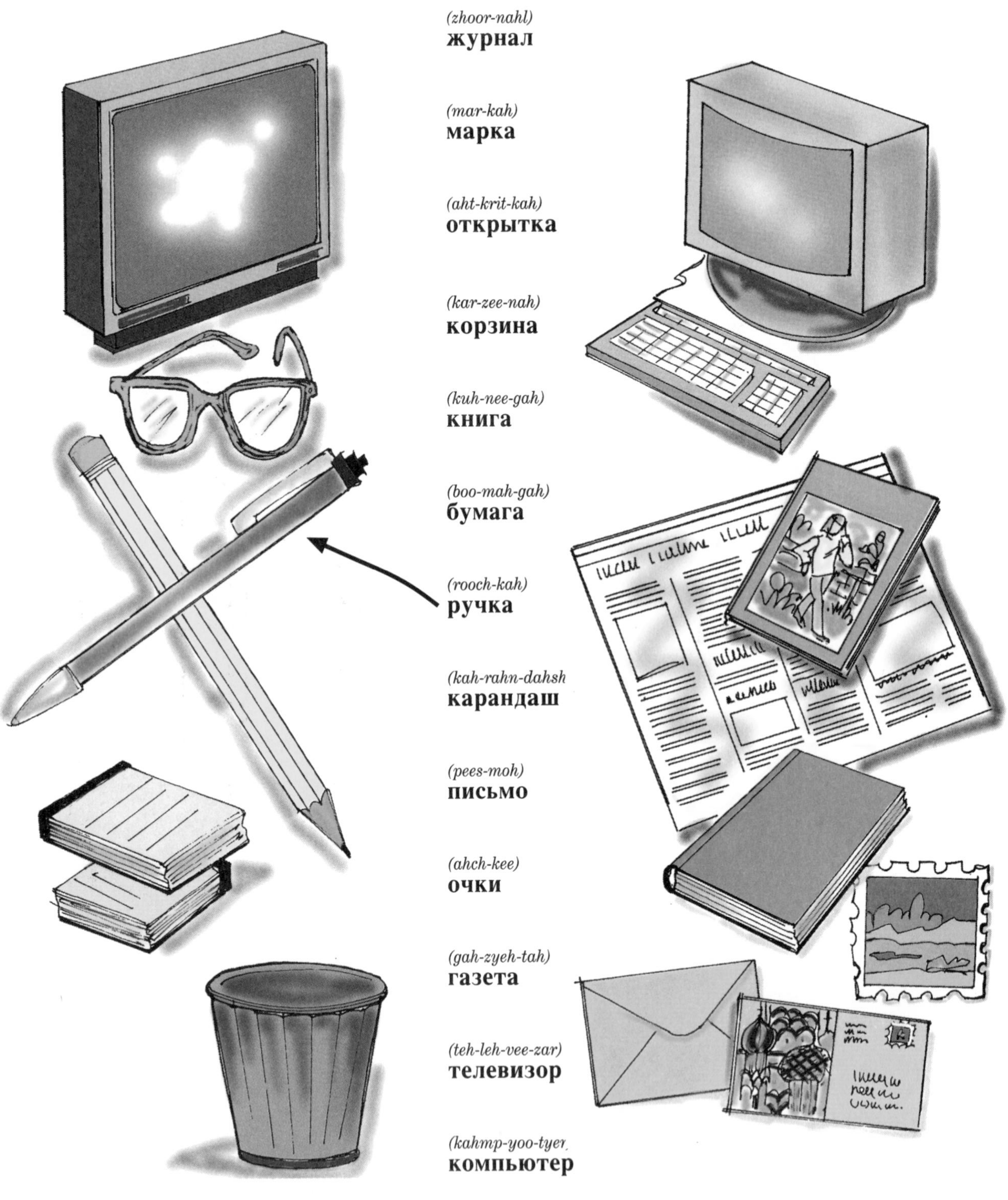

- ☐ **опера** *(oh-pyair-ah)* . . . . opera
- ☐ **органист** *(ar-gah-neest)* . . . . organist
- ☐ **оркестр** *(ar-kyes-tair)* . . . . orchestra
- ☐ **офицер** *(ah-feet-syair)* . . . . officer
- ☐ **официальный** *(ah-feet-see-ahl-nee)* . . . . official

О

16 Почта (poach-tah)

mail, post office

Теперь вы (vwee) know, **как** (kahk) to count, **как** to ask **вопросы** (vah-proh-sih), **как** to use verbs **с** (suh) the "plug-in" formula, **как** to make statements **и как** to describe something, be it the location of **гостиница или цвет** (tsvet) [color (of)] **дома** [house]. Let's take the basics that **вы** have learned **и** expand them in special areas that will be most helpful in your travels. What does everyone do on a holiday? Send **открытки** (aht-krit-kee), of course! Let's learn exactly **как почта** (poach-tah) works because **почта в России** has everything.

Почта is where **вы** buy **марки** (mar-kee) **и конверты** (kahn-vyair-tih) [envelopes], send **посылки** (pah-sil-kee) [packages], **письма** (pees-mah) [letters] **и открытки** (aht-krit-kee). **Вы** can send **телеграмму** (teh-leh-grahm-moo) [telegram] or use **междугородний** (myezh-doo-gah-rohd-nee) [long-distance] **и международный** (myezh-doo-nah-rohd-nee) [international] **телефон на почте.** On **субботам** [Saturdays] **и воскресеньям** (vah-skree-syen-yahm) [Sundays] **почта закрыта** (zah-krih-tah) [closed].

☐ **павильон** *(pah-veel-yohn)*	pavilion	
☐ **пакет** *(pah-kyet)*	package	
☐ **Пакистан** *(pah-kee-stahn)*	Pakistan	**П**
☐ **парад** *(pah-rahd)*	parade	
☐ **парк** *(park)*	park	

(voht) **Вот** *(here are)* the necessary **слова** *(dil-yah)* **для** *(for)* *(poach-tih)* **почты.** *(post office)* Practice them aloud **и** write **слова** in the blanks.

(kahn-vyairt)
конверт
envelope

____

(aht-krit-kah)
открытка
postcard

____

(pah-sil-kah)
посылка
package

____

(teh-leh-grahm-mah)
телеграмма
telegram

____

(ah-vee-ah-poach-toy)
авиапочтой
by airmail

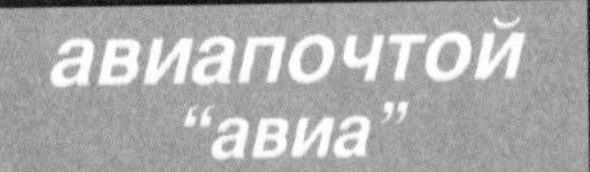

____

(fahks)
факс
fax

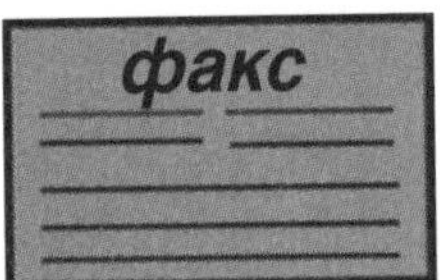

____

(mar-kah)
марка
stamp

____

(teh-leh-fohn-ahv-tah-maht)
телефон-автомат
public telephone

____

(pahch-toh-vee) *(yahsh-chik)*
почтовый ящик
mailbox

____

(teh-leh-fohn)
телефон
telephone

____

☐ **парламент** *(par-lah-myent)* .... parliament _______________
☐ **партия** *(par-tee-yah)* .... party _______________
☐ **паспорт** *(pahs-part)* .... passport **П** _______________
☐ **пассажир** *(pahs-sah-zheer)* .... passenger _______________
☐ **позиция** *(pah-zeet-see-yah)* .... position _______________

Next step — **вы** ask **вопросы** like those **внизу**, depending on what **вы** *(hah-teet-yeh)* **хотите** (would like). Repeat these sentences aloud many times.

Где я (I) *(mah-goo)* **могу** (can) *(koo-peet)* **купить** (buy) *(mar-kee)* **марки?** ____________________

Где я могу купить *(aht-krit-koo)* **открытку?** ____________________

Где телефон? ____________________

Где *(pahch-toh-vee)* *(yahsh-chik)* **почтовый ящик** (mailbox)**?** ____________________

Где телефон-автомат (public telephone)**?** ____________________

Где я могу *(pah-slaht)* **послать** *(pah-sil-koo)* **посылку** (package)**?** ____________________

Где я могу *(pahz-vah-neet)* **позвонить в** *(seh-sheh-ah)* **США** (U.S.A.)**?** ____________________

Сколько это *(stoy-eet)* **стоит** (costs)**?** ____________________

Теперь, quiz yourself. Can **вы** can translate the following thoughts **на русский?**

1. Where is a public telephone? ____________________
2. Where can I phone to the U.S.A.? ____________________
3. Where can I phone to St. Petersburg? ____________________
4. Where is the post office? ____________________
5. Where can I buy stamps? ____________________
6. Airmail envelopes? ____________________
7. Where can I send a package? ____________________
8. Where can I send a fax? ____________________

ОТВЕТЫ

1. **Где телефон-автомат?**
2. **Где я могу позвонить в США?**
3. **Где я могу позвонить в Санкт-Петербург?**
4. **Где почта?**
5. **Где я могу купить марки?**
6. **Конверты авиа?**
7. **Где я могу послать посылку?**
8. **Где я могу послать факс?**

(voht)
Вот are more verbs.

(die-tee) (men-yeh)
дайте мне ______________________
give me

(pee-saht)
писать ______________________
to write

(pah-kah-zih-vaht)
показывать ______________________
to show

(zah-plah-teet) (zah)
заплатить за ______________________
to pay for

Practice these verbs by not only filling in the blanks, but by saying them aloud many, many times until you are comfortable with the sounds and the words.

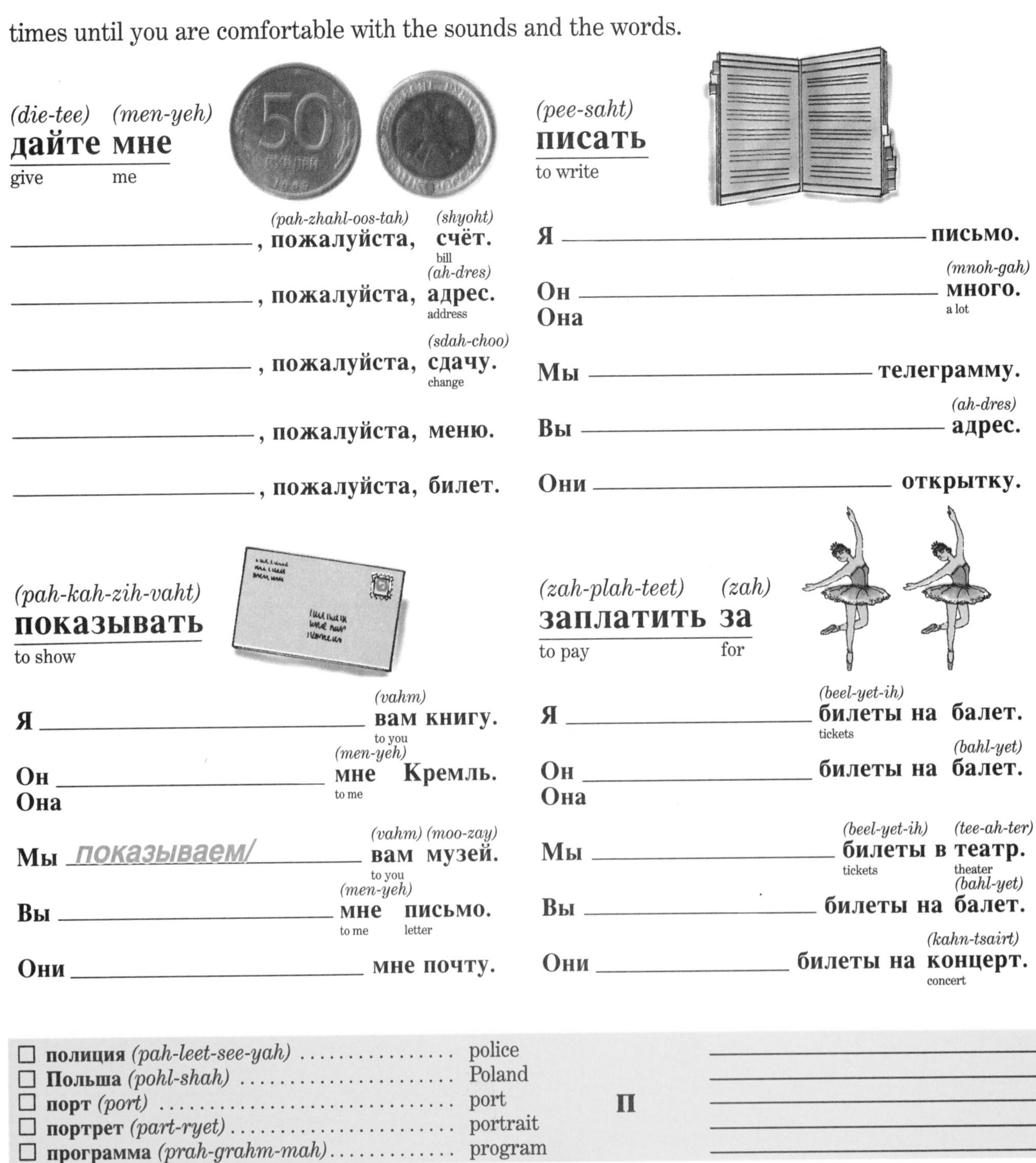

(die-tee) (men-yeh)
дайте мне
give me

______________, *(pah-zhahl-oos-tah)* **пожалуйста,** *(shyoht)* **счёт.** (bill)

______________, **пожалуйста,** *(ah-dres)* **адрес.** (address)

______________, **пожалуйста,** *(sdah-choo)* **сдачу.** (change)

______________, **пожалуйста, меню.**

______________, **пожалуйста, билет.**

(pee-saht)
писать
to write

Я ______________ **письмо.**

Он / Она ______________ *(mnoh-gah)* **много.** (a lot)

Мы ______________ **телеграмму.**

Вы ______________ *(ah-dres)* **адрес.**

Они ______________ **открытку.**

(pah-kah-zih-vaht)
показывать
to show

Я ______________ *(vahm)* **вам** (to you) **книгу.**

Он / Она ______________ *(men-yeh)* **мне** (to me) **Кремль.**

Мы *показываем/*______________ *(vahm)* **вам** (to you) *(moo-zay)* **музей.**

Вы ______________ *(men-yeh)* **мне** (to me) **письмо.** (letter)

Они ______________ **мне почту.**

(zah-plah-teet) (zah)
заплатить за
to pay for

Я ______________ *(beel-yet-ih)* **билеты** (tickets) **на балет.**

Он / Она ______________ **билеты на** *(bahl-yet)* **балет.**

Мы ______________ *(beel-yet-ih)* **билеты** (tickets) **в** *(tee-ah-ter)* **театр.** (theater)

Вы ______________ **билеты на** *(bahl-yet)* **балет.**

Они ______________ **билеты на** *(kahn-tsairt)* **концерт.** (concert)

☐ **полиция** *(pah-leet-see-yah)* .... police
☐ **Польша** *(pohl-shah)* .... Poland
☐ **порт** *(port)* .... port
☐ **портрет** *(part-ryet)* .... portrait
☐ **программа** *(prah-grahm-mah)*............. program

П ______________

17 Basic Traffic Signs and Conversions

Some of these signs you probably recognize, but take a couple of minutes to review them anyway.

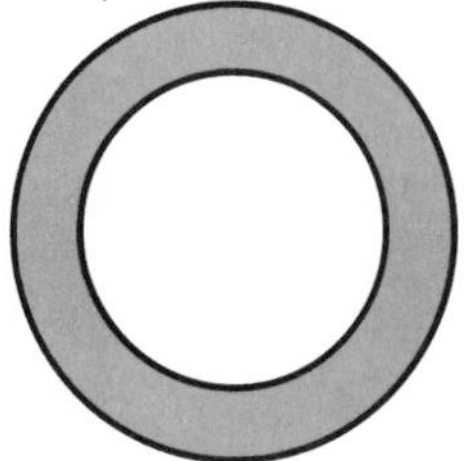

(dvee-zhen-ee-yeh) (zah-presh-chen-oh)
движение запрещено
road closed to vehicles

(tah-mohzh-nyah)
таможня
customs

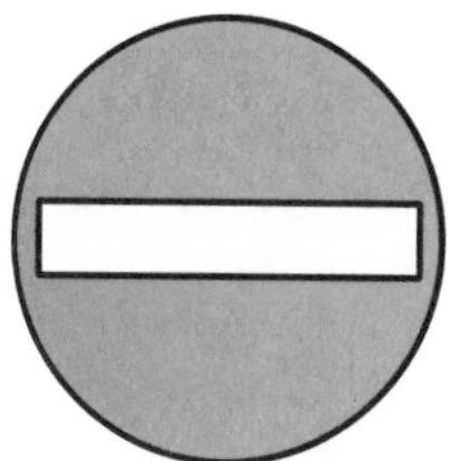

(vyezd) (zah-presh-chyohn)
въезд запрещён
no entrance

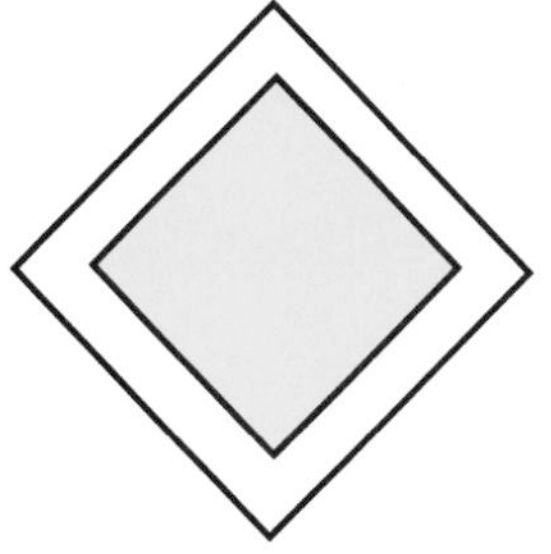

(glahv-nah-yah) (dah-roh-gah)
главная дорога
main road, you have the right of way

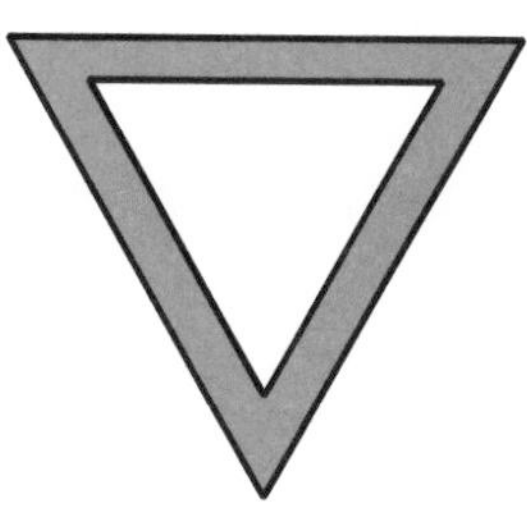

(oo-stoo-peet-yet) (dah-roh-goo)
уступите дорогу
yield

(mahk-see-mahl-nah-yah) (skoh-rahst)
максимальная скорость
speed limit

(stah-yahn-kah) (zah-presh-chen-ah)
стоянка запрещена
no parking

(ahb-gohn) (zah-presh-chyohn)
обгон запрещён
no passing

(stohp)
стоп
stop

(ahb-yezd)
ОБЪЕЗД
detour

What follows are approximate conversions, so when you order something by liters, kilograms or grams you will have an idea of what to expect and not find yourself being handed one piece of candy when you thought you ordered an entire bag.

To Convert		Do the Math		
liters (l) to gallons,	multiply by 0.26	4 liters x 0.26	=	1.04 gallons
gallons to liters,	multiply by 3.79	10 gal. x 3.79	=	37.9 liters
kilograms (kg) to pounds,	multiply by 2.2	2 kilograms x 2.2	=	4.4 pounds
pounds to kilos,	multiply by 0.46	10 pounds x 0.46	=	4.6 kg
grams (g) to ounces,	multiply by 0.035	100 grams x 0.035	=	3.5 oz.
ounces to grams,	multiply by 28.35	10 oz. x 28.35	=	283.5 g.
meters (m) to feet,	multiply by 3.28	2 meters x 3.28	=	6.56 feet
feet to meters,	multiply by 0.3	6 feet x 0.3	=	1.8 meters

For fun, take your weight in pounds and convert it into kilograms. It sounds better that way, doesn't it? How many kilometers is it from your home to school, to work, to the post office?

The Simple Versions		
one liter	=	approximately one US quart
four liters	=	approximately one US gallon
one kilo	=	approximately 2.2 pounds
100 grams	=	approximately 3.5 ounces
500 grams	=	slightly more than one pound
one meter	=	slightly more than three feet

The distance between **Москва и Петербург** is approximately 400 miles. How many kilometers would that be?				
kilometers (km.) to miles,	multiply by 0.62	1000 km. x 0.62	=	620 miles
miles to kilometers,	multiply by 1.6	1000 miles x 1.6	=	1,600 km.

Inches 1	2	3	4	5	6	7

To convert centimeters into inches, multiply by 0.39 Example: 9 cm. x 0.39 = 3.51 in.

To convert inches into centimeters, multiply by 2.54 Example: 4 in. x 2.54 = 10.16 cm.

cm 1	2	3	4	5	6	7	8	9	10	11	12	13	14	15	16	17	18

Bilingual Books' Unique Pocket Pal™
Cut it out, fold it up, and carry it with you at all times.

POLITE ESSENTIALS

good morning	**доброе утро**	*(doh-brah-yeh) (oo-trah)*
good afternoon/day	**добрый день**	*(doh-brih) (dyen)*
good evening	**добрый вечер**	*(doh-brih) (vyeh-cher)*
good night	**спокойной ночи**	*(spah-koy-nay)(noh-chee)*
hello	**алло** or **привет**	*(ahl-loh)* or *(pree-vyet)*
please	**пожалуйста**	*(pah-zhahl-oos-tah)*
thank you	**спасибо**	*(spah-see-bah)*
you're welcome	**не за что** or **пожалуйста**	*(nyeh) (zah) (shtah)* or *(pah-zhahl-oos-tah)*
excuse me	**извините**	*(eez-vee-neet-yeh)*
I'm sorry.	**простите**	*(prahs-tyet-yeh)*
yes	**да**	*(dah)*
no	**нет**	*(nyet)*
male/man	**мужчина**	*(moozh-chee-nah)*
female/woman	**женщина**	*(zhen-shchee-nah)*
My name is . . .	**Меня зовут . . .**	*(men-yah) (zah-voot)*
What is your name?	**Как вас зовут?**	*(kahk) (vahs) (zah-voot)*
I'm from the U.S.A.	**Я из США.**	*(yah) (eeez)(seh-sheh-ah)*
Where are you from?	**Вы откуда?**	*(vwee) (aht-koo-dah)*
I would like . . .	**Я хочу . . .**	*(yah) (hah-choo)*
I have . . .	**У меня есть . . .**	*(oo)(men-yah) (yest)*
Do you speak English?	**Вы говорите по-английски?**	*(vwee) (gah-vah-reet-yeh) (pah-ahn-glee-skee)*
I understand.	**Я понимаю.**	*(yah) (pah-nee-mah-yoo)*
I do not understand.	**Я не понимаю.**	*(yah)(nyeh) (pah-nee-mah-yoo)*
Please repeat.	**Повторите, пожалуйста.**	*(pahv-tah-reet-yeh) (pah-zhahl-oos-tah)*

ESSENTIAL NUMBERS

zero	**ноль**	*(nohl)*
one	**один**	*(ah-deen)*
two	**два** or **две**	*(dvah)* or *(dveh)*
three	**три**	*(tree)*
four	**четыре**	*(cheh-tir-ee)*
five	**пять**	*(pyaht)*
six	**шесть**	*(shest)*
seven	**семь**	*(syem)*
eight	**восемь**	*(voh-syem)*
nine	**девять**	*(dyev-yet)*
ten	**десять**	*(dyes-yet)*
11	**одиннадцать**	*(ah-deen-nud-tset)*
12	**двенадцать**	*(dveh-nahd-tset)*
13	**тринадцать**	*(tree-nahd-tset)*
14	**четырнадцать**	*(cheh-tir-nud-tset)*
15	**пятнадцать**	*(pyaht-nahd-tset)*
16	**шестнадцать**	*(shest-nahd-tset)*
17	**семнадцать**	*(sim-nahd-tset)*
18	**восемнадцать**	*(vah-sim-nahd-tset)*
19	**девятнадцать**	*(div-yet-nahd-tset)*
20	**двадцать**	*(dvahd-tset)*
30	**тридцать**	*(treed-tset)*
40	**сорок**	*(so-rahk)*
50	**пятьдесят**	*(peed-dyes-yaht)*
60	**шестьдесят**	*(shest-dyes-yaht)*
70	**семьдесят**	*(syem-dyes-yet)*
80	**восемьдесят**	*(voh-syem-dyes-yet)*
90	**девяносто**	*(dyev-yah-noh-stah)*
100	**сто** or **сот**	*(stoh)* or *(soht)*
500	**пятьсот**	*(pyet-soht)*
1,000	**тысяча**	*(tih-syah-chah)*
5,000	**пять тысяч**	*(pyaht)(tih-syahch)*

KEY QUESTIONS

who	**кто**	*(ktoh)*
Who is that?	**Кто это?**	*(ktoh) (et-tah)*
what	**что**	*(shtoh)*
What is that?	**Что это?**	*(shtoh) (et-tah)*
why	**почему**	*(pah-chee-moo)*
when	**когда**	*(kahg-dah)*
how	**как**	*(kahk)*
How are you?	**Как дела?**	*(kahk) (dee-lah)*
how much	**сколько**	*(skohl-kah)*
How much does that cost?	**Сколько это стоит?**	*(skohl-kah) (et-tah) (stoy-eet)*
where	**где**	*(gdyeh)*
Where is the	**Где**	*(gdyeh)*
bank?	**банк?**	*(bahnk)*
hotel?	**гостиница?**	*(gah-stee-neet-sah)*
restaurant?	**ресторан?**	*(res-tah-rahn)*
lavatory?	**туалет?**	*(too-ahl-yet)*
taxi?	**такси?**	*(tahk-see)*
mailbox?	**почтовый ящик?**	*(pahch-toh-vee) (yahsh-chik)*

EMERGENCY ESSENTIALS

do not enter	**входа нет**	*(vhoh-dah)(nyet)*
I'm lost.	**Я заблудился.**	*(yah)(zah-bloo-deel-syah)*
I lost my . . .	**Я потерял . . .**	*(yah)(pah-tyair-yahl)*
help	**на помощь**	*(nah)(poh-mahshch)*
police	**милиция**	*(mee-leet-see-yah)*
doctor	**врач**	*(vrahch)*

TIME ESSENTIALS

Monday	**понедельник**	*(pah-nee-dyel-neek)*
Tuesday	**вторник**	*(vtor-neek)*
Wednesday	**среда**	*(sree-dah)*
Thursday	**четверг**	*(chet-vyairg)*
Friday	**пятница**	*(pyaht-neet-sah)*
Saturday	**суббота**	*(soo-boh-tah)*
Sunday	**воскресенье**	*(vah-skree-syen-yeh)*
today	**сегодня**	*(see-vohd-nyah)*
yesterday	**вчера**	*(vchee-rah)*
tomorrow	**завтра**	*(zahv-trah)*
morning	**утро**	*(oo-trah)*
afternoon	**день**	*(dyen)*
evening	**вечер**	*(vyeh-cher)*
night	**ночь**	*(nohch)*
January	**январь**	*(yahn-var)*
February	**февраль**	*(fyev-rahl)*
March	**март**	*(mart)*
April	**апрель**	*(ahp-ryel)*
May	**май**	*(my)*
June	**июнь**	*(ee-yoon)*
July	**июль**	*(ee-yool)*
August	**август**	*(ahv-goost)*
September	**сентябрь**	*(syen-tyah-bair)*
October	**октябрь**	*(ahk-tyah-bair)*
November	**ноябрь**	*(nah-yah-bair)*
December	**декабрь**	*(dee-kah-bair)*
What time is it?	**Сколько времени?**	*(skohl-kah)(vreh-mee-nee)*
hour	**час**	*(chahs)*
day	**день**	*(dyen)*
week	**неделя**	*(nee-dyel-yah)*
month	**месяц**	*(myeh-syets)*
year	**год**	*(gohd)*

EATING OUT ESSENTIALS

breakfast	**завтрак**	*(zahv-trahk)*
lunch	**обед**	*(ah-byed)*
dinner	**ужин**	*(oo-zheen)*
I'm hungry.	**Я хочу есть.**	*(yah)(hah-choo)(yest)*
I'm thirsty.	**Я хочу пить.**	*(yah)(hah-choo)(peet)*
Where is a restaurant?	**Где ресторан?**	*(gdyeh)(res-tah-rahn)*
Where is a cafeteria?	**Где столовая?**	*(gdyeh)(stah-loh-vah-yah)*
I have a reservation.	**У меня есть заказ.**	*(oo)(men-yah)(yest) (zah-kahz)*
My name is . . .	**Меня зовут . . .**	*(men-yah)(zah-voot)*
I would like to make a reservation.	**Я хочу сделать заказ.**	*(yah)(hah-choo) (sdyeh-laht)(zah-kahz)*
I would like to order . . .	**Я хочу заказать . . .**	*(yah)(hah-choo) (zah-kah-zaht)*
appetizer	**закуски**	*(zah-koo-skee)*
soup	**суп**	*(soop)*
salad	**салат**	*(sah-laht)*
fish	**рыба**	*(rih-bah)*
meat	**мясо**	*(myah-sah)*
poultry	**птица**	*(pteet-sah)*
dessert	**десерт**	*(dyes-yairt)*
beverages	**напитки**	*(nah-peet-kee)*
knife	**нож**	*(nohzh)*
fork	**вилка**	*(veel-kah)*
spoon	**ложка**	*(lohzh-kah)*
napkin	**салфетка**	*(sahl-fyet-kah)*
plate	**тарелка**	*(tar-yel-kah)*
waiter	**официант**	*(ah-feet-see-ahnt)*
menu	**меню**	*(men-yoo)*
bill	**счёт**	*(shyoht)*
Enjoy your meal!	**Приятного аппетита!**	*(pree-yaht-nah-vah) (ah-peh-tee-tah)*

TRANSPORTATION ESSENTIALS

map	**карта**	*(kar-tah)*
subway	**метро**	*(myeh-troh)*
bus	**автобус**	*(ahv-toh-boos)*
taxi	**такси**	*(tahk-see)*
car	**машина**	*(mah-shee-nyah)*
train	**поезд**	*(poh-yezd)*
train station	**вокзал**	*(vahk-zahl)*
plane	**самолёт**	*(sah-mahl-yoht)*
airport	**аэропорт**	*(ah-air-ah-port)*
ticket	**билет**	*(beel-yet)*
one-way	**в одном направлении**	*(vuh)(ahd-nohm) (nah-prahv-lyen-ee-ee)*
round-trip	**туда и обратно**	*(too-dah)(ee) (ahb-raht-nah)*
arrival	**прибытие**	*(pree-bit-ee-yeh)*
departure	**отправление**	*(aht-prahv-lyen-ee-yeh)*
foreign	**иностранный**	*(ee-nah-strahn-nee)*
domestic (internal)	**местный**	*(myes-nee)*
occupied	**занято**	*(zahn-yah-tah)*
service station	**автостанция**	*(ahv-tah-stahnt-see-yah)*
I would like a ticket to . . .	**Я хочу билет в . . .**	*(yah)(hah-choo) (beel-yet)(vuh)*
How much is a ticket to . . .	**Сколько стоит билет в . . .**	*(skohl-kah)(stoy-eet) (beel-yet)(vuh)*
Where is the bus stop?	**Где остановка автобуса?**	*(gdyeh) (ahs-tah-nohv-kah) (ahv-toh-boo-sah)*
subway station?	**станция метро?**	*(stahnt-see-yah) (myeh-troh)*
museum?	**музей?**	*(moo-zay)*
bank?	**банк?**	*(bahnk)*
post office?	**почта?**	*(poach-tah)*

SLEEPING ESSENTIALS

hotel	**гостиница**	*(gah-stee-neet-sah)*
home	**дом**	*(dohm)*
bedroom	**спальня**	*(spahl-nyah)*
expensive	**дорогая**	*(dah-rah-gah-yah)*
inexpensive	**дешёвая**	*(dyeh-shyoh-vah-yah)*
bed	**кровать**	*(krah-vaht)*
pillow	**подушка**	*(pah-doosh-kah)*
blanket	**одеяло**	*(ah-dee-yah-lah)*
towel	**полотенце**	*(pah-lah-tyent-seh)*
I would like a	**Я хочу**	*(yah)(hah-choo)*
single room.	**номер на одного.**	*(nohm-yair)(nah) (ahd-nah-voh)*
double room.	**номер на двоих.**	*(nohm-yair)(nah) (dvah-eehk)*
room with a bath.	**номер с ванной.**	*(nohm-yair)(suh) (vahn-noy)*
room with a shower.	**номер с душем.**	*(nohm-yair)(suh) (doo-shem)*
room for one night.	**номер на сутки.**	*(nohm-yair)(nah) (soot-kee)*
room for two nights.	**номер на двое суток.**	*(nohm-yair)(nah) (dvah-yeh)(soo-tahk)*
I have a reservation.	**У меня заказ.**	*(oo)(men-yah)(zah-kahz)*
I do not have a reservation.	**У меня нет заказа.**	*(oo)(men-yah)(nyet) (zah-kahz-ah)*

The *"10 minutes a day®"* series is available from your local bookseller or from:
Bilingual Books, Inc.
1719 West Nickerson Street, Seattle, WA 98119 USA
1-800-488-5068 or 1-206-284-4211

SHOPPING ESSENTIALS

Where is a	**Где**	*(gdyeh)*
department store?	**универмаг?**	*(oo-nee-vyair-mahg)*
laundromat?	**прачечная?**	*(prahch-yech-nah-yah)*
pharmacy?	**аптека?**	*(ahp-tyek-ah)*
supermarket?	**гастроном?**	*(gah-strah-nohm)*
newstand?	**киоск?**	*(kee-ohsk)*
bakery?	**булочная?**	*(boo-lahch-nah-yah)*
I need . . .	**Мне нужно . . .**	*(men-yeh)(noozh-nah)*
Do you have . . .?	**У вас есть . . .?**	*(oo)(vahs)(yest)*
How much does it cost?	**Сколько это стоит?**	*(skohl-kah)(et-tah) (stoy-eet)*
too expensive	**очень дорого**	*(oh-chen)(doh-rah-gah)*
I'll take it.	**Я возьму это.**	*(yah)(vahz-moo)(et-tah)*
Do you take credit cards?	**Вы принимаете кредитные карточки?**	*(vwee)(pree-nee-mah-yet-yeh) (kreh-deet-nih-yeh) (kar-tahch-kee)*
traveler's checks?	**дорожные чеки?**	*(dah-rohzh-nih-yeh) (cheh-kee)*
I would like to buy	**Я хочу купить**	*(yah)(hah-choo)(koo-peet)*
stamps.	**марки.**	*(mar-kee)*
postcards.	**открытки.**	*(aht-krit-kee)*
souvenirs.	**сувениры.**	*(soo-veh-neer-ih)*
socks.	**носки.**	*(nah-skee)*
deodorant.	**дезодорант.**	*(dyeh-zah-dah-rahnt)*
aspirin.	**аспирин.**	*(ah-spee-reen)*
toothpaste.	**зубную пасту.**	*(zoob-noo-yoo)(pahs-too)*

U.S. Patent No. 5,063,637. Manufactured and sold under license from Wood-Howard Products, Inc., and FastMark, Inc., Palo Alto, CA USA.

Как платить

(kahk) (plah-teet)
how to pay

Да, there are also **счета** (shyeh-tah) [bills] to pay **в России. Вы** have just finished your delicious dinner **и вы хотите** (hah-teet-yeh) [would like] **счёт** (shyoht) [bill]. **Как вы можете** (mohzh-yet-yeh) [can] **платить** [pay]? **Вы** call for **официанта** (ah-feet-see-ahn-tah) [waiter]: **"Официант!"** **Официант** (ah-feet-see-ahnt) [waiter] will normally reel off what **вы** have eaten while writing rapidly. **Он** will then place **счёт** (shyoht) **на стол** (stohl) **"Вот счёт. Восемьсот тысяч рублей** (roo-blay)**."** **Вы** will pay **официанту** (ah-feet-see-ahn-too) **или** perhaps **вы** will pay **кассиру** (kahs-see-roo).

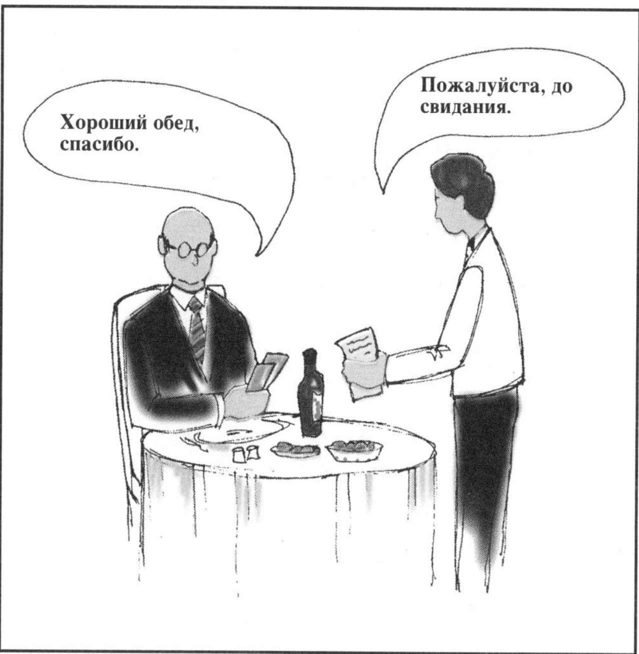

Being a seasoned traveler, **вы** know that tipping as **мы** (mwee) know it **в США** (seh-sheh-ah) **и Канаде** can vary from country to country. If the service is not included **в счёте** (shyoht-yeh), round the bill up **или** simply leave what you consider an appropriate amount for your **официанта** (ah-feet-see-ahn-tah). When **вы** dine out **в России,** always make a reservation. It can be very difficult to get into a popular **ресторан** (res-tah-rahn). Nevertheless, the experience is well worth the trouble **вы** will encounter to obtain a reservation. **И** remember, **вы** know enough **русский** to make a reservation. Just speak slowly and clearly.

☐ **прогресс** *(prahg-ryes)*	progress		________
☐ **продукт** *(prah-dookt)*	product		________
☐ **проект** *(prah-yekt)*	project	**П**	________
☐ **профессия** *(prah-fyes-see-yah)*	profession		________
☐ **профессор** *(prah-fyes-sar)*	professor		________

Remember these key **слова** when dining out **в России.**

(ah-feet-see-ahnt)
официант ______________________
waiter

(ah-feet-see-ahnt-kah)
официантка ______________________
waitress

(shyoht)
счёт ______________________
bill

(sdah-chah)
сдача ______________________
change

(men-yoo)
меню меню, меню, меню
menu

(kvee-tahn-tsee-yah)
квитанция ______________________
receipt

(eez-vee-neet-yeh)
извините ______________________
excuse me

(spah-see-bah)
спасибо ______________________
thank you

(pah-zhahl-oos-tah)
пожалуйста ______________________
please

(die-tee) (men-yeh)
дайте мне ______________________
give me

Вот a sample conversation involving paying *(shyoht)* **счёт.** Practice by writing it in the blanks.

(zee-nah) Зина: *(ah-plah-teet)* **Извините. Я хочу оплатить счёт.** (оплатить = to pay)

____

(ahd-mee-nee-strah-tor) Администратор: *(nohm-yair) (pah-zhahl-oos-tah)* **Номер, пожалуйста?** (Номер = number (room))

____

Зина: *(nohm-yair) (tree-stah) (dyes-yet)* **Номер триста десять.** (Номер = number)

____

Администратор: *(ahd-noo)* **Спасибо. Одну минуту.**

____

Администратор: **Вот счёт.**

____

If **вы** have any problems **с** *(chee-slah-mee)* **числами,** (numbers) just ask someone to write out *(chee-slah)* **числа,** so that **вы** can be sure you understand everything correctly, **Пожалуйста,** *(nah-pee-sheet-yeh)* **напишите** (write out) *(soom-moo)* **сумму.** ((the) sum) **Спасибо.**

Practice: ______________________
(Please write out the sum. Thank you.)

☐ **процент** *(praht-syent)*	percent	**п**	______________
☐ **радио** *(rah-dee-oh)*..................	radio		______________
☐ **ракета** *(rah-kyet-ah)*..................	rocket	**р**	______________
☐ **ранг** *(rahng)*	rank		______________
☐ **рапорт** *(rah-port)*	report		______________

Теперь, let's take a break from **счетов** *(shyeh-tohv)* **и** **денег** *(dyen-yeg)* money **и** learn some **новые** *(noh-vih-yeh)* new fun **слова. Вы** can always practice these **слова** by using your flash cards at the back of this **книга.** *(kuh-nee-gah)* Carry these flash cards in your purse, pocket, briefcase **или** knapsack **и** *use them!*

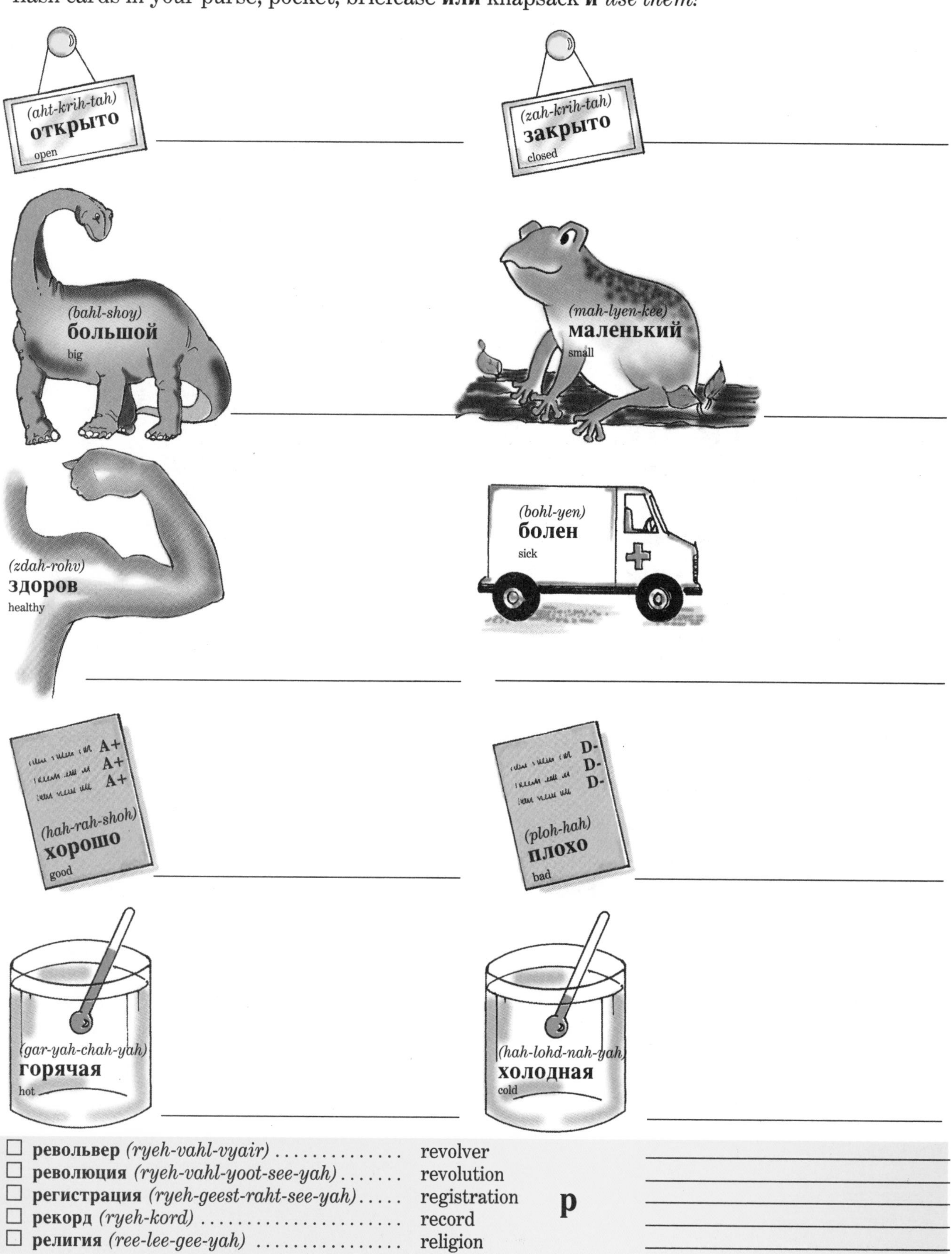

- ☐ **револьвер** *(ryeh-vahl-vyair)* .... revolver
- ☐ **революция** *(ryeh-vahl-yoot-see-yah)* .... revolution
- ☐ **регистрация** *(ryeh-geest-raht-see-yah)* ..... registration
- ☐ **рекорд** *(ryeh-kord)* .... record
- ☐ **религия** *(ree-lee-gee-yah)* .... religion

р

(kah-roht-kah-yah)
короткая ________________________
short

(dleen-nah-yah)
длинная ________________________
long

(myed-lyen-nah)
медленно ________________________
slow

(bis-trah)
быстро ________________________
fast

(vwee-soh-kah-yah)
высокая ________________________
tall

(mah-lyen-kah-yah)
маленькая ________________________
short, small

(stah-ree)
старый ________________________
old

(mah-lah-doy)
молодой ________________________
young

(dah-rah-gah-yah)
дорогая ________________________
expensive

(dyeh-shyoh-vah-yah)
дешёвая ________________________
inexpensive

(bah-gaht)
богат ________________________
rich

(byed-yen)
беден ________________________
poor

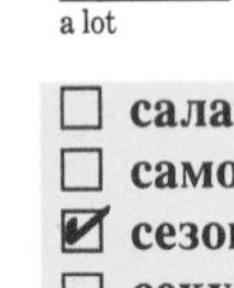

(mnoh-gah)
много ________________________
a lot

(mah-lah)
мало ________________________
a little

- ☐ **салат** *(sah-laht)* . . . . salad — ____________________
- ☐ **самовар** *(sah-mah-var)* . . . . samovar — ____________________
- ☑ **сезон** *(syeh-zone)* . . . . season — **с** — *сезон, сезон, сезон, сезон, сезон*
- ☐ **секунда** *(see-koon-dah)* . . . . second — ____________________
- ☐ **семинар** *(syem-ee-nar)* . . . . seminar — ____________________

Вот новые verbs.

(znaht) **знать** to know (fact, address)	________________	*(mohch)* **мочь** to be able to, can	*мочь, мочь, мочь*
(chee-taht) **читать** to read	________________	*(poot-yeh-shest-vah-vaht)* **путешествовать** to travel	________________

Study the patterns **внизу** closely, as **вы** will use these verbs a lot.

(znaht)
знать
to know

Я ________________ **всё.** *(vsyoh)* everything

Он / **Она** ________________ **адрес.** *(ah-dres)* address

Мы ________________, **как говорить по-русски.** *(gah-vah-reet)* how to speak

Вы ________________ **название гостиницы.** *(nahz-vah-nee-yeh)* name

Они ________________ **название ресторана.** *(res-tah-rah-nah)*

(mohch)
мочь
to be able to, can

Я ________________ **говорить по-русски.** *(gah-vah-reet)* speak

Он / **Она** ________________ **понимать по-английски.** *(pah-nee-maht)* understand

Мы ________________ **понимать по-русски.**

Вы ________________ **говорить по-английски.**

Они ________________ **говорить по-русски тоже.** *(toh-zheh)* also

(chee-taht)
читать
to read

Я ________________ **книгу.**

Он / **Она** ________________ **журнал.** magazine

Мы ________________ **меню.**

Вы ________________ **много.** a lot

Они ________________ **газету.** newspaper

(poot-yeh-shest-vah-vaht)
путешествовать
to travel

Я ________________ **в январе.** *(vuh) (yahn-var-yeh)* January

Он / **Она** ________________ **зимой.** *(zee-moy)* in winter

Мы ________________ **в июле.** *(ee-yool-yeh)* July

Вы ________________ **летом.** *(lyet-ahm)* in summer

Они ________________ **весной.** *(vees-noy)* in spring

с

- ☐ **сигара** *(see-gah-rah)* . . . . cigar ________________
- ☐ **сигарета** *(see-gah-ryet-ah)* . . . . cigarette ________________
- ☐ **симфония** *(seem-foh-nee-yah)* . . . . symphony ________________
- ☐ **советский** *(sah-vyet-skee)* . . . . Soviet ________________
- ☐ **стадион** *(stah-dee-ohn)* . . . . stadium ________________

Some verbs change slightly by adding a **"за-" или "по-."** Don't panic. This does not change the basic meaning of the word. **Вот два** examples. Learn to listen for the core of the verb. For example, note the word **"платить"** within **"заплатить за."**

(plah-teet) **платить** (to pay) — *(ah-plah-teet)* **оплатить** (to pay) — *(zah-plah-teet)* **заплатить** (to pay) *(zah)* **за** (for)

Я *(plah-choo)* **плачу пять тысяч рублей.**

Я хочу оплатить *(shyoht)* **счёт.**

Я *(zah-plah-choo)* **заплачу за** *(ah-byed)* **обед** (meal)**.**

(koo-peet) **купить** (to buy) — *(pah-koo-paht)* **покупать** (to buy)

Я хочу купить *(mar-kee)* **марки.**

Я хочу купить *(kuh-nee-goo)* **книгу.**

Я *(pah-koo-pah-yoo)* **покупаю** *(zhoor-nahl)* **журнал.**

Вы *(mohzh-yet-yeh)* **можете** (can) translate the sentences **внизу на** (into) **русский? Ответы внизу.**

1. I can speak Russian. __________
2. They can pay the bill. __________
3. He needs to pay the bill. __________
4. We know the address. Мы знаем адрес.
5. She knows a lot. __________
6. We can read Russian. __________
7. I can pay the bill. __________
8. We are not able to (cannot) understand English. __________
9. I would like to go to Russia. __________
10. She reads the newspaper. __________

ОТВЕТЫ

1. Я могу говорить по-русски.
2. Они могут оплатить счёт.
3. Ему нужно оплатить счёт.
4. Мы знаем адрес.
5. Она знает много.
6. Мы можем читать по-русски.
7. Я могу оплатить счёт.
8. Мы не можем понимать по-английски.
9. Я хочу поехать в Россию.
10. Она читает газету.

Теперь, draw **линию** *(lee-nee-yoo)* (lines) **между** *(myezh-doo)* (between) the opposites **внизу.** **Не** forget to say them out loud. Use **эти** *(et-tee)* **слова** every day to describe **вещи** *(vesh-chee)* **в доме** (home), **в школе** *(shkohl-yeh)* (school), **и** at work.

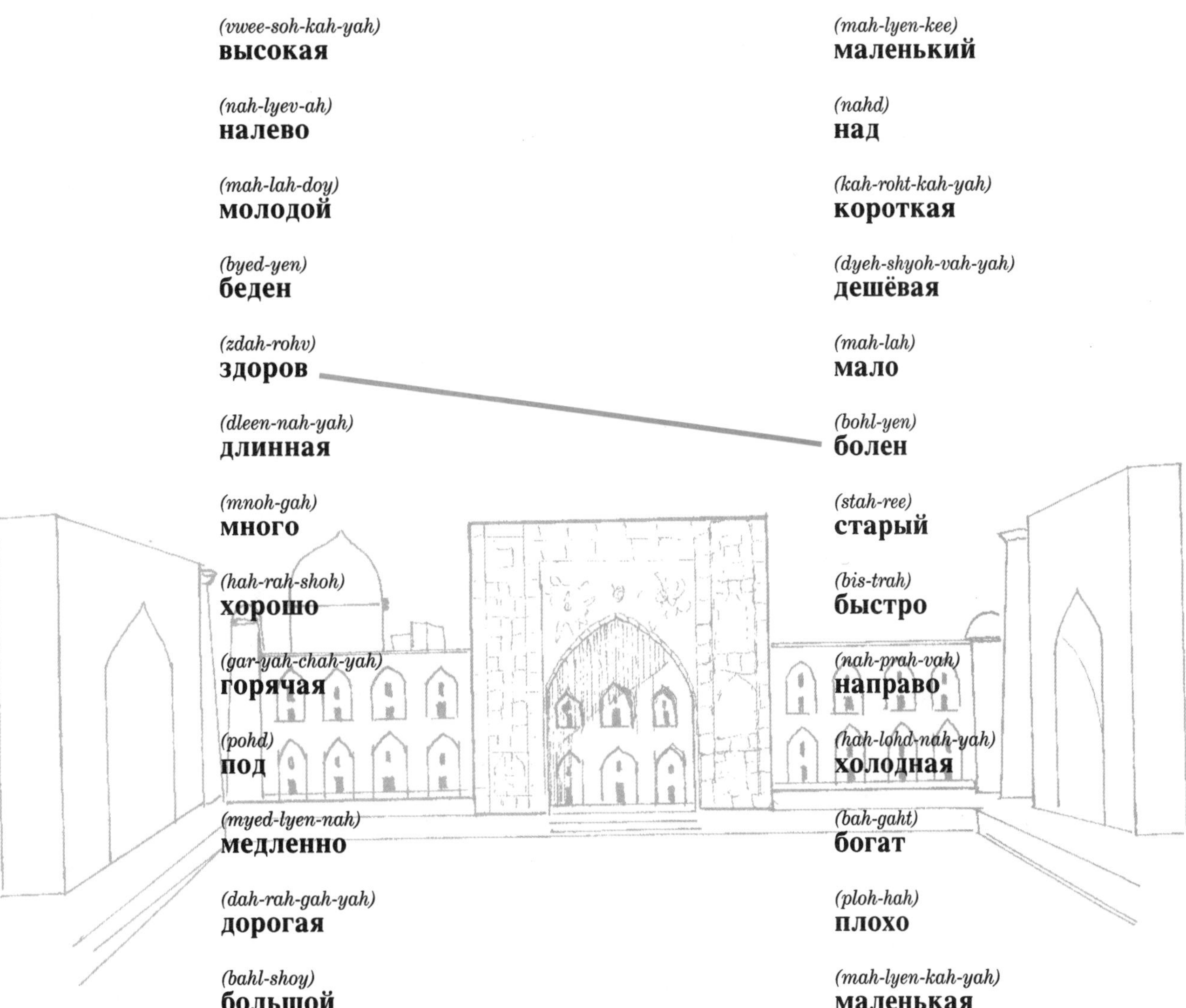

(vwee-soh-kah-yah) **высокая**	*(mah-lyen-kee)* **маленький**
(nah-lyev-ah) **налево**	*(nahd)* **над**
(mah-lah-doy) **молодой**	*(kah-roht-kah-yah)* **короткая**
(byed-yen) **беден**	*(dyeh-shyoh-vah-yah)* **дешёвая**
(zdah-rohv) **здоров**	*(mah-lah)* **мало**
(dleen-nah-yah) **длинная**	*(bohl-yen)* **болен**
(mnoh-gah) **много**	*(stah-ree)* **старый**
(hah-rah-shoh) **хорошо**	*(bis-trah)* **быстро**
(gar-yah-chah-yah) **горячая**	*(nah-prah-vah)* **направо**
(pohd) **под**	*(hah-lohd-nah-yah)* **холодная**
(myed-lyen-nah) **медленно**	*(bah-gaht)* **богат**
(dah-rah-gah-yah) **дорогая**	*(ploh-hah)* **плохо**
(bahl-shoy) **большой**	*(mah-lyen-kah-yah)* **маленькая**

Теперь вы знаете, что (that) **"большой"** means "large" **по-русски.** Have **вы** heard of the famous **"Большой театр"?** In addition to being one of the world's foremost ballet companies, it is also **старейший** *(star-yeh-shee)* (oldest) **московский театр.** It is a must to see, **когда вы** are **в Москве.**

If **вы** travel **в Петербург, тогда** visit **"Мариинский** *(mah-reen-skee)* **театр,"** formerly **"Театр Кирова** *(kee-rah-vah)***,"** where traditional opera and ballet productions are staged.

☐ **старт** *(start)*	start		________
☐ **студент** *(stoo-dyent)*	student	**С**	________
☐ **суп** *(soop)*	soup		________
☐ **табак** *(tah-bahk)*	tobacco	**Т**	________
☐ **такси** *(tahk-see)*	taxi		________

19 Путешествовать

(poot-yeh-shest-vah-vaht) **Путешествовать** — to travel

(vchee-rah) **Вчера** (yesterday) **в** *(pyeh-tyair-boorg-yeh)* **Петербурге!**

(see-vohd-nyah) **Сегодня** (today) **в** *(nohv-gah-rahd-yeh)* **Новгороде!**

(zahv-trah) **Завтра** (yesterday) **в** *(smahl-yensk-yeh)* **Смоленске!**

If you know a few key **слова**, traveling can be easy **в России. Россия и** the nations of the Commonwealth of Independent States span almost 6,000 miles which is equivalent to the distance *(myezh-doo)* **между** (between) California **и** France. **Россия** has *(ah-deen-nud-tset)* **одиннадцать** time zones. The map below should give you a rough idea of the size of this area and help you to understand why traveling **в России** can be a major undertaking.

Иван (Ivan) *(yed-yet)* **едет** (goes) **на машине.**

Борис *(lee-teet)* **летит** (flies) **на** *(sah-mahl-yoht-yeh)* **самолёте** (airplane)**.**

(ee-ree-nah) **Ирина едет на** *(mah-tah-tsee-kul-yeh)* **мотоцикле** (motorcycle)**.**

Нина едет (goes) **на** *(poh-yezd-yeh)* **поезде** (train)**.**

Зина едет на *(myeh-troh)* **метро** (subway)**.**

(veek-tor) **Виктор едет на автобусе.**

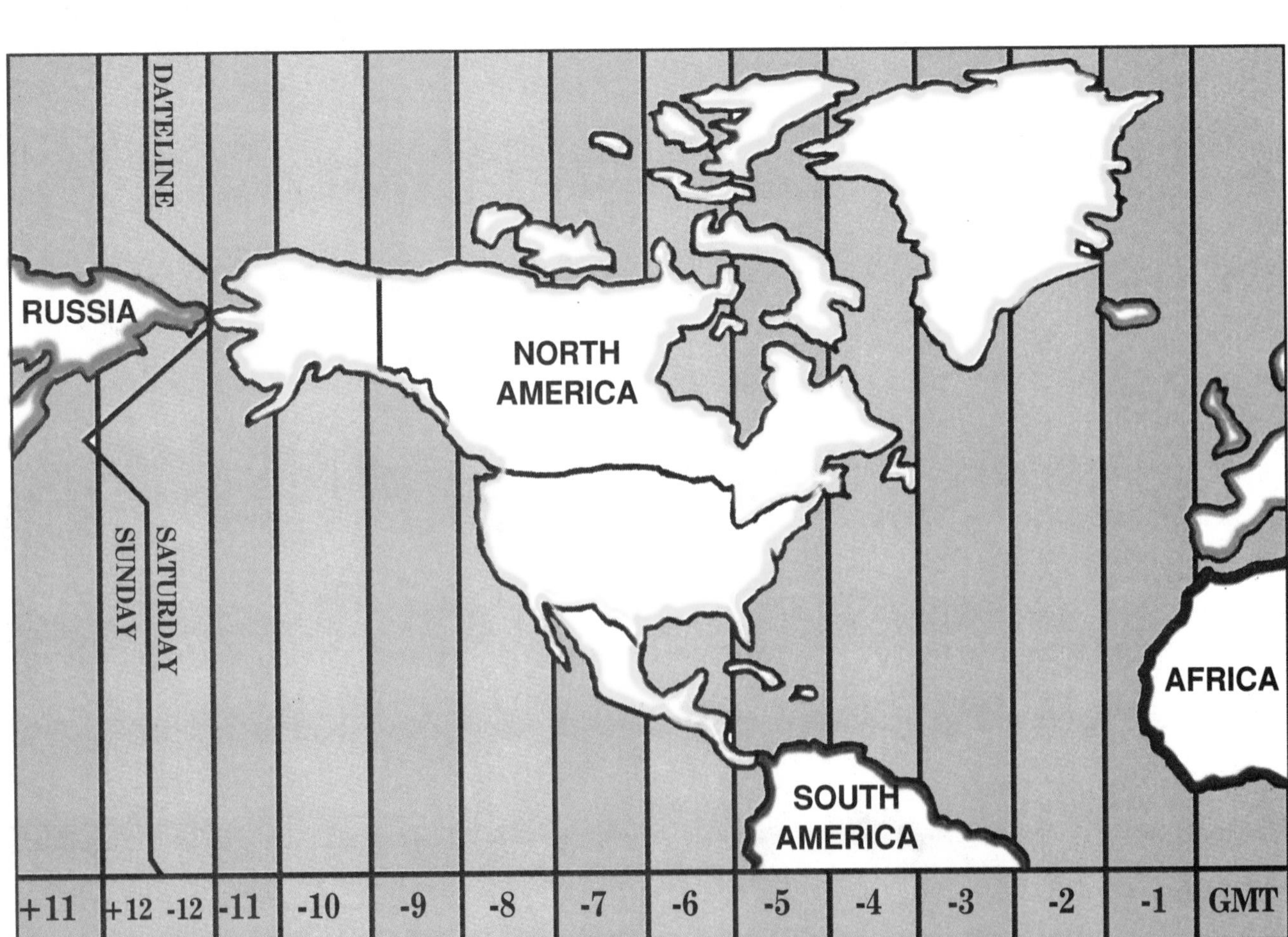

When **вы** are traveling, **вы** will want to tell others your nationality **и вы** will meet people from all corners of the world. Can you guess where someone is from if they say one of the following? **Ответы** are in your glossary beginning on page 110.

(ah-zyair-by-dzah-nyets)
Я азербайджанец. ______________________

(ah-myeh-ree-kah-nyets)
Я американец. ______________________

(ar-myah-neen)
Я армянин. ______________________

(ahn-glee-chah-neen)
Я англичанин. ______________________

(byeh-lah-roos)
Я белорус. Я белорус. Я белорус.

(kah-nah-dyets)
Я канадец. ______________________

(es-toh-nyets)
Я эстонец. ______________________

(groo-zeen)
Я грузин. ______________________

(kah-zahk)
Я казах. ______________________

(kir-geez)
Я кыргыз. ______________________

(lah-tish)
Я латыш. ______________________

(lee-toh-vyets)
Я литовец. ______________________

(mahl-dah-vah-neen)
Я молдованин. ______________________

(roos-skee)
Я русский. ______________________

(tahd-zheek)
Я таджик. ______________________

(toork-myen)
Я туркмен. ______________________

(oo-kry-nyets)
Я украинец. ______________________

(ooz-bek)
Я узбек. ______________________

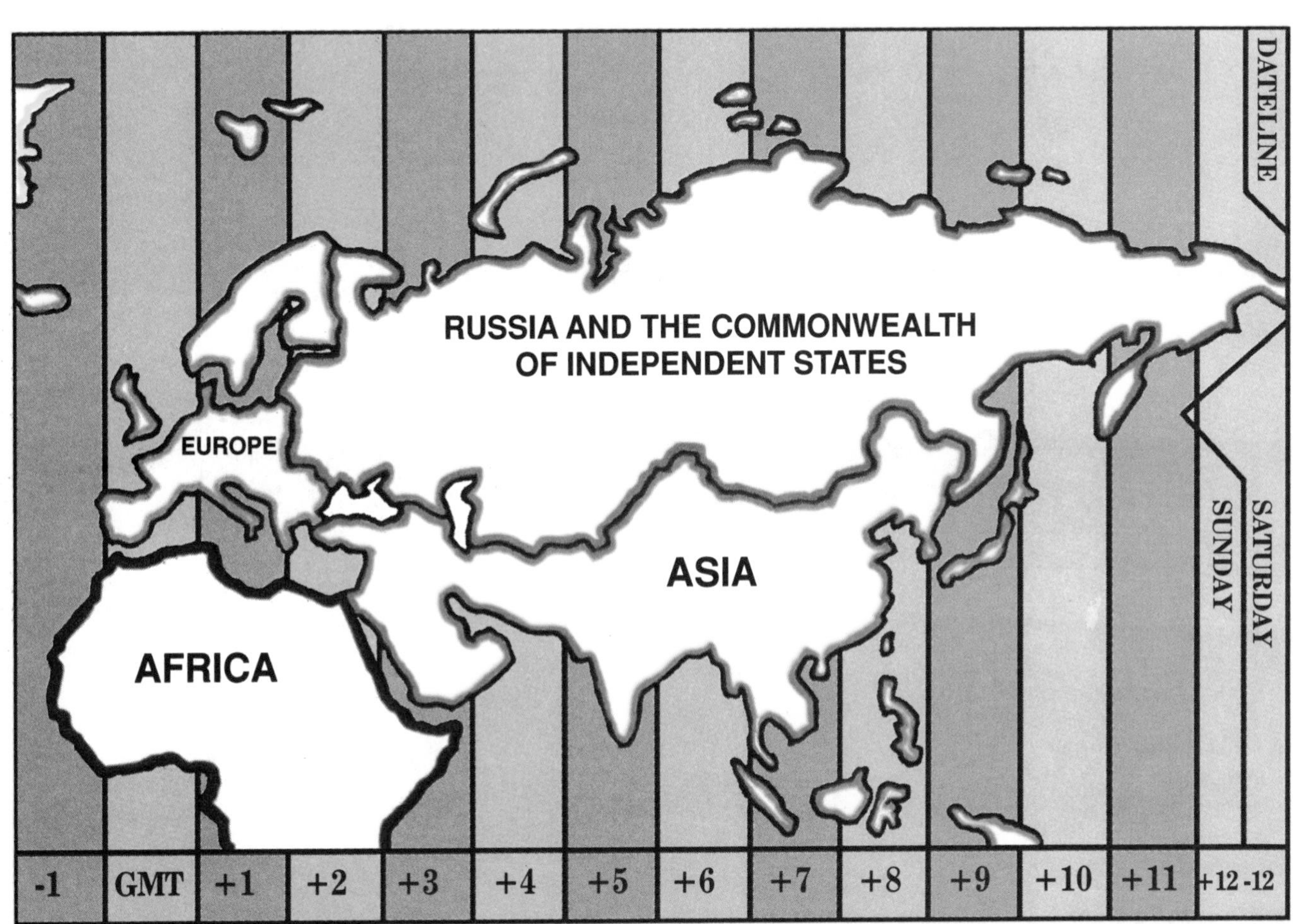

Русские *(loob-yaht)* **любят** (love) *(poot-yeh-shest-vah-vaht)* **путешествовать.** It should *(nyeh)* **не** be a surprise to find **много слов** revolving around the concept of travel which is exactly what **вы** *(hah-teet-yeh)* **хотите** (want) to do. Practice the following **слова** many times. **Вы** will see them *(chah-stah)* **часто** (often).

(poot-yeh-shest-vah-vaht)
путешествовать ______________
to travel

(byoo-roh) (poot-yeh-shest-vee-ee)
бюро путешествий ______________
travel agency

(poot-yeh-shest-vyen-neek)
путешественник ______________
traveler

(pah-yezd-kah)
поездка ______________
journey, trip

If **вы** choose **ехать на машине, вот** a few key **слов.**

(shàhs-syeh)
шоссе шоссе, шоссе, шоссе
main road

(mah-shee-nah) (nah-prah-kaht)
машина напрокат ______________
rental car

(dah-roh-gah)
дорога ______________
road

(byoo-roh) (prah-kah-tah)
бюро проката ______________
rental agency

(oo-leet-sah)
улица ______________
street

(ahv-tah-stahnt-see-yah)
автостанция ______________
service station

(vnee-zoo) **Внизу** some basic signs which *(vahm)* **вам** *(noozh-nah)* **нужно** *(znaht)* **знать** (to know).

(vhah-deet)
входить ______________
to enter

(vwee-hah-deet)
выходить ______________
to exit

ВХОД

ВЫХОД

(vhohd)
вход ______________
entrance

(vwee-hahd)
выход ______________
exit

(glahv-nee)
главный вход ______________
main entrance

(zah-pahs-noy)
запасной выход ______________
emergency exit

ОТ СЕБЯ

К СЕБЕ

(aht) (syeb-yah)
от себя ______________
push (doors)

(kuh) (syeb-yeh)
к себе ______________
pull (doors)

☐ **театр** *(tee-ah-ter)*	theater		______________
☐ **телевизор** *(teh-leh-vee-zar)*	television		______________
☐ **телеграмма** *(teh-leh-grahm-mah)*	telegram	**т**	______________
☐ **телескоп** *(teh-leh-skope)*	telescope		______________
☐ **телефон** *(teh-leh-fohn)*	telephone		______________

Let's learn the basic travel verbs. Take out a piece of paper **и** make up your own sentences with these new **слова.** Follow the same pattern **вы** have in previous Steps.

(lee-tyet) **лететь** to fly ______

(yek-aht) (nah) (mah-shee-nyeh) **ехать на машине** to drive ______

(pree-hah-deet) **приходить** to arrive (vehicles) ______

(aht-hah-deet) **отходить** to depart (vehicles) ______

(oo-yez-zhaht) **уезжать** to leave ______

(oo-klah-dih-vaht) **укладывать** to pack ______

(dyeh-laht) **делать** to make ______

(dyeh-laht) (pyair-yeh-sahd-koo) **делать пересадку** to make a transfer ______

Вот some *(noh-vih-yeh)* **новые слова** *(dil-yah)* **для** *(pah-yezd-kee)* **поездки.** (journey)

(ah-air-ah-port) **аэропорт** airport

______

(plaht-for-mah) **платформа** platform

______

(rah-spee-sah-nee-yeh) **расписание поездов** timetable

Санкт-Петербург ---		Москва
Отправление	Поезд	Прибытие
00:41	50	12:41
07:40	19	19:40
12:15	10	00:15
14:32	04	02:32
21:40	22	09:40

______

(vahk-zahl) **вокзал** train station

______

☐ **теннис** *(tyen-nees)*........................ tennis ______
☐ **три** *(tree)*........................ three ______
☐ **томат** *(tah-maht)*........................ tomato **Т** ______
☐ **тост** *(toast)*........................ toast ______
☐ **турист** *(too-reest)*........................ tourist ______

С these words **вы** are ready for any trip, anywhere. **Вы** should have no problem **с** these verbs, just remember the basic "plug-in" formula **вы** have already learned. Use that knowledge to translate the following thoughts **на** (into) **русский. Ответы внизу.** *Hint:* If **вы** have forgotten the words for "to reserve" **и** "to arrive," review pages 40 **и** 42 again.

1. I fly to Russia. ____________________
2. I make a transfer in Moscow. ____________________
3. He arrives in Yalta. ____________________
4. We leave tomorrow. *Мы уезжаем завтра.*
5. We reserve tickets to Kiev. ____________________
6. They drive to Novgorod. ____________________
7. Where is the train to Odessa? ____________________
8. How can I fly to Russia? On British Airways or Aeroflot? ____________________

Вот some **очень** important words for the traveler.

Санкт-Петербург ---		Москва
Отправление	Поезд	Прибытие
00:41	50	12:41
07:40	19	19:40
12:15	10	00:15
14:32	04	02:32
21:40	22	09:40

(zahn-yah-tah)
занято ____________________
occupied

(svah-bohd-nah)
свободно ____________________
free

(vah-gohn)
вагон ____________________
compartment, wagon

(myes-tah)
место ____________________
seat, place

(aht-prahv-lyen-ee-yeh)
отправление ____________________
departure

(pree-bit-ee-yeh)
прибытие ____________________
arrival

(ee-nah-strahn-nee)
иностранный ____________________
foreign

(myes-nee)
местный ____________________
domestic, internal

ОТВЕТЫ

1. **Я лечу в Россию.**
2. **Я делаю пересадку в Москве.**
3. **Он приезжает в Ялту.**
4. **Мы уезжаем завтра.**
5. **Мы заказываем билеты в Киев.**
6. **Они едут на машине в Новгород.**
7. **Где поезд в Одессу?**
8. **Как я могу лететь в Россию? Британской авиакомпанией или Аэрофлотом?**

Increase your travel **слова** by writing out **слова внизу и** practicing the sample sentences out loud. Practice asking **"где"** questions. It will help you *(pohzh-yeh)* **позже** (later).

(vuh)
в ____________________
to
Где поезд в Москву?

(poot)
путь ____________________
line, route
Где путь номер семь?

(kah-myair-ah) (hrah-nyen-ee-yah)
камера хранения ____________________
left-luggage office
Где камера хранения?

(nah-seel-shcheek)
носильщик ____________________
porter
Где носильщик?

(sprah-vahch-nah-yeh) (byoo-roh)
справочное бюро ____________________
information bureau
Где справочное бюро?

(tah-mohzh-nyah)
таможня Где таможня? Где таможня? Где таможня?
customs
Где таможня?

(kahs-sah)
касса ____________________
ticket office, cashier
Где касса?

(myes-tah)
место ____________________
seat, place
Это место занято?

(vah-gohn)
вагон ____________________
compartment, wagon
Этот вагон свободен?

(vah-gohn-res-tah-rahn)
вагон-ресторан ____________________
dining compartment
Где вагон-ресторан?

(spahl-nee)
спальный вагон ____________________
sleeping compartment
Где спальный вагон?

(boo-fyet)
буфет ____________________
snack car
Где буфет?

__________ (when) __________ (when) **касса открыта?**

__________ (what) __________ (what) **вы делаете?**

- ☐ **февраль** *(fyev-rahl)* .... February ____________
- ☐ **фильм** *(feelm)* .... film ____________
- ☐ **фотограф** *(fah-toh-grahf)* .... photographer **ф** ____________
- ☐ **Франция** *(frahn-tsee-yah)* .... France ____________
- ☐ — where they speak **по-французски** *(pah-frahn-tsoo-skee)* ____________

(mohzh-yet-yeh) (prah-chee-taht)
Вы можете прочитать the following paragraph?
can read

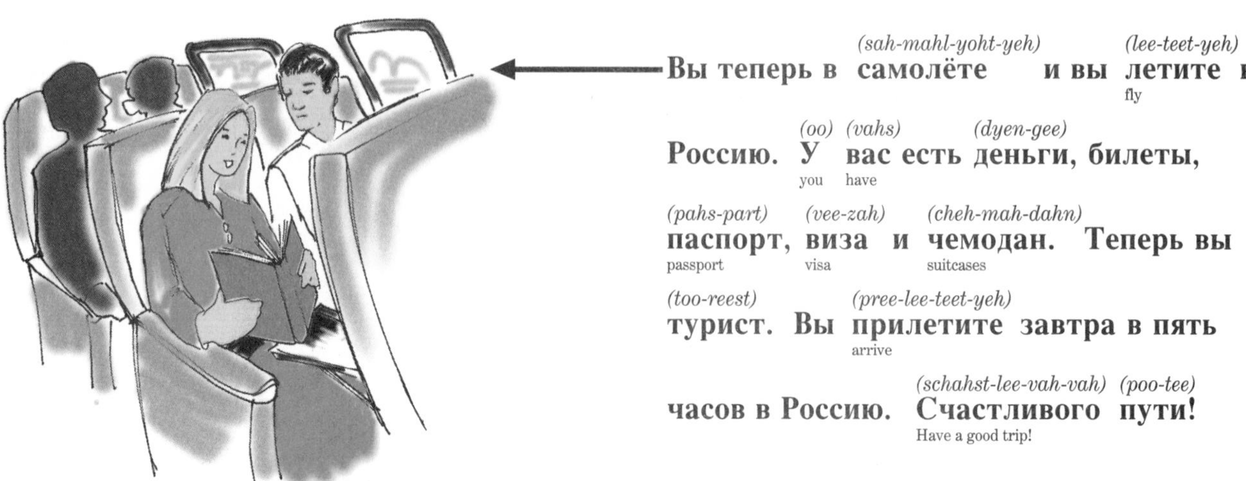

Вы теперь в (sah-mahl-yoht-yeh) **самолёте и вы** (lee-teet-yeh) **летите** (fly) **в России.** (oo) **У** (you) (vahs) **вас есть** (have) (dyen-gee) **деньги, билеты,** (pahs-part) **паспорт,** (passport) (vee-zah) **виза** (visa) **и** (cheh-mah-dahn) **чемодан.** (suitcases) **Теперь вы** (too-reest) **турист. Вы** (pree-lee-teet-yeh) **прилетите** (arrive) **завтра в пять часов в Россию.** (schahst-lee-vah-vah) **Счастливого** (poo-tee) **пути!** (Have a good trip!)

В России there are different types of trains – (pree-gah-rahd-nee-yeh) **пригородные** (suburban) **поезда,** called "(el-ek-treech-kee) **электрички,**" provide the main transportation from (pree-gah-rah-dahv) **пригородов** (suburbs) to (tsen-trah) **центра** (center (of)) (go-rah-dah) **города;** (city) (myezh-doo-gah-rohd-nee-yeh) **междугородные** (inter-city) **поезда** travel longer distances, **между** (gah-rah-dah-mee) **городами.** (cities) If **вы** travel **из** (from) **Москвы в Петербург или из Москвы во Владивосток, вы** may wish to catch an express train which would travel faster **и** make fewer intermediate stops.

☐ **фрукт** *(frookt)*	fruit	**ф**	______
☐ **футбол** *(foot-bohl)*	soccer, football		______
☐ **царь** *(tsar)*	czar, tsar	**ц**	______
☐ **цирк** *(tseerk)*	circus		______
☐ **Чили** *(chee-lee)*	Chile	**ч**	______

Knowing these travel **слова** will make your holiday twice as enjoyable **и** at least three times as easy. Review these **новые слова** by doing the crossword puzzle *(vnee-zoo)* **внизу.** Drill yourself on this Step by selecting other destinations **и** ask your own *(vah-proh-sih)* **вопросы** about *(poh-yez-dahk)* **поездах,** *(ahv-toh-boo-sahk)* **автобусах** **или** *(sah-mahl-yoh-tahk)* **самолётах** that go there. Select **новые слова из** (from) *(slah-var-yah)* **словаря и** ask your own questions beginning with **где, когда,** and **сколько стоит. Ответы** to the crossword puzzle are at the bottom of the next page. **Удачи!**

ACROSS

1. to arrive
2. page
3. platform
4. excuse me
5. main road
6. compartment
7. to eat
8. one
9. thank-you
10. why
11. east
13. customs
14. trip, journey
15. fast
16. domestic, internal
17. to order, to reserve
18. street
19. bank
20. motorcycle

DOWN

3. traveler
8. departure
14. to drink
16. menu
21. restaurant
22. Jewish man
23. or
24. tomorrow
25. over
26. timetable
27. airport
28. hour, o'clock
30. open
31. porter
32. give!
33. taxi
34. toilet

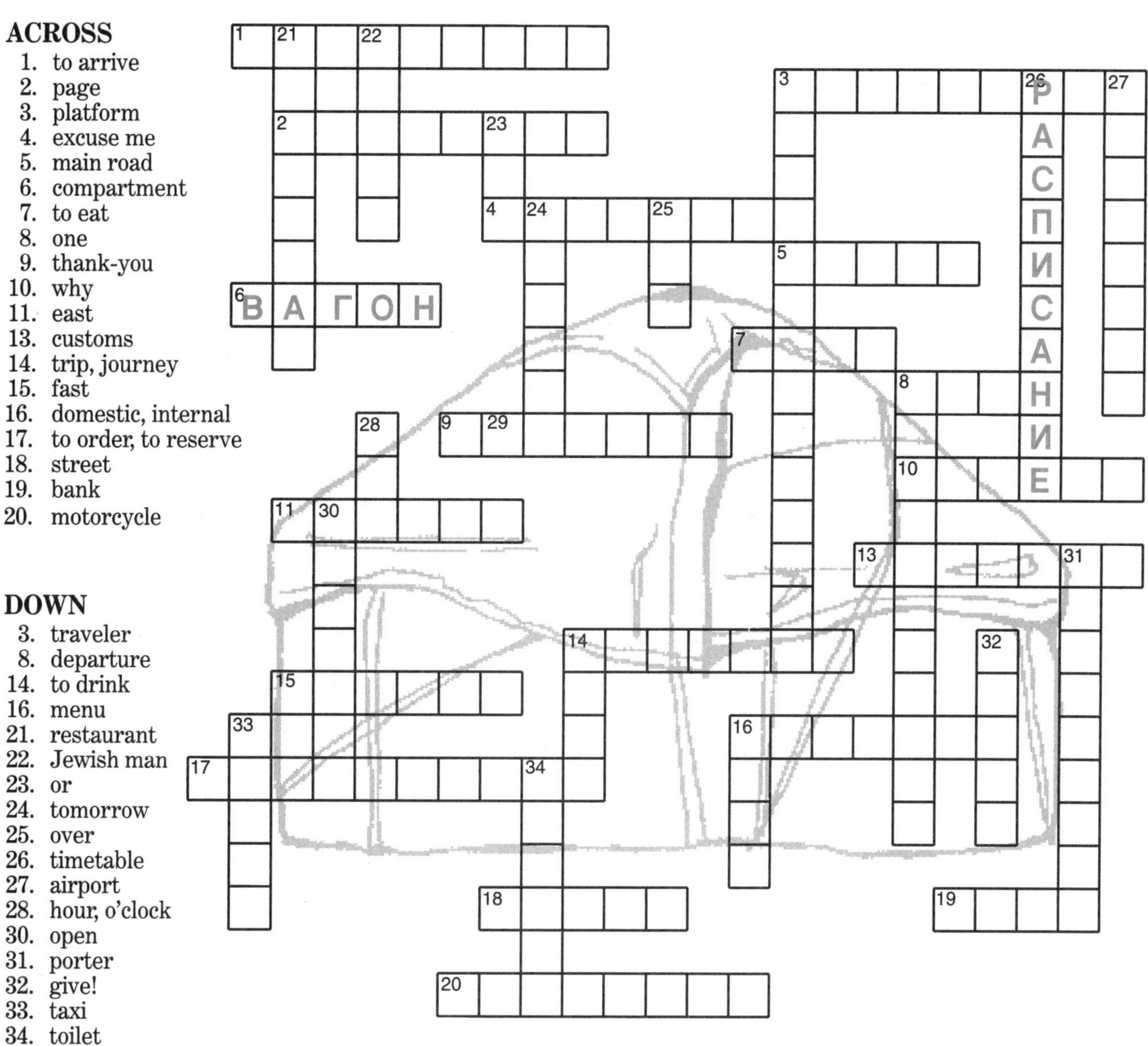

юрта – yurt, the traditional nomadic 'home' of Central Asia. The flag of the Kyrgyz Republic depicts a birds-eye view of these felt-covered structures which have no sharp edges and protect their owners from the harsh elements throughout the year.

☐ **шарф** *(sharf)*	scarf	________
☐ **Швеция** *(shvet-see-yah)*	Sweden	________
☐ — where they speak **по-шведски** *(pah-shved-skee)*	**Ш**	________
☐ **штат** *(shtaht)*	state	________
☐ **шторм** *(shtorm)*	storm	________

What about inquiring about the price of **билетов?** *(beel-yet-tohv)* tickets **Вы можете** *(mohzh-yet-yeh)* can ask these **вопросы.**

Сколько стоит билет *(beel-yet)* **в Петербург?** ______________________

Сколько стоит билет в Одессу? *(ah-des-soo)* ______________________

Сколько стоит билет в Москву? *(mahsk-voo)* ______________________

в одном направлении *(ahd-nohm) (nah-prahv-lyen-ee-ee)* one-way ______________________

туда и обратно *(too-dah) (ahb-raht-nah)* there and back, round trip ______________________

What about times of **отправления** *(aht-prahv-lyen-ee-yah)* departure **и прибытия?** *(pree-bit-ee-yah)* arrival **Вы тоже** *(toh-zheh)* **можете** ask these **вопросы.**

Когда *(kahg-dah)* when **отходит** *(aht-hah-deet)* departs **поезд в Ташкент?** *(tahsh-kyent)* Tashkent ______________________

Когда улетает *(oo-lee-tah-yet)* flies away **самолёт** *(sah-mahl-yoht)* **в Москву?** ______________________

Когда улетает самолёт во *(voh)* to **Владивосток?** *(vlah-dee-vah-stohk)* ______________________

Когда приходит *(pree-hoh-deet)* arrives **поезд из** from **Риги?** *(ree-gee)* Riga ______________________

Когда приходит поезд из Баку? *(bah-koo)* Baku ______________________

Вы have just arrived **в Россию. Вы теперь на** at **вокзале.** *(vahk-zahl-yeh)* **Вы хотите** *(hah-teet-yeh)* want **ехать** to go **в Петербург?** **или в Киев?** *(kee-yev)* Kiev **или в Москву? или в Одессу?** Tell that to the person at **окне** window selling **билеты.**

Я хочу поехать в Одессу. *(ah-des-soo)* Odessa ______________________

Когда отходит поезд в Одессу? ______________________

Сколько стоит билет в Одессу? ______________________

ОТВЕТЫ

ACROSS

1. приезжать
2. страница
3. платформа
4. извините
5. шоссе
6. вагон
7. есть
8. один
9. спасибо
10. почему
11. восток
13. таможня
14. поездка
15. быстро
16. местный
17. заказывать
18. улица
19. банк
20. мотоцикл

DOWN

3. путешественник
8. отправление
14. пить
16. меню
21. ресторан
22. еврей
23. или
24. завтра
25. над
26. расписание
27. аэропорт
28. час
30. открыта
31. носильщик
32. дайте
33. такси
34. туалет

Теперь that **вы** know the words essential for traveling – be it throughout **Россия**, **Украина** *(oo-krah-ee-nah)* Ukraine, **Туркменистан** *(toork-men-ee-stahn)* Turkmenistan **или** **Казахстан** *(kah-zahk-stahn)* Kazakstan – what are some speciality items **вы** might go in search of?

(mah-tryohsh-kah)
матрёшка
nesting dolls

(bah-lah-lie-kah)

балалайка
balalaika

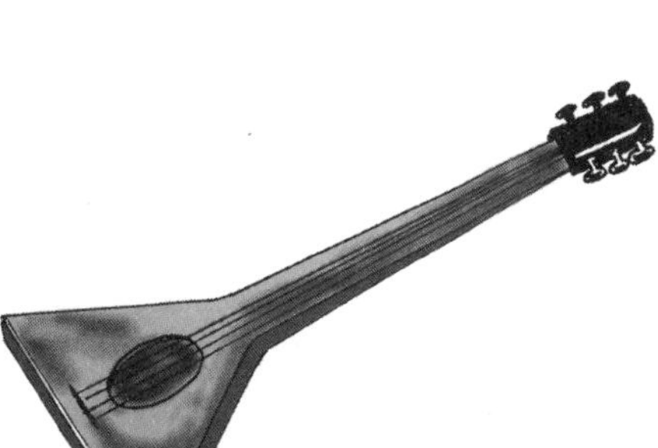

(sah-mah-var)
самовар
samovar

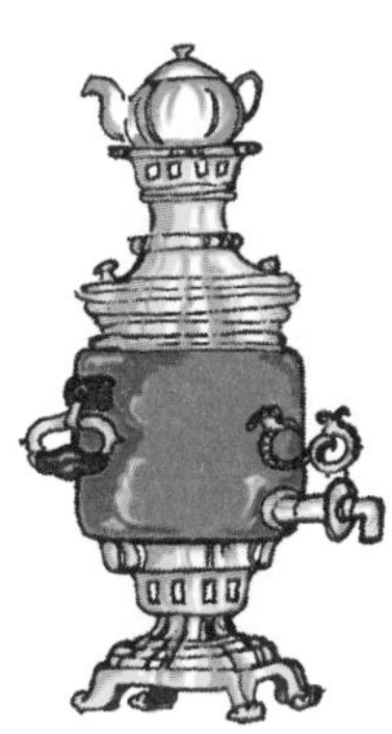

самовар, самовар

(shkah-tool-kah)

шкатулка
lacquer box

(plah-tohk)
платок
shawl

(dyair-yev-yahn-nah-yah) *(pah-soo-dah)*
деревянная посуда
village-style wooden dishes

Your Pocket Pal™ can be found on page 69. Each section focuses on essentials for your **поездка.** Cut out your Pocket Pal™, fold it **и** carry it with you at all times. It does not matter whether **вы** carry it in your pocket, briefcase, knapsack **или** wallet. Do not pack it in your luggage as it will not be much help to you in your suitcase. Your Pocket Pal™ is not meant to replace learning Russian, but will help you in the event **вы** forget something and need a little bit of help.

- ☐ **экватор** *(ek-vah-tar)* .... equator
- ☐ **экзамен** *(ek-zah-myen)* .... exam
- ☐ **экономика** *(ek-ah-noh-mee-kah)* .... economics
- ☐ **экспресс** *(ek-spres)* .... express
- ☐ **эра** *(air-ah)* .... era

Э

20 Меню (men-yoo) menu

Вы теперь в России и у (oo) вас (vahs) [you have] есть номер. Вы [you] хотите (hah-teet-yeh) [are hungry] есть (yest). Где хороший (hah-roh-shee) [good] ресторан (res-tah-rahn)?

First of all, there are different types of places to eat. Let's learn them.

(res-tah-rahn)
ресторан ______________________________
the most expensive of **русских** restaurants — frequently a dinner-and-dance establishment

(stah-loh-vah-yah)
столовая ______________________________
generally self-service, similar to a cafeteria **или** canteen, and yes it also means "dining room"

(boo-fyet)
буфет ______________________________
a snack bar generally found in **гостиницах**, theaters, **музеях**, bus **и** train stations

(bar)
бар ______________________________
exactly that, a place, **где** drinks are served – this is where you come for Russian **водка!**

(kah-fyeh)
кафе ______________________________
similar to a restaurant, meals are served thoughout the evening

If **вы** look around you **в русском ресторане, вы** will see that some **русские** customs might be different from ours. **Хлеб** (hlyeb) [bread] may be set directly on the tablecloth, elbows are often rested **на** (nah) **столе и** please **не** (nyeh) forget to mop up your **соус** (soh-oos) [sauce] **хлебом** (hlyeb-ahm) [with your bread]. Before beginning your **обед** (ah-byed), be sure to wish those sharing your table – **"Приятного аппетита."** (pree-yaht-nah-vah)(ah-peh-tee-tah) [enjoy your meal] Your turn to practice now.

____
(enjoy your meal)

And at least one more time for practice!

____
(enjoy your meal)

- ☐ **эскалатор** *(es-kah-lah-tor)* . . . . escalator ______________
- ☐ **январь** *(yahn-var)* . . . . January ______________
- ☐ **Япония** *(yah-pohn-ee-yah)* . . . . Japan ______________
- ☐ — where they speak **по-японски** *(pah-yah-pohn-skee)* ______________
- ☐ **яхта** *(yahk-tah)* . . . . yacht ______________

Э

Я

There are some **рестораны** whose names are indicative of the foods they serve.

Here you will find – **шашлык** *(shahsh-leek)* shashlik, kebabs — **пирожки** *(pee-rahzh-kee)* pastries, small cakes — **блины** *(blee-nee)* pancakes — **пельмени** *(pyel-myen-ee)* pelmeni, dumplings — **закуски!** *(zah-koo-skee)* snacks

Try them all. Experiment. **Теперь вы** have found **хороший** *(hah-roh-shee)* **ресторан.** *(res-tah-rahn)* **Вы входите** *(vhah-deet-yeh)* enter **в ресторан и находите** *(nah-hoh-deet-yeh)* find **место.** *(myes-tah)* seat Sharing **столы** *(stoh-lih)* tables **с** others is a common **и очень** *(oh-chen)* pleasant custom. If **вы видите** *(vee-deet-yeh)* see a vacant **стул,** *(stool)* chair be sure to ask,

Извините. Это место занято? *(zahn-yah-tah)* occupied

If **вам** *(vahm)* **нужно** *(noozh-nah)* you need **меню,** catch the attention of **официант,** *(ah-feet-see-ahnt)* waiter

Официант! Дайте *(die-tee)* **мне меню, пожалуйста.** *(pah-zhahl-oos-tah)*

____
(Waiter! Please, give me a menu.)

If your **официант** asks if **вы** enjoyed your **обед,** *(ah-byed)* a smile **и "Да, спасибо,"** will tell him that **вы** did.

Most **русские рестораны** *(res-tah-rahn-ih)* post **меню** outside **или** inside. Do not hesitate to ask to see **меню** before being seated so **вы знаете** *(znah-yet-yeh)* know what type of **обеды** *(ah-byed-ih)* meals **и цены** *(tsyen-ih)* prices **вы** will encounter. Most **рестораны** offer a special meal of the day. This is a complete **обед** *(ah-byed)* meal at a fair **цене.** *(tsyen-yeh)* price Be fore-warned that frequently all items **в меню** are **не** available. Have a second choice in mind.

Вот a few special greetings **по-русски.**

- ☐ **С Рождеством Христовым!** *(suh)(rahzh-dyest-vohm)(hrees-toh-vim)* . . . . Merry Christmas!
- ☐ **С Новым годом!** *(suh)(noh-vim)(go-dahm)* . . . . Happy New Year!
- ☐ **С днём рождения!** *(suh)(den-yohm)(rahzh-dyen-ee-yah)* . . . . Happy Birthday!
- ☐ **Поздравления!** *(pahz-drahv-lyen-ee-yah)* . . . . Congratulations!

В России there are **три** main meals to enjoy every day, plus **кофе** (koh-fyeh) **и** perhaps pastry **для** (dil-yah) for the tired traveler late in **днём** (den-yohm) afternoon.

завтрак (zahv-trahk) breakfast ____________________

can mean much more than **чай или кофе, хлеб, масло и** jam. It may include ham **и яйца,** (yight-sah) **сыр** (seer) cheese **или сосиски** (sah-see-skee). Check serving times before **вы** retire for the night or you might miss out!

обед (ah-byed) mid-day meal ____________________

generally served from 14:00 to 16:00. For most, this is the main meal of the day.

ужин (oo-zheen) evening meal ____________________

generally served from 19:00 to 22:30; frequently, after 22:30, only cold items are served.

Most **рестораны** have a standard **меню.** Don't expect to get a separate wine list – it is usually printed on **меню.** Service can be slow, so be prepared to wait between courses. **Теперь** for a preview of delights to come . . . At the back of this **книги,** (kuh-nee-gee) **вы** will find a sample **русское меню.** Read **меню** **сегодня** (see-vohd-nyah) today **и** learn **новые слова! Когда вы** are ready to leave for **Россию** cut out **меню,** fold it **и** carry it in your pocket, wallet **или** purse. Before you go, how do **вы** say these **три** phrases which are so very important for the hungry traveler?

Excuse me. Is this seat occupied? ____________________

Waiter! Please, give me a menu. ____________________

Enjoy your meal! ____________________

____________ (who) **ест суп?** eats

____________ (who) **пьёт чай?** drinks

____________ (who)

____________ (who) **путешествует в Одессу?**

Learning the following should help you to identify what kind of meat **вы** have ordered **и как** it will be prepared.

- ☐ **говядина** *(gahv-yah-dee-nah)* . . . . beef ____________
- ☐ **телятина** *(tyel-yah-tee-nah)* . . . . veal ____________
- ☐ **свинина** *(svee-nee-nah)* . . . . pork ____________
- ☐ **баранина** *(bah-rah-nee-nah)* . . . . mutton ____________

The **меню внизу** has the main categories **вы** will find in most restaurants. Learn them **сегодня** *(see-vohd-nyah)* today so that **вы** will easily recognize them when you dine **в России.** Be sure to write the words in the blanks below.

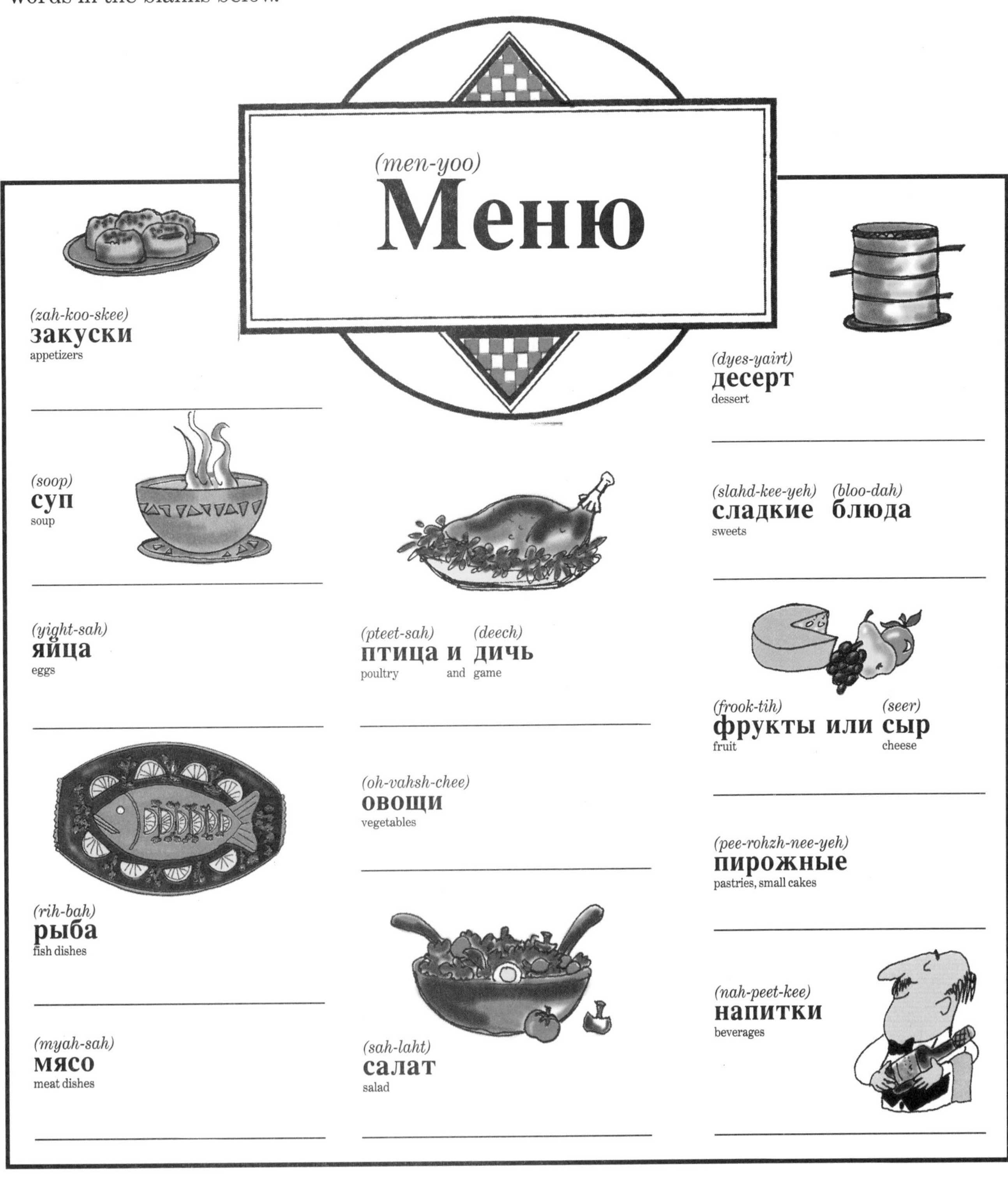

(men-yoo)
Меню

(zah-koo-skee)
закуски
appetizers

(soop)
суп
soup

(yight-sah)
яйца
eggs

(rih-bah)
рыба
fish dishes

(myah-sah)
мясо
meat dishes

(pteet-sah) (deech)
птица и дичь
poultry and game

(oh-vahsh-chee)
овощи
vegetables

(sah-laht)
салат
salad

(dyes-yairt)
десерт
dessert

(slahd-kee-yeh) (bloo-dah)
сладкие блюда
sweets

(frook-tih) (seer)
фрукты или сыр
fruit cheese

(pee-rohzh-nee-yeh)
пирожные
pastries, small cakes

(nah-peet-kee)
напитки
beverages

- ☐ **домашняя птица** *(dah-mahsh-nyah-yah)(pteet-sah)* . . . . poultry ____________
- ☐ **молодая баранина** *(mah-lah-dah-yah)(bah-rah-nee-nah)* . . . . lamb ____________
- ☐ **оленина** *(ahl-yeh-nee-nah)* . . . . venison ____________
- ☐ **отварное** *(aht-var-noh-yeh)* . . . . boiled ____________
- ☐ **жареное** *(zhar-yen-ah-yeh)* . . . . roasted, fried ____________

Вы will also get **овощи** *(oh-vahsh-chee)* vegetables with your **обедом** *(ah-byed-ahm)* meal **и** perhaps **салат.** One day at an open-air **рынке** *(rin-kyeh)* market will teach you **названия** *(nahz-vah-nee-yah)* names for all the different kinds of **овощей** *(ah-vahsh-chay)* **и фруктов** *(frook-tahv)* fruit, plus it will be a delightful experience for you. **Вы можете** *(mohzh-yet-yeh)* always consult your menu guide at the back of **книги** *(kuh-nee-gee)* if **вы** forget the correct **название. Теперь вы** are seated **и официант** *(ah-feet-see-ahnt)* arrives.

Завтрак *(zahv-trahk)* breakfast can vary from a light continental breakfast to a hearty breakfast of eggs **или** cold cuts **или** vegetables. **Внизу** is a sample of what **вы можете** *(mohzh-yet-yeh)* expect to greet you **утром** *(oo-trahm)* in morning.

Напитки
чай с лимоном
кофе чёрный
кофе с молоком
апельсиновый (orange) сок (juice)
какао
Яйца
омлет с сыром (cheese)
взбитая (scrambled) яичница (eggs)
И . . .
сыр (cheese)
пирожные (pastry)
булочки (rolls)
масло
варенье (jam)
Мясо
сосиски (small sausages, hot dogs)
колбаса (sausage)

- ☐ **тушёное** *(toosh-yoh-nah-yeh)* . . . . stewed ____________
- ☐ **запечённое** *(zahp-yeh-chyohn-nah-yeh)* . . . . baked ____________
- ☐ **мясо-гриль** *(myah-sah-greel)* . . . . grilled ____________
- ☐ **фаршированый** *(far-shee-roh-vah-nee)* . . . . stuffed ____________
- ☐ **фри** *(free)* . . . . fried ____________

Вот an example of what **вы** might select for your evening meal. Using your menu guide on pages 119 and 120, as well as what **вы** have learned in this Step, fill in the blanks *in English* with what **вы** believe your **официант** will bring you. **Ответы внизу.**

Супы

Традиционный русский суп "Рыбная солянка"

____

Салаты и закуски

Фрукты с йогуртом

____

Основные блюда

Шашлык из баранины со сладким перцем, луком и рис "Шафран"

____

Десерты

Десерт из бананов и мороженого

____

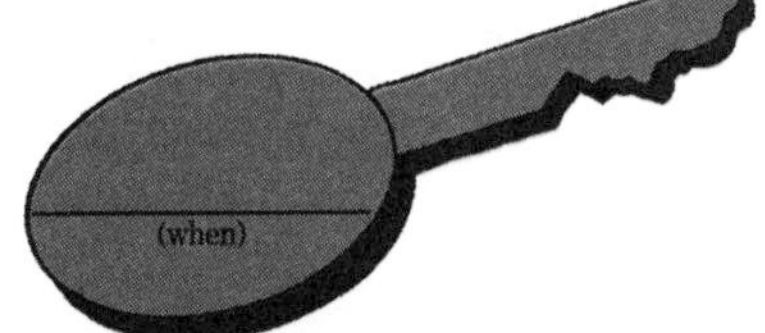

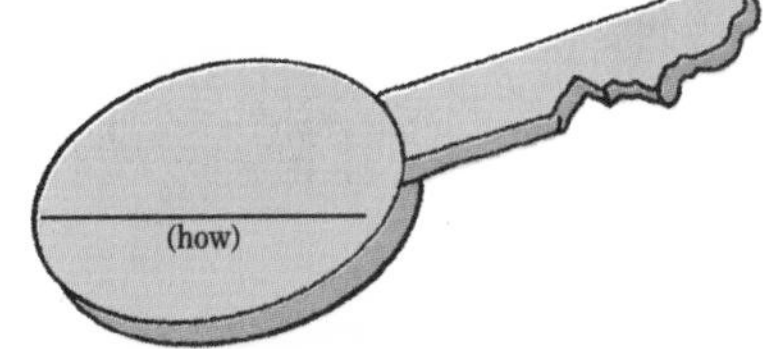

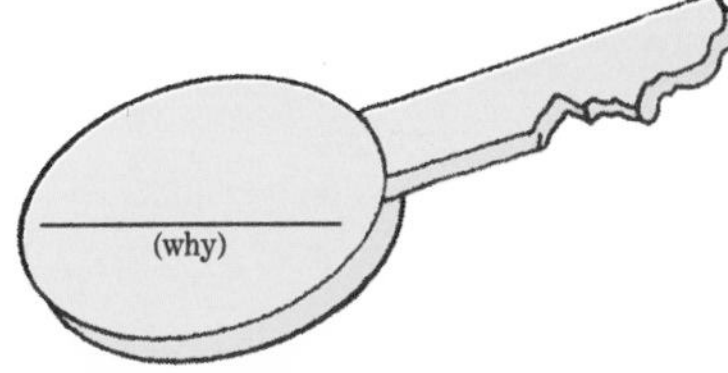

ОТВЕТЫ

Soups: Traditional Russian Fish Solyanka
Salads and Appetizers: Selection of Fruits with Yogurt
Entrees: Lamb, Sweet Pepper and Onion Shashlik with Saffron Rice
Desserts: Banana Split

Теперь it is a good time for a quick review. Draw lines between the *(roos-skee-mee) (slah-vah-mee)* **русскими словами** **и** their English equivalents.

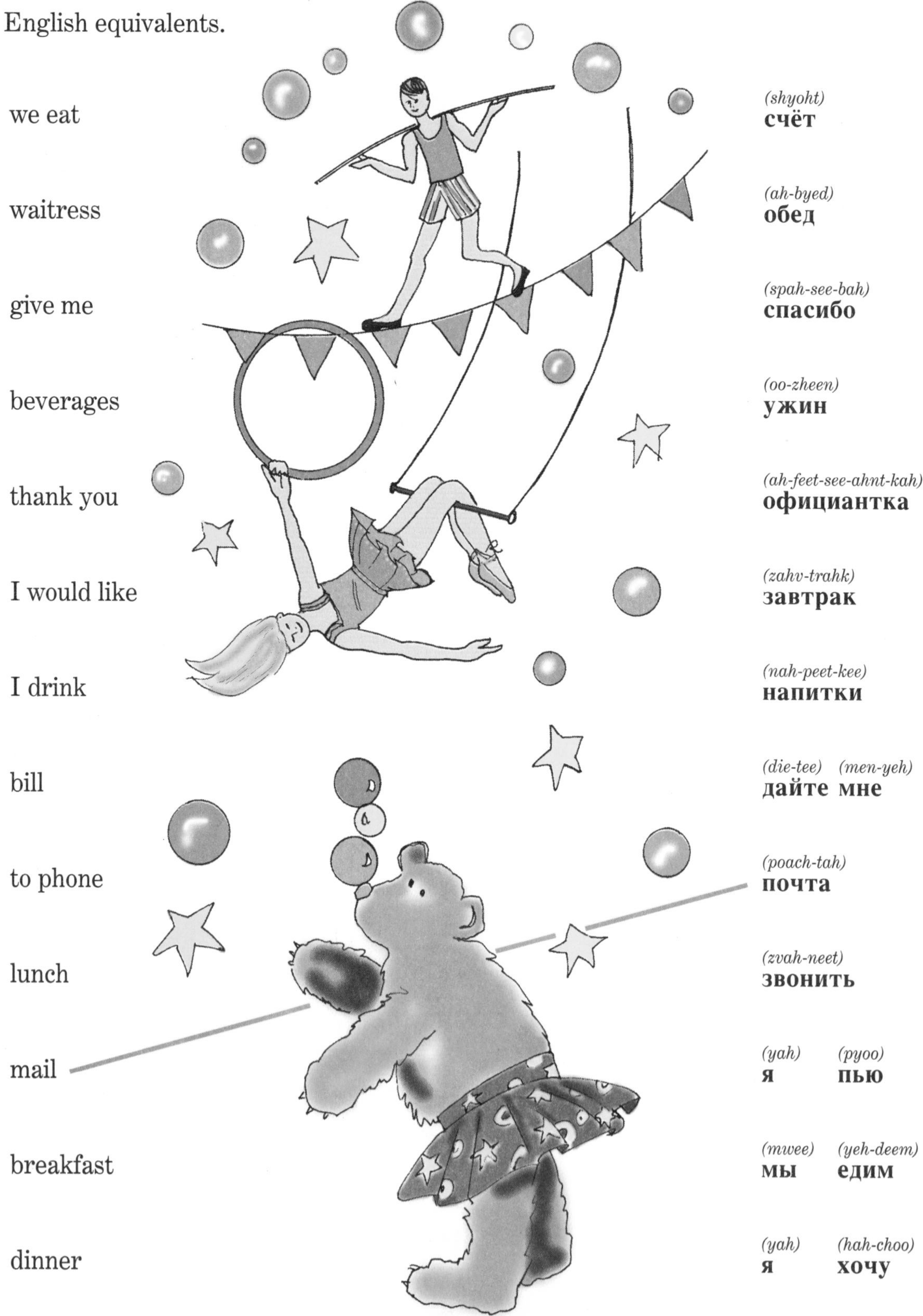

we eat	*(shyoht)* **счёт**
waitress	*(ah-byed)* **обед**
give me	*(spah-see-bah)* **спасибо**
beverages	*(oo-zheen)* **ужин**
thank you	*(ah-feet-see-ahnt-kah)* **официантка**
I would like	*(zahv-trahk)* **завтрак**
I drink	*(nah-peet-kee)* **напитки**
bill	*(die-tee) (men-yeh)* **дайте мне**
to phone	*(poach-tah)* **почта**
lunch	*(zvah-neet)* **звонить**
mail	*(yah) (pyoo)* **я пью**
breakfast	*(mwee) (yeh-deem)* **мы едим**
dinner	*(yah) (hah-choo)* **я хочу**

Вот a few more holidays which you might experience during your visit.

- ☐ **День победы** *(dyen)(pah-byeh-dee)* . . . . Victory Day
- ☐ **День независимости России** *(dyen)(nyeh-zah-vee-see-mah-stee)(rahs-see-ee)* . Russian Independence Day
- ☐ **День Конституции** *(dyen)(kahn-stee-toot-see-ee)* . . . . Constitution Day
- ☐ **Праздник весны** *(prah-zneek)(vees-nee)* . . . . Spring Holiday

Телефон

(teh-leh-fohn) telephone

What is different about телефон (teh-leh-fohn) в России? Well, вы never notice such things until вы want to use them. Be warned теперь that телефоны (teh-leh-fohn-ih) в России are much less numerous than в США (seh-sheh-ah) или в Канаде. Nevertheless, телефон allows you to call друзьям (drooz-yahm) friends, reserve билеты (beel-yet-ih) в театр (tee-ah-ter), на балет (bahl-yet) и концерт (kahn-tsairt), make emergency calls, check on the hours of a музея (moo-zyeh-yah), rent машину (mah-shee-noo) и all those other things which нам (nahm) we need нужно (noozh-nah) сделать to do on a daily basis. It also gives you a certain amount of freedom, когда вы можете (mohzh-yet-yeh) позвонить (pah-zvah-neet) phone on your own.

Having телефон в номере гостиницы не as common в России as в США. That means that вам (vahm) нужно (noozh-nah) знать (znaht) to know, как to find телефон: на почте (poach-teh), на (nah) улице (oo-leet-seh) street, в баре (bar-yeh) и in the lobby of гостиницы.

So, let's learn how to operate телефон.

Инструкции (een-strook-tsee-ee) instructions can look complicated, but remember, some of these слова вы should be able to recognize already. Ready? Well, before you turn the page it would be a good idea to go back и review all your numbers one more time.

To dial from the United States to any other country вы need that country's international area code. Your телефонная книга at home should have a listing of international area codes. When

Вот some **очень** useful words built around the word, **"телефон."**

- ☐ **телефонист** *(teh-leh-fahn-eest)* .... operator ____________
- ☐ **телефон-автомат** *(teh-leh-fohn-ahv-tah-maht)* .... public telephone booth ____________
- ☐ **телефонная книга** *(teh-leh-fohn-nah-yah)(kuh-nee-gah)*.. telephone book ____________
- ☐ **разговор по телефону** *(rahz-gah-vor)(pah)(teh-leh-foh-noo)* telephone conversation ____________

вы leave your contact numbers with friends, family **или** business colleagues, **вы** should include your destination country's area code **и** city code whenever possible . For example,

Country Codes		City Codes	
Russia	7	Moscow	095
		St. Petersburg	812
Ukraine	7	Kiev	044
		Odessa	0482
Lithuania	370	Kaunas	7

To call from one city to another city **в России**, you may need to go **на почту** *(poach-too)* **или звонить телефонисту** (operator) **из гостиницы. На почте** tell **телефонисту "Мне нужно позвонить в США,"** **или "Мне нужно позвонить в Англию."**

Now you try it: ______________________________
(I need to call to the U.S.A.)

Do not be surprised if **вы** have to pay for your call in advance. Sometimes it is even necessary to order your call a day in advance.

When answering **телефон, вы** pick up the receiver **и** say, *(ahl-loh)* **Алло. Это**__________ (your name).

When saying goodbye, you say **"До свидания"** or **"До завтра."** (until tomorrow) Your turn —

____
(Hello. This is . . .)

______________ (goodbye) ______________ (until tomorrow)

Не forget that **вы можете** *(mohzh-yet-yeh)* (can) ask . . .

Сколько стоит позвонить в США? *(seh-sheh-ah)* (U.S.A.) ______________________________

Сколько стоит позвонить в Англию? ______________________________

Вот free telephone calls.
- ☐ **пожарная охрана** *(pah-zhar-nah-yah)(ah-hrah-nah)* . . fire 01 __________
- ☐ **милиция** *(mee-leet-see-yah)* . . . . police 02 __________
- ☐ **скорая помощь** *(skoh-rah-yah)(poh-mashch)* . . . . emergency medical help 03 __________
- ☐ **служба газа** *(sloozh-bah)(gah-zah)* . . . . heating gas service 04 __________

(voht) *(teh-leh-foh-noo)*
Вот some sample sentences **по телефону.** Write them in the blanks **внизу.**

(hah-choo) *(chee-kah-goh)*
Я хочу позвонить в Чикаго. ______________________
to call · Chicago

(kahs-soo) *(ah-air-ah-floh-tah)* *(ah-air-ah-par-too)*
Я хочу позвонить в кассу "Аэрофлота" в аэропорту. ______________________
booking office of

(lohn-dahn)
Я хочу позвонить в Лондон. *Я хочу позвонить в Лондон.*

(moy) *(nohm-yair)*
Мой номер 344-21-89. ______________________
my

(vahsh) *(pah-zhahl-oos-tah)*
Ваш номер телефона, пожалуйста? ______________________
your · number

(naht-see-oh-nahl)
Номер телефона гостиницы "Националь," пожалуйста? ______________________
hotel

(ee-vahn) *(ee-vah-nah-veech)* *(pah-gah-vah-reet)* *(ahn-noy)*
Иван: **Алло. Это Иван Иванович. Я хочу поговорить с Анной Петровной.**
to speak

____

(syek-ryair-tar) *(noh)* *(lee-nee-yah)* *(zahn-yah-tah)*
Секретарь: **Одну минуту. Извините, но линия занята.**
one · but · line · busy

____

(pahv-tah-reet-yeh) *(myed-lyen-nah)*
Иван: **Повторите, пожалуйста. Говорите медленно, пожалуйста.**
repeat · speak · slowly

____

Секретарь: **Извините, но линия занята.**

____

Иван: **Спасибо. До свидания.**

____

(myed-lyen-nah)
Вы теперь ready to use any **телефон в России.** Just take it **медленно и** speak clearly.
slowly

Вот countries, **где русский язык,** as well as other languages, is spoken that **вы** may wish to call.

- ☐ **Азербайджан** *(ah-zyair-by-dzhan)* .... Azerbaijan ______
- ☐ **Армения** *(ar-myeh-nee-yah)* .... Armenia ______
- ☐ **Беларусь** *(byeh-lah-roos)* .... Belarus ______
- ☐ **Грузия** *(groo-zee-yah)* .... Georgia ______

22 Метро

(myeh-troh) subway

An excellent means of transportation **в России** is **метро** (myeh-troh). In many cities, **метро** is an extensive system with express lines to the suburbs. **Трамвай** (trahm-vy) (streetcar) is also a good means of transportation, plus **вы можете** see your surroundings **на трамвае** (trahm-vah-yeh).

(myeh-troh) **метро** subway

(trahm-vy) **трамвай** streetcar, trolley

_______________ _______________

(stahnt-see-yah) **станция** (station) **метро**

(ahs-tah-nohv-kah) **остановка** (stop) *(trahm-vah-yah)* **трамвая**

остановка (stop) *(ahv-toh-boo-sah)* **автобуса**

_______________ _______________ _______________

Maps displaying the various **линии** (lee-nee-ee) (lines) **и** **остановки** (ahs-tah-nohv-kee) (stops) are generally posted inside **станции** (stahnt-see-ee) **метро.** Almost every **карта Москвы и Петербурга** has **метро** map. **Линии** (lee-nee-ee) (lines) are color-coded to facilitate reading just like your example on the next page. **Метро в Москве** is famous for its elaborate stations with mosaics **и** sculptures. Enjoy them as **вы** pass through. Don't forget, **вы** need tokens for **метро**!

- ☐ **Казахстан** *(kah-zahk-stahn)* .... Kazakstan _______________
- ☐ **Кыргызская республика** *(kir-geez-skah-yah)(rehs-poo-blee-kah)* Kyrgyz Republic _______________
- ☐ **Латвия** *(laht-vee-yah)* .... Latvia _______________
- ☐ **Литва** *(leet-vah)* .... Lithuania _______________
- ☐ **Молдова** *(mahl-doh-vah)* .... Moldova _______________

Other than having foreign words, the Russian **метро** functions just like **метро в США, в Канаде или в Англии.** Locate your destination, select the correct line on your practice **метро и** hop on board.

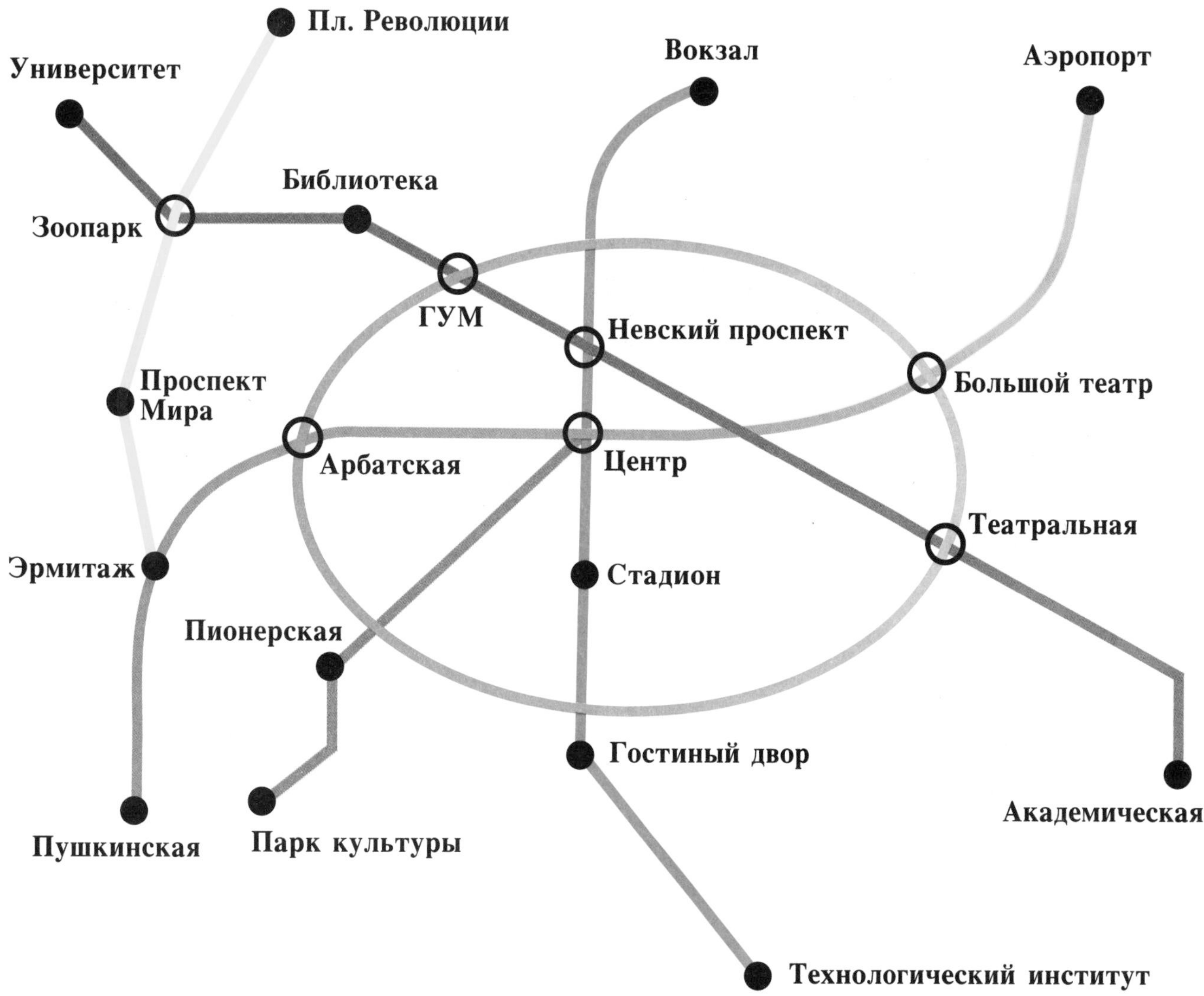

Say these questions aloud many times and don't forget your tokens for **метро.**

Где *(stahnt-see-yah)* **станция метро?**	**Где** *(ahs-tah-nohv-kah)* **остановка автобуса?**
Где *(stah-yahn-kah)* **стоянка такси?**	**Где остановка** *(trahm-vah-yah)* **трамвая?**

- ☐ **Таджикистан** *(tahd-zheek-ee-stahn)* . . . . Tajikistan ________________
- ☐ **Туркменистан** *(toork-men-ee-stahn)* . . . . . . Turkmenistan ________________
- ☐ **Украина** *(oo-krah-ee-nah)* . . . . Ukraine ________________
- ☐ **Узбекистан** *(ooz-bek-ee-stahn)* . . . . Uzbekistan ________________
- ☐ **Эстония** *(es-toh-nee-yah)* . . . . Estonia ________________

Practice the following basic **вопросы** out loud **и** then write them in the blanks below.

1. **Как** (how) *(chahs-tah)* **часто** (often) *(hoh-deet)* **ходит** (goes) **автобус номер 36?** ____________________

Как часто ходит *(trahm-vy)* **трамвай номер 20?** ____________________

2. *(ee-dyoht)* **Идёт** (goes) **автобус до Большого театра?** ____________________

Идёт трамвай до зоопарка? ____________________

Идёт поезд до гостиницы "Метрополь"? ____________________

3. **Сколько стоит билет в метро?** Сколько стоит билет в метро?

Сколько стоит билет в автобусе? ____________________

Сколько стоит билет на поезд? ____________________

Сколько стоит билет в трамвае? ____________________

4. **Где я** *(mah-goo)* **могу** (can) **купить** (buy) **билет на метро?** ____________________

Где я могу купить билет на автобус? ____________________

Где я могу купить билет на поезд? ____________________

Let's change directions **и** learn **три** new verbs. **Вы** know the basic "plug-in" formula, so write out your own sentences using these new verbs.

(stee-raht) **стирать** to wash (clothes) ____________________

(tyair-yaht) **терять** to lose ____________________

(zah-nee-mah-yet) **занимает** it takes ____________________

Вот a few holidays to keep in mind.

- ☐ **Пасха** *(pahs-hkah)* .... Easter
- ☐ **Новый год** *(noh-vee)(gohd)* .... New Year's Day
- ☐ **Рождество** *(rahsh-dyest-voh)* .... Russian Orthodox Christmas
- ☐ **Международный женский день** *(myezh-doo-nah-rohd-nee)(zhen-skee)(dyen)* . International Women's Day

23 Продавать и покупать

(prah-dah-vaht) Продавать — to sell; (pah-koo-paht) покупать — to buy

Shopping abroad is exciting. The simple everyday task of buying **литр** (lee-ter) liter **молока** (mah-lah-kah) milk **или** **яблоко** (yah-blah-kah) apple becomes a challenge that **вы** (vwee) should **теперь** be able to meet quickly **и** easily. Of course, **вы** will purchase **сувениры** (soo-veh-neer-ih) souvenirs, **марки и открытки**, but **не** forget those many other items ranging from shoelaces to **аспирина** (ah-spee-ree-nah) aspirin that **вы** might need unexpectedly. Locate your store, draw a line to it **и**, as always, write your new words in the blanks provided.

(oo-nee-vyair-mahg) **универмаг** ______________________ department store

(kee-noh) **кино** ______________________ cinema

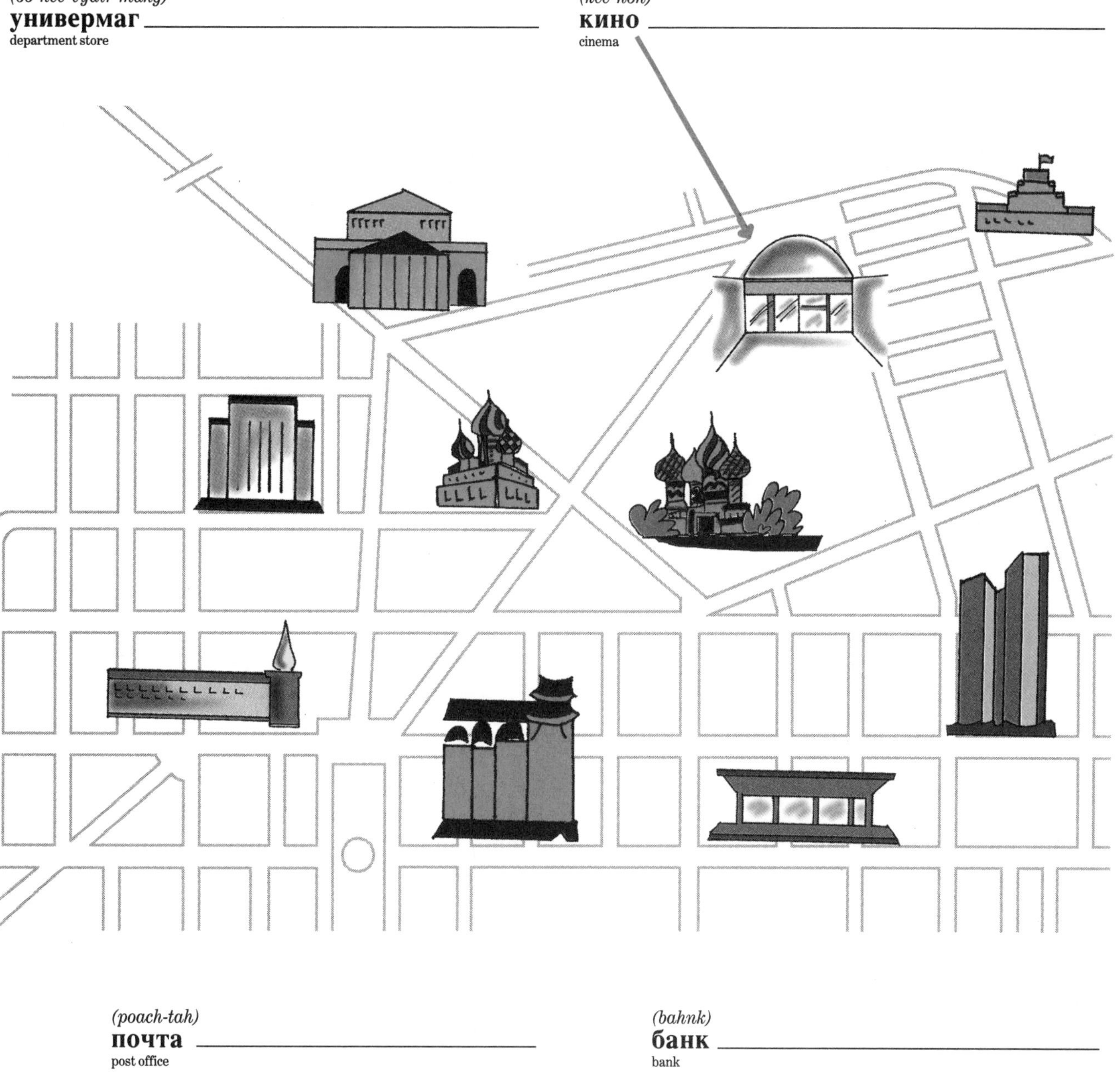

(poach-tah) **почта** ______________________ post office

(bahnk) **банк** ______________________ bank

(gah-stee-neet-sah) **гостиница** ______________________ hotel, inn

(byen-zah-kah-lohn-kah) **бензоколонка** ______________________ service station *(mah-gah-zeen-ih)* **Магазины** are generally *(aht-krih-tih)* **открыты** (open) from 8:00 or 10:00 until 19:00 or 20:00. Keep in mind, many shops close over the lunch hour.

(myahs-noy) **мясной** (butcher) *(mah-gah-zeen)* **магазин** (shop) ____________

(kuh-nee-gee) **книги** (bookstore) ____________

____________ *(heem-cheest-kah)* **химчистка** (dry cleaner's)

____________ *(oh-vahsh-chee)* **овощи** (greengrocer)

____________ *(ahp-tyek-ah)* **аптека** (pharmacy)

____________ *(stah-yahn-kah)* **стоянка** (parking lot)

____________ *(kee-ohsk)* **киоск** (newsstand)

____________ *(gah-strah-nohm)* **гастроном** (grocery store, delicatessen)

____________ *(tah-bahk)* **табак** (tobacco)

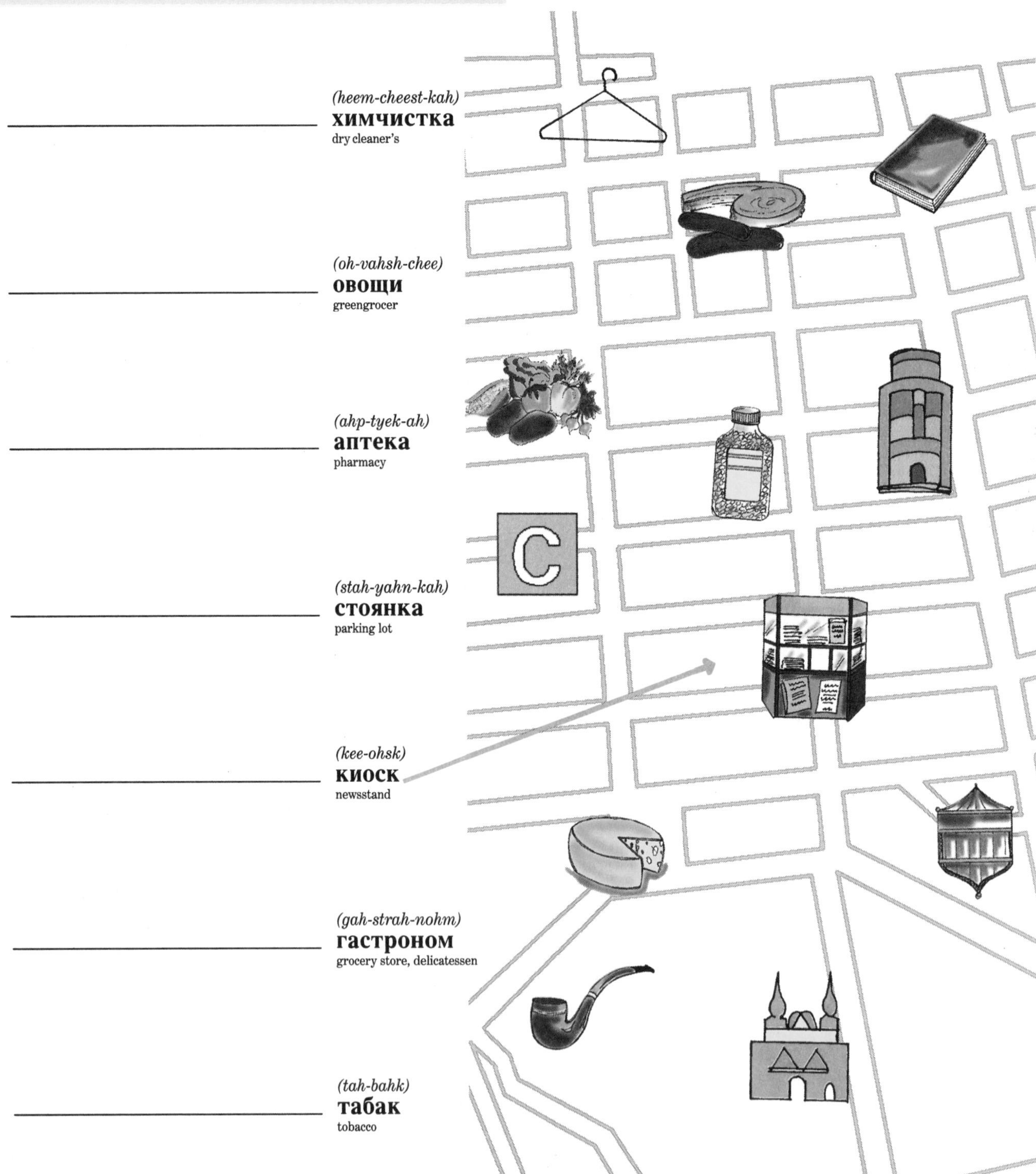

While **в Москве вы** will want to visit **ГУМ**, short for **"Государственный** *(gah-soo-darst-vyen-nee)* **универсальный** *(oo-nee-vyair-sahl-nee)* **магазин." ГУМ** sells everything!

(byoo-roh) **бюро** *(poot-yeh-shest-vee-ee)* **путешествий** (travel agency) ____________

(mee-leet-see-yah) **милиция** (police) ____________

(mah-lah-koh)
молоко
dairy

(tsvet-ih)
цветы
flowers

(rib-nee) (rin-ahk)
рыбный рынок
fish market

(foh-tah-tah-vah-rih)
фототовары
camera supplies

(rin-ahk)
рынок
market

(prahd-mahg)
продмаг
food store

(chah-sih)
часы
watchmaker

(boo-lahch-nah-yah)
булочная булочная, булочная
bakery

(kah-fyeh)
кафе
cafe

(prahch-yech-nah-yah)
прачечная
laundry

(kahnt-stah-vah-rih)
канцтовары
stationery store

(pah-reek-mahk-yairs-kah-yah)
парикмахерская
hairdresser

While **Москва** has (goom) **ГУМ**, **Санкт-Петербург** has "(gah-stee-nee) **Гостиный** (dvor) **двор**". **Гостиный двор** is the city's largest shopping mall. Enjoy shopping, browsing or just people-watching.

(oo-nee-vyair-sahl-nee) Универсальный *(mah-gah-zeen)* магазин

department store

At this point, **вы** should just about be ready for your **поездки. Вы** have gone shopping for those last-minute odds 'n ends. Most likely, the store directory at your local **универсальный** *(oo-nee-vyair-sahl-nee)* (department) **магазин** (store) did not look like the one **внизу. Вы знаете**, that **"женщина"** *(zhen-shchee-nah)* is Russian for "woman" so if **вам нужно** something for a woman, **вы** would probably look **на втором** *(vtah-rohm)* (second) **этаже**, *(eh-tahzh-yeh)* (floor) wouldn't you?

5. этаж	Хрусталь Фарфор Керамика Товары для кухни	Кафе Вино Фрукты Овощи	Мороженое Булочная Спиртные напитки Ресторан
4. этаж	Кровати Постельное Бельё Зеркала Мебель	Лампы Ковры Картины Электроприборы	Телевизоры Фототовары Радио
3. этаж	Детский отдел Детская обувь Купальные костюмы	Спортивные товары Кожаные товары Перчатки	Принадлежности туалета Ювелирные изделия Часы
2. этаж	Женская одежда Женские головные уборы Женская обувь	Мужская одежда Мужские головные уборы Мужская обувь	Носки, чулки Пояса Зонты
1. этаж	Книги Табак Газеты Журналы	Карты Конфеты Игрушки Духи	Косметика Музыкальные товары Канцтовары

Let's start a checklist **для поездки.** Besides **одежды,** *(ah-dyezh-dih)* (clothes) **что вам нужно?** As you learn these **слова**, assemble these items **в углу** (corner) of your **дома.** Check **и** make sure that **они** are clean **и** ready **для поездки.** *(pah-yezd-kee)* (trip) Be sure to do the same **с** the rest of **вещами** *(vesh-chah-mee)* (things) that **вы** pack. On the next pages, match each item to its picture, draw a line to it and write out the word many times. As **вы** organize these things, check them off on this list. Do not forget to take the next group of sticky labels and label **эти** *(et-tee)* **вещи сегодня.** *(see-vohd-nyah)*

(pahs-part)
паспорт
passport

(beel-yet)
билет
ticket

(cheh-mah-dahn)
чемодан
suitcase

(soom-kah)
сумка
handbag

сумка, сумка, сумка ✔

(boo-mahzh-neek)
бумажник
wallet

(dyen-gee)
деньги
money

(kreh-deet-nah-yah) *(kar-tahch-kah)*
кредитная карточка
credit card

(dah-rohzh-nih-yeh) *(cheh-kee)*
дорожные чеки
traveler's checks

(foh-tah-ahp-pah-raht)
фотоаппарат
camera

(foh-tah-plyohn-kah)
фотоплёнка
film

(koo-pahl-nee) *(kahst-yoom)*
купальный костюм
swimsuit

(koo-pahl-nee) *(kahst-yoom)*
купальный костюм
swimsuit

(sahn-dahl-ee-ee)
сандалии
sandals

(tyohm-nih-yeh) *(ahch-kee)*
тёмные очки
sunglasses

(zoob-nah-yah) *(shchoht-kah)*
зубная щётка
toothbrush

(zoob-nah-yah) *(pahs-tah)*
зубная паста
toothpaste

(mwee-lah)
мыло
soap

(breet-vah)
бритва
razor

(dyeh-zah-dah-rahnt)
дезодорант
deodorant

(rahs-chohs-kah)
расчёска
comb

расчёска, расчёска

(pahl-toh)
пальто
overcoat

(zohn-teek)
зонтик
umbrella

(plahshch)
плащ
raincoat

(pyair-chaht-kee)
перчатки
gloves

(shlyah-pah)
шляпа
hat

(shlyah-pah)
шляпа
hat

(sah-pah-gee)
сапоги
boots

(too-flee)
туфли
shoes

(krahs-sohv-kee)
кроссовки
tennis shoes

(kahst-yoom)
костюм
suit

(gahl-stook)
галстук
tie

(roo-bahsh-kah)
рубашка
shirt

(plah-tohk)
платок
handkerchief

(peed-zhahk)
пиджак
jacket, blazer

(bryoo-kee)
брюки
trousers

(dzheen-sih)
джинсы
jeans

(shohr-tih)
шорты
shorts

(my-kah)
майка
t-shirt

(troo-sih)
трусы
underpants

(my-kah)
майка
undershirt

(plaht-yeh)
платье
dress

(blooz-kah)
блузка
blouse

(yoob-kah)
юбка
skirt

юбка, юбка, юбка ✔

(svee-tyair)
свитер
sweater

(kahm-bee-naht-see-yah)
комбинация
slip

(leef-cheek)
лифчик
brassiere

(troo-sih)
трусы
underpants

(nah-skee)
носки
socks

(kahl-goht-kee)
колготки
pantyhose

(pee-zhah-mah)
пижама
pajamas

(nahch-nah-yah) (roo-bahsh-kah)
ночная рубашка
night shirt

(bahn-nee) (hah-laht)
банный халат
bathrobe

(tah-poach-kee)
тапочки
slippers

From now on, (oo) (vahs) **у вас** (you have) (zoob-nah-yah) (pahs-tah) **"зубная паста"** (ah) **а** (and) **не** "toothpaste." Having assembled (et-tee) **эти** (these) **вещи, вы** are ready (yek-hakt) **ехать** (to go). Let's add these important shopping phrases to your basic repetoire.

(kah-koy) (rahz-myair)
Какой размер? ____________
what size

(hah-rah-shoh) (see-deet)
Хорошо сидит. ____________
well it fits

(ploh-hah) (see-deet)
Плохо сидит. ____________
badly it fits

Treat yourself to a final review. **Вы знаете** the names for **русских магазинов,** *(mah-gah-zee-nahv)* so let's practice shopping. Just remember your basic **вопросы** that you learned in Step 2. Whether **вы** need to buy **женские** *(zhen-skee-yeh)* **брюки** *(bryoo-kee)* **или книги** the necessary **слова** are the same.

1. First step — **Где?**

Где кино? **Где молоко?** **Где банк?** **Где булочная?** *(boo-lahch-nah-yah)* **Где кафе?**

____
(Where is the department store?)

____
(Where is the grocery store/delicatessen?)

____
(Where is the market?)

2. Second step — tell them what **вы** are looking for, need **или хотите!**

(men-yeh) *(noozh-nah)*
Мне нужно . . .
I need

(yah) *(hah-choo)*
Я хочу . . .
I would like

(oo) *(vahs)* *(yest)*
У вас есть . . .?
do you have

____
(Do you have postcards?)

____
(I would like four stamps.)

____
(I need toothpaste.)

____
(I would like to buy film.)

____
(Do you have coffee?)

Go through the glossary at the end of (et-toy) **этой** (this) **книги и** select (dvahd-tset) **двадцать слов.** Drill the above patterns **с** (et-tee-mee) **этими** (these) twenty **словами.** Don't cheat. Drill them (see-vohd-nyah) **сегодня. Теперь** take (dvahd-tset) **двадцать** more **слов из** your glossary **и** do the same.

3. Third step — find out (skohl-kah) **сколько** (et-tah) **это** (stoy-eet) **стоит.**

Сколько стоит марка? **Сколько стоит** (aht-krit-kah) **открытка?** **Сколько стоит** (kee-loh) **кило** (kilo) (yah-blahk) **яблок?** (apples)

____
(How much does the toothpaste cost?)

____
(How much does the soap cost?)

____
(How much does a cup of tea cost?)

4. Fourth step — success! I found it!

Once **вы** find what **вы** would like, (gah-vah-reet-yeh) **говорите,** (say)

Я хочу это, пожалуйста. ____

or

Дайте мне это, пожалуйста. Дайте мне это, пожалуйста.

Или if **вы** would not like it

Я не хочу (et-tah-vah) **этого,** (that) **спасибо.** ____

or

Спасибо, не (nah-dah) **надо.** ((it is) not right) ____

Congratulations! You have finished. By now you should have stuck your labels, flashed your cards, cut out your menu guide and Pocket Pal™, and packed your suitcases. You should be very pleased with your accomplishment. You have learned what it sometimes takes others years to achieve and you hopefully had fun doing it. **Счастливого пути!**

Glossary

This glossary contains words used in this book only. It is not meant to be a dictionary. Consider purchasing a dictionary which best suits your needs - small for traveling, large for reference, or specialized for specific vocabulary needs.

The words here are all presented in *Russian* alphabetical order followed by the pronunciation guide used in this book. Remember that Russian words change their endings depending upon how they are used. Not all variations of a word will be given. Learn to look for the core of the word.

А

а *(ah)* ... but, and
абрикос *(ah-bree-kohs)* ... apricot
август *(ahv-goost)* ... August
авиа *(ah-vee-ah)* ... airmail
авиапочта *(ah-vee-ah-poach-tah)* ... by airmail
авиация *(ah-vee-aht-see-yah)* ... aviation
Австралия *(ahv-strah-lee-yah)* ... Australia
Австрия *(ahv-stree-yah)* ... Austria
автобиография *(ahv-tah-bee-ah-grah-fee-yah)* ... autobiography
автобус *(ahv-toh-boos)* ... bus
автобусы *(ahv-toh-boo-sih)* ... buses
автограф *(ahv-toh-grahf)* ... autograph
автомат *(ahv-tah-maht)* ... automat
автомобиль *(ahv-tah-mah-beel)* ... automobile, car
автор *(ahv-tar)* ... author
автостанция *(ahv-tah-stahnt-see-yah)* ... service station
агент *(ah-gyent)* ... agent
адвокат *(ahd-vah-kaht)* ... advocate, lawyer
адрес *(ah-dres)* ... address
Азербайджан *(ah-zyair-by-dzhahn)* ... Azerbaijan
азербайджанец *(ah-zyair-by-dzhah-nyets)* ... Azerbaijanian
Азия *(ah-zee-yah)* ... Asia
академия *(ah-kah-dyeh-mee-yah)* ... academy
аккуратный *(ahk-koo-raht-nee)* ... accurate, fastidious, neat
акробат *(ah-krah-baht)* ... acrobat
акт *(ahkt)* ... act
актёр *(ahk-tyor)* ... actor
акцент *(ahkt-syent)* ... accent
алгебра *(ahl-gyeh-brah)* ... algebra
алкоголь *(ahl-kah-gohl)* ... alcoholic drinks, alcohol
алло *(ahl-loh)* ... hello
алфавит *(ahl-fah-veet)* ... alphabet
Америка *(ah-myeh-ree-kah)* ... America
Америке *(ah-myeh-ree-kyeh)* ... America
Америку *(ah-myeh-ree-koo)* ... America
американец *(ah-myeh-ree-kah-nyets)* ... American male
американка *(ah-myeh-ree-kahn-kah)* ... American female
Англия *(ahn-glee-yah)* ... England
Англию *(ahn-glee-yoo)* ... England
английский *(ahn-glee-skee)* ... English
англичанин *(ahn-glee-chah-neen)* ... Englishman
англичанка *(ahn-glee-chahn-kah)* ... Englishwoman
анекдот *(ah-nyek-doht)* ... anecdote, joke
антенна *(ahn-tyen-nah)* ... antenna
антибиотики *(ahn-tee-bee-oh-tee-kee)* ... antibiotics
аппетит *(ah-peh-teet)* ... appetite
апрель *(ahp-ryel)* ... April
аптека *(ahp-tyek-ah)* ... pharmacy, drugstore
арена *(ar-yen-ah)* ... arena
арест *(ar-yest)* ... arrest
Армения *(ar-myeh-nee-yah)* ... Armenia
армянин *(ar-myah-neen)* ... Armenian
армия *(ar-mee-yah)* ... army
аспирин *(ah-spee-reen)* ... aspirin
астронавт *(ah-strah-nahvt)* ... astronaut
атлет *(aht-lyet)* ... athlete
Африка *(ah-free-kah)* ... Africa
аэродром *(ah-air-ah-drohm)* ... airfield
аэропорт *(ah-air-ah-port)* ... airport

Б

бабушка *(bah-boosh-kah)* ... grandmother
багаж *(bah-gahzh)* ... baggage
базар *(bah-zar)* ... bazaar
Баку *(bah-koo)* ... Baku
бал *(bahl)* ... ball (dance)
балалайка *(bah-lah-lie-kah)* ... balalaika
балерина *(bah-leh-ree-nah)* ... ballerina
банан *(bah-nahn)* ... banana
бандит *(bahn-deet)* ... bandit, robber
банк *(bahnk)* ... bank
банный халат *(bahn-nee)(hah-laht)* ... bathrobe
бар *(bar)* ... bar (restaurant)
баранина *(bah-rah-nee-nah)* ... mutton
баржа *(bar-zhah)* ... barge
барьер *(bar-yair)* ... barrier
бас *(bahs)* ... bass (voice)
баскетбол *(bah-sket-bohl)* ... basketball
батальон *(bah-tahl-yohn)* ... battalion
батарея *(bah-tar-yeh-yah)* ... battery
беден *(byed-yen)* ... poor
без *(byez)* ... minus, without
Беларусь *(byeh-lah-roos)* ... Belarus
беларус *(byeh-lah-roos)* ... Belarussian
белый *(byeh-lee)* ... white
Бельгия *(byel-gee-yah)* ... Belgium
бензоколонка *(byen-zah-kah-lohn-kah)* . sevice station, gas pump
библиотека *(bee-blee-ah-tyeh-kah)* ... library
Библия *(bee-blee-yah)* ... Bible
билет *(beel-yet)* ... ticket
билеты *(beel-yet-ih)* ... tickets
бинокль *(bee-noh-kil)* ... binoculars
бланк *(blahnk)* ... blank (form)
блузка *(blooz-kah)* ... blouse
блюда *(bloo-dah)* ... dishes (food)
богат *(bah-gaht)* ... rich
бокал *(bah-kahl)* ... wine glass, glass
бокс *(bohks)* ... boxing
Болгария *(bahl-gar-ee-yah)* ... Bulgaria
болен *(bohl-yen)* ... sick
Боливия *(bah-lee-vee-yah)* ... Bolivia
больше *(bohl-shee)* ... more
большой *(bahl-shoy)* ... big, large
Большой театр *(bahl-shoy)(tee-ah-ter)* ... Bolshoi Theater
бомба *(bohm-bah)* ... bomb
борщ *(borshch)* ... borsch (beet soup)
брат *(braht)* ... brother
бритва *(breet-vah)* ... razor
бронза *(brohn-zah)* ... bronze
брюки *(bryoo-kee)* ... trousers
брюнет *(broo-nyet)* ... brunette (male)
будете пить *(boo-dyet-yeh)(peet)* ... (you) will drink
будильник *(boo-deel-neek)* ... alarm clock
булочки *(boo-lahch-kee)* ... rolls
булочная *(boo-lahch-nah-yah)* ... bakery
бульвар *(bool-var)* ... boulevard
бумага *(boo-mah-gah)* ... paper
бумажник *(boo-mahzh-neek)* ... wallet
буфет *(boo-fyet)* ... snack bar, snack car
было *(bih-lah)* ... was
быстро *(bis-trah)* ... fast
бюро *(byoo-roh)* ... bureau, office
бюро проката *(byoo-roh)(prah-kah-tah)* ... rental agency
бюро путешествий *(byoo-roh)(poot-yeh-shest-vee-ee)* travel agency
бюрократ *(byoo-rah-kraht)* ... bureaucrat

В

в *(vuh)* ... at, in, on, to
в августе *(vuh)(ahv-goost-yeh)* ... in August
в апреле *(vuh)(ahp-ryel-yeh)* ... in April
в декабре *(vuh)(dee-kah-bryeh)* ... in December
в июле *(vuh)(ee-yool-yeh)* ... in July

в июне *(vuh)(ee-yoon-yeh)* ... in June
в мае *(vuh)(mah-yeh)* ... in May
в марте *(vuh)(mart-yeh)* ... in March
в ноябре *(vuh)(nah-yah-bryeh)* ... in November
в одном направлении *(vuh)(ahd-nohm)(nah-prahv-lyen-ee-ee)* ... one-way
в октябре *(vuh)(ahk-tyah-bryeh)* ... in October
в сентябре *(vuh)(syen-tyah-bryeh)* ... in September
в феврале *(vuh)(fyev-rahl-yeh)* ... in February
в январе *(vuh)(yahn-var-yeh)* ... in January
вагон *(vah-gohn)* ... compartment, wagon
вагон-ресторан *(vah-gohn-res-tah-rahn)* ... dining compartment
важно *(vahzh-nah)* ... important
ваза *(vah-zah)* ... vase
вальс *(vahls)* ... waltz
вам *(vahm)* ... to you
вам нужно *(vahm)(noosh-nah)* ... you need
ванная *(vahn-nah-yah)* ... bathroom
ванной *(vahn-noy)* ... bathroom
ванную *(vahn-noo-yoo)* ... bathroom
варенье *(var-yen-yeh)* ... jam (food)
вас *(vahs)* ... you
вас зовут *(vahs)(zah-voot)* ... your name is
Ватикан *(vah-tee-kahn)* ... Vatican
ваш *(vahsh)* ... your
велосипед *(vyeh-lah-see-pyed)* ... bicycle
веранда *(vee-rahn-dah)* ... veranda
весной *(vees-noy)* ... in spring
ветрено *(vyet-ren-ah)* ... windy
вечер *(vyeh-cher)* ... evening
вещи *(vesh-chee)* ... things
видеть *(vee-dyet)* ... to see
виза *(vee-zah)* ... visa
вилка *(veel-kah)* ... fork
вино *(vee-noh)* ... wine
витамин *(vee-tah-meen)* ... vitamin
Владивосток *(vlah-dee-vah-stohk)* ... Vladivostok
внизу *(vnee-zoo)* ... downstairs, below
во *(voh)* ... to
вода *(vah-dah)* ... water
воды *(vah-dih)* ... water
водка *(vohd-kah)* ... vodka
вокзал *(vahk-zahl)* ... train station
Волга *(vohl-gah)* ... Volga River
волейбол *(vah-lay-bohl)* ... volleyball
вопрос *(vah-prohs)* ... question
вопросы *(vah-proh-sih)* ... questions
восемь *(voh-syem)* ... eight
восемнадцать *(vah-sim-nahd-tset)* ... eighteen
восемьдесят *(voh-syem-dyes-yet)* ... eighty
воскресенье *(vah-skree-syen-yeh)* ... Sunday
восток *(vah-stohk)* ... east
вот *(voht)* ... here is, here are
врач *(vrahch)* ... doctor
всё *(vsyoh)* ... everything
вторник *(vtor-neek)* ... Tuesday
втором этаж *(vtah-rohm)(eh-tahzh-yeh)* ... second floor
вход *(vhohd)* ... entrance
входить *(vhah-deet)* ... to enter
вчера *(vchee-rah)* ... yesterday
въезд запрещён *(vyezd)(zah-presh-chyohn)* ... no entrance
вы *(vwee)* ... you
высокая *(vwee-soh-kah-yah)* ... high, tall
выход *(vwee-hahd)* ... exit
выходить *(vwee-hah-deet)* ... to go out, to exit

Г

газ *(gahz)* ... natural gas
газета *(gah-zyeh-tah)* ... gazette, newspaper
газету *(gah-zyeh-too)* ... newspaper
газетчик *(gah-zyet-cheek)* ... newspaper man
галерея *(gahl-yair-eh-yah)* ... gallery
галстук *(gahl-stook)* ... tie
гараж *(gah-rahzh)* ... garage
гастроном *(gah-strah-nohm)* ... delicatessen, grocery store
где *(gdyeh)* ... where
генерал *(gee-nee-rahl)* ... general
география *(gee-ah-grah-fee-yah)* ... geography
геолог *(gee-oh-lahg)* ... geologist
геология *(gee-ah-loh-gee-yah)* ... geology
геометрия *(gee-ah-myet-ree-yah)* ... geometry
Гибралтар *(gee-brahl-tar)* ... Gibraltar
гид *(geed)* ... guide
гимнастика *(geem-nah-stee-kah)* ... gymnastics
гитара *(gee-tah-rah)* ... guitar
главная дорога *(glahv-nah-yah)(dah-roh-gah)* ... right of way
главный вход *(glahv-nee)(vhohd)* ... main entrance
говорить *(gah-vah-reet)* ... to speak, to say
говядина *(gahv-yah-dee-nah)* ... beef
год *(gohd)* ... year
года *(go-dah)* ... year
году *(gah-doo)* ... year
голубой *(gah-loo-boy)* ... light blue
города *(go-rah-dah)* ... city
городами *(gah-rah-dah-mee)* ... cities
горячая *(gar-yah-chah-yah)* ... hot
гостиная *(gah-stee-nah-yah)* ... living room
гостиница *(gah-stee-neet-sah)* ... hotel, inn
гостинице *(gah-stee-neet-seh)* ... hotel, inn
Гостиный двор *(gah-stee-nee)(dvor)* ... department store in St. Petersburg
градусы *(grah-doo-sih)* ... degrees
грамм *(grahm)* ... gram
гранит *(grah-neet)* ... granite
Греция *(gret-see-yah)* ... Greece
Грузия *(groo-zee-yah)* ... Georgia
грузин *(groo-zeen)* ... Georgian
группа *(groop-pah)* ... group
ГУМ *(goom)* ... department store in Moscow
гусь *(goose)* ... goose

Д

да *(dah)* ... yes
дайте *(die-tee)* ... give!
дайте мне *(die-tee)(men-yeh)* ... give me
дама *(dah-mah)* ... dame, lady, woman
Дания *(dah-nee-yah)* ... Denmark
дата *(dah-tah)* ... date
два, две *(dvah),(dveh)* ... two
двадцать *(dvahd-tset)* ... twenty
двенадцать *(dveh-nahd-tset)* ... twelve
дверь *(dvyair)* ... door
движение запрещено *(dvee-zhen-ee-yeh)(zah-presh-chen-oh)* ... road closed to vehicles
девять *(dyev-yet)* ... nine
девяносто *(dyev-yah-noh-stah)* ... ninety
девятнадцать *(div-yet-nahd-tset)* ... nineteen
дедушка *(dyeh-doosh-kah)* ... grandfather
дедушку *(dyeh-doosh-koo)* ... grandfather
дезодорант *(dyeh-zah-dah-rahnt)* ... deodorant
декабрь *(dee-kah-bair)* ... December
делать *(dyeh-laht)* ... to do, to make
делать пересадку *(dyeh-laht)(pyair-yeh-sahd-koo)* ... to transfer
делегат *(dyeh-leh-gaht)* ... delegate
демонстрация *(dyeh-mahn-straht-see-yah)* ... demonstration
день *(dyen)* ... day, afternoon
деньги *(dyen-gee)* ... money
денег *(dyen-yeg)* ... money
деревянная посуда *(dyair-yev-yahn-nah-yah)(pah-soo-dah)* ... village-style wooden dishes
десерт *(dyes-yairt)* ... dessert
десять *(dyes-yet)* ... ten
дети *(dyeh-tee)* ... children
детская обувь *(dyet-skah-yah)(oh-boov)* ... children's footware
детский отдел *(dyet-skee)(aht-dyel)* ... children's department
дешёвая *(dyeh-shyoh-vah-yah)* ... inexpensive
джаз *(dzhahz)* ... jazz
джин *(dzheen)* ... gin
джинсы *(dzheen-sih)* ... jeans
диагноз *(dee-ahg-nahz)* ... diagnosis
диаграмма *(dee-ah-grahm-mah)* ... diagram, blueprint
диалог *(dee-ah-lohg)* ... dialogue, conversation
диалоги *(dee-ah-loh-gee)* ... dialogues, conversations
диван *(dee-vahn)* ... divan, sofa
дизель *(dee-zyel)* ... diesel
диплом *(dee-plohm)* ... diploma
дипломат *(dee-plah-maht)* ... diplomat
директор *(dee-rek-tar)* ... director
дискуссия *(dee-skoos-see-yah)* ... discussion
дичь *(deech)* ... game (food)

длинная *(dleen-nah-yah)* .... long
для *(dil-yah)* .... for
днём *(den-yohm)* .... afternoon
дня *(den-yah)* .... day
дни *(dnee)* .... days
дней *(dnay)* .... days
до *(doh)* .... to, until
до завтра *(dah)(zahv-trah)* .... until tomorrow
до свидания *(dah)(svee-dahn-ee-yah)* .... goodbye
доброе утро *(doh-brah-yeh)(oo-trah)* .... good morning
добрый вечер *(doh-brih)(vyeh-cher)* .... good evening
добрый день *(doh-brih)(dyen)* .... good day, good afternoon
дождь *(dohzhd)* .... rain
доктор *(dohk-tar)* .... doctor
документ *(dah-koo-myent)* .... document
доллар *(dohl-lar)* .... dollar
дом *(dohm)* .... house
дома *(doh-mah)* .... house
доме *(doh-myeh)* .... house
домашняя птица *(dah-mahsh-nyah-yah)(pteet-sah)* .... poultry
дорога *(dah-roh-gah)* .... road
дорогая *(dah-rah-gah-yah)* .... expensive
дорогу *(dah-roh-goo)* .... directions
дорожные чеки *(dah-rohzh-nih-yeh)(cheh-kee)* . traveler's checks
дочь *(dohch)* .... daughter
драма *(drah-mah)* .... drama
друзьям *(drooz-yahm)* .... friends
духи *(doo-hkee)* .... perfume
душ *(doosh)* .... shower
дядя *(dyah-dyah)* .... uncle

Е

еврей *(yev-ray)* .... Jewish man
еврейка *(yev-ray-kah)* .... Jewish woman
его зовут *(yee-voh)(zah-voot)* .... his name is
её зовут *(yee-yoh)(zah-voot)* .... her name is
есть *(yest)* .... to eat
ехать *(yek-haht)* .... to go, to ride (with a means of transportation)
ехать на машине *(yek-haht)(nah)(mah-shee-nyeh)* ..... to drive

Ж

жакет *(zhah-kyet)* .... jacket
жареное *(zhar-yen-ah-yeh)* .... roasted, fried
жарко *(zhar-kah)* .... hot
жасмин *(zhahs-meen)* .... jasmine
ждать *(zhdaht)* .... to wait for
желе *(zhel-yeh)* .... jelly
женский *(zhen-skee)* .... ladies' (restroom)
женщина *(zhen-shchee-nah)* .... woman
женская обувь *(zhen-skah-yah)(oh-boov)* .... ladies' footware
женская одежда *(zhen-skah-yah)(ah-dyezh-dah)*. ladies' clothing
женские головные уборы *(zhen-skee-yeh)(gah-lahv-nih-yeh)(oo-bohr-ih)* .... ladies' hats
жёлтый *(zhyol-tee)* .... yellow
жить *(zheet)* .... to live, to reside
журнал *(zhoor-nahl)* .... journal, magazine
журналы *(zhoor-nah-lih)* .... journals, magazines
журналист *(zhoor-nah-leest)* .... journalist

З

за *(zah)* .... behind
завтра *(zahv-trah)* .... tomorrow
завтрак *(zahv-trahk)* .... breakfast
заказ *(zah-kahz)* .... reservations
заказывать *(zah-kah-zih-vaht)* .... to order, to reserve
закрывается *(zah-krih-vah-yet-syah)* .... closes
закрыта *(zah-krih-tah)* .... closed
закуски *(zah-koo-skee)* .... appetizers, snacks
занавес *(zah-nahv-yes)* .... curtain
занимает *(zah-nee-mah-yet)* .... it occupies, it takes up
занято *(zahn-yah-tah)* .... busy, occupied
запад *(zah-pahd)* .... west
запасной выход *(zah-pahs-noy)(vwee-hahd)* ..... emergency exit
запечённое *(zahp-yeh-chyohn-nah-yeh)* .... baked
заплатить за *(zah-plah-teet)(zah)* .... to pay for
звонить *(zvah-neet)* .... to phone
здесь *(zdyes)* .... here
здоров *(zdah-rohv)* .... healthy
зелёный *(zyel-yoh-nee)* .... green
зеркало *(zyair-kah-lah)* .... mirror
зеркала *(zyair-kah-lah)* .... mirrors
зимой *(zee-moy)* .... in winter
знать *(znaht)* .... to know
вы знаете *(vwee)(znah-yet-yeh)* .... you know
зовут *(zah-voot)* .... is called
как зовут *(kahk)(zah-voot)* .... what is (someone's) name
меня зовут *(men-yah)(zah-voot)* .... I am called, my name is
зона *(zoh-nah)* .... zone
зонтик *(zohn-teek)* .... umbrella
зонты *(zahn-tih)* .... umbrellas
зоопарк *(zah-ah-park)* .... zoo
зубная паста *(zoob-nah-yah)(pahs-tah)* .... toothpaste
зубная щётка *(zoob-nah-yah)(shchoht-kah)* .... toothbrush

И

и *(ee)* .... and
игрушки *(ee-groosh-kee)* .... toys
идти *(eed-tee)* .... to go, to walk (to a destination)
он/она идёт *(ee-dyoht)* .... he/she goes, walks
идёт дождь *(ee-dyoht)(dohzhd)* .... it rains
идёт снег *(ee-dyoht)(snyeg)* .... it snows
из *(eez)* .... out of, from
извините *(eez-vee-neet-yeh)* .... excuse me
изучать *(ee-zoo-chaht)* .... to learn
изучайте! *(ee-zoo-chay-tee)* .... learn!
икра *(ee-krah)* .... caviar
или *(ee-lee)* .... or
имена *(ee-myen-ah)* .... names
импортный *(eem-part-nee)* .... imported
Индия *(een-dee-yah)* .... India
индустриальный *(een-doo-stree-ahl-nee)* .... industrial
инженер *(een-zhyen-yair)* .... engineer
иностранный *(ee-nah-strahn-nee)* .... foreign
инспектор *(een-spyek-tar)* .... inspector
институт *(een-stee-toot)* .... institute
инструктор *(een-strook-tar)* .... instructor
инструкции *(een-strook-tsee-ee)* .... instructions
инструмент *(een-stroo-myent)* .... instrument
интеллигент *(een-tyel-lee-gyent)* .... intellectual
интервью *(een-tyair-view)* .... interview
интерес *(een-tyair-yes)* .... interest
интернациональный *(een-tyair-naht-see-ah-nahl-nee)* international
информация *(een-far-maht-see-yah)* .... information
искать *(ees-kaht)* .... to look for
Исландия *(ees-lahn-dee-yah)* .... Iceland
Испания *(ee-spahn-ee-yah)* .... Spain
Испанию *(ee-spahn-ee-yoo)* .... Spain
история *(ees-toh-ree-yah)* .... history
Италия *(ee-tah-lee-yah)* .... Italy
Италию *(ee-tah-lee-yoo)* .... Italy
их зовут *(eehk)(zah-voot)* .... their name is
июль *(ee-yool)* .... July
июле *(ee-yool-yeh)* .... July
июнь *(ee-yoon)* .... June

К

к себе *(kuh)(syeb-yeh)* .... pull (doors)
кабина *(kah-bee-nah)* .... cabin, booth
кабинет *(kah-bee-nyet)* .... study
Казахстан *(kah-zahk-stahn)* .... Kazakstan
казах *(kah-zahk)* .... Kazak
как *(kahk)* .... how
Как дела? *(kahk)(dee-lah)* .... how are things? how are you?
Как вас зовут? *(kahk)(vahs)(zah-voot)* ..... what is your name?
какая *(kah-kah-yah)* .... what kind of, how is
какао *(kah-kah-oh)* .... cocoa
какой *(kah-koy)* .... what
календарь *(kah-lyen-dar)* .... calendar
камера *(kah-myair-ah)* .... cell, chamber
камера хранения *(kah-myair-ah)(hrah-nyen-ee-yah)* .... left-luggage office
Канада *(kah-nah-dah)* .... Canada
Канаду *(kah-nah-doo)* .... Canada
канадец *(kah-nah-dyets)* .... Canadian
канал (кан.) *(kah-nahl)* .... canal
канарейка *(kah-nah-ray-kah)* .... canary
кандидат *(kahn-dee-daht)* .... candidate
канцтовары *(kahnt-stah-vah-rih)* .... stationery store
капитал *(kah-pee-tahl)* .... capital (money)
капиталист *(kah-pee-tah-leest)* .... capitalist

карамель *(kah-rah-myel)* caramel
карандаш *(kah-rahn-dahsh)* pencil
карие *(kah-ree-yeh)* light brown
карта *(kar-tah)* map
карту *(kar-too)* map
карты *(kar-tih)* maps
картина *(kar-tee-nah)* picture
касса *(kahs-sah)* ticket machine, cashier, tickets
кассу *(kahs-soo)* booking office, cashier
кассиру *(kahs-see-roo)* cashier
католик *(kah-toh-leek)* Catholic man
католичка *(kah-tah-leech-kah)* Catholic woman
кафе *(kah-fyeh)* cafe
квитанция *(kvee-tahn-tsee-yah)* receipt
керамика *(kee-rahm-ee-kah)* ceramics
Киев *(kee-yev)* Kiev
кило *(kee-loh)* kilo
кино *(kee-noh)* cinema
киоск *(kee-ohsk)* newsstand
класс *(klahs)* class
классик *(klahs-seek)* classic
клоун *(kloh-oon)* clown
книга *(kuh-nee-gah)* book
книги *(kuh-nee-gee)* book, bookstore
книгу *(kuh-nee-goo)* book
ковёр *(kahv-yor)* carpet
ковры *(kahv-rih)* carpets
когда *(kahg-dah)* when
кожаные товары *(koh-zhah-nih-yeh)(tah-var-ih)* leather goods
колбаса *(kahl-bah-sah)* sausage
колготки *(kahl-goht-kee)* pantyhose
коллекция *(kahl-yekt-see-yah)* collection
командир *(kah-mahn-deer)* commander
комбинация *(kahm-bee-naht-see-yah)* slip
комедия *(kah-myeh-dee-yah)* comedy
комиссар *(kah-mees-sar)* commissar
коммунист *(kahm-moo-neest)* communist
комната *(kohm-nah-tah)* room
комнате *(kohm-nah-tyeh)* room
комнаты *(kohm-nah-tih)* room
компас *(kohm-pahs)* compass
композитор *(kahm-pah-zee-tar)* composer
компьютер *(kahmp-yoo-tyer)* computer
кому *(koh-moo)* to whom (on envelopes)
конверт *(kahn-vyairt)* envelope
конверты *(kahn-vyair-tih)* envelopes
конверты-авиа *(kahn-vyair-tih-ah-vee-ah)* airmail envelopes
коньяк *(kahn-yahk)* cognac
конференция *(kahn-fyair-yent-see-yah)* conference
концерт *(kahn-tsairt)* concert
корзина *(kar-zee-nah)* basket
коричневый *(kah-reech-nyeh-vwee)* brown
короткая *(kah-roht-kah-yah)* short
корт *(kort)* court (tennis)
косметика *(kahs-myeh-tee-kah)* cosmetics
костюм *(kahst-yoom)* suit
кот *(koht)* cat
который час? *(kah-toh-ree)(chahs)* what time is it?
кофе *(koh-fyeh)* coffee
кошка *(kohsh-kah)* cat
кошку *(kohsh-koo)* cat
краб *(krahb)* crab
красивых *(krah-see-vik)* pretty
красный *(krahs-nee)* red
кредитная карточка *(kreh-deet-nah-yah)(kar-tahch-kah)* credit card
Кремль *(kreml)* Kremlin
кровать *(krah-vaht)* bed
кровати *(krah-vah-tee)* bed
кроссовки *(krahs-sohv-kee)* tennis shoes
кто *(ktoh)* who
Куба *(koo-bah)* Cuba
куда *(koo-dah)* where (on envelopes)
культуры *(kool-toor-ih)* cultural
купальный костюм *(koo-pahl-nee)(kahst-yoom)* swimsuit
купальные костюмы *(koo-pahl-nih-yeh)(kahst-yoom-ih)* swimsuits
купить *(koo-peet)* to buy
кухня *(koohk-nyah)* kitchen
кухне *(koohk-nyeh)* kitchen
Кыргызская республика *(kir-geez-skah-yah)(rehs-poo-blee-kah)* Kyrgyz Republic
кыргыз *(kir-geez)* Kyrgyz

Л

лаборатория *(lah-bah-rah-toh-ree-yah)* laboratory
лампа *(lahm-pah)* lamp, light
лампы *(lahm-pih)* lamps
Латвия *(laht-vee-yah)* Latvia
латыш *(lah-tish)* Latvian
Ленинград *(lyen-een-grahd)* Leningrad (now St. Petersburg)
лететь *(lee-tyet)* to fly
летом *(lyet-ahm)* in summer
лимон *(lee-mohn)* lemon
лимонад *(lee-mah-nahd)* lemonade
линия *(lee-nee-yah)* line
линии *(lee-nee-ee)* lines (transportation)
линию *(lee-nee-yoo)* lines
литература *(lee-tyair-ah-too-rah)* literature
Литва *(leet-vah)* Lithuania
литовец *(lee-toh-vyets)* Lithuanian
литр *(lee-ter)* liter
лифчик *(leef-cheek)* brassiere
ложка *(lohzh-kah)* spoon
любят *(loob-yaht)* (they) love
люди *(loo-dee)* people

М

магазин *(mah-gah-zeen)* store
магазины *(mah-gah-zeen-ih)* stores
май *(my)* May
майка *(my-kah)* t-shirt, undershirt
максимальная скорость *(mahk-see-mahl-nah-yah)(skoh-rahst)* speed limit
маленькая *(mah-lyen-kah-yah)* small
маленькие *(mah-lyen-kee-ee)* small
маленький *(mah-lyen-kee)* small
мало *(mah-lah)* little
Мариинский театр *(mah-reen-skee)(tee-ah-ter)* Mariinsky Theater
марка *(mar-kah)* stamp
марки *(mar-kee)* stamps
марок *(mar-ahk)* stamps
март *(mart)* March
масло *(mah-slah)* butter
масса *(mahs-sah)* mass
мастер *(mahs-tyair)* master
математика *(mah-tyeh-mah-tee-kah)* mathematics
материя *(mah-tyair-ee-yah)* material
матрёшки *(mah-tryohsh-kah)* Russian dolls
матч *(mahtch)* match (game)
мать *(maht)* mother
машина *(mah-shee-nah)* machine (car)
машина напрокат *(mah-shee-nah)(nah-prah-kaht)* rental car
мебель *(myeh-byel)* furniture
медаль *(myeh-dahl)* medal
медик *(myeh-deek)* medic
медицина *(myeh-deet-see-nah)* medicine
медленно *(myed-lyen-nah)* slow, slowly
между *(myezh-doo)* between
междугородний *(myezh-doo-gah-rohd-nee)* long-distance, inter-city
международный *(myezh-doo-nah-rohd-nee)* international (calls)
Международный женский день *(myezh-doo-nah-rohd-nee)(zhen-skee)(dyen)* International Women's Day
мелодия *(myeh-loh-dee-yah)* melody
меню *(men-yoo)* menu
меня зовут *(men-yah)(zah-voot)* I am called, my name is
местный *(myes-nee)* domestic, internal
место *(myes-tah)* seat, place
месяц *(myeh-syets)* month
месяцев *(myeh-syet-syev)* months
месяцы *(myeh-syet-sih)* months
металл *(myeh-tahl)* metal
метод *(myeh-tahd)* method
метро *(myeh-troh)* metro, subway
механик *(myeh-hah-neek)* mechanic
микрофон *(mee-krah-fohn)* microphone
милиция *(mee-leet-see-yah)* police
миллион *(meel-lee-ohn)* million
миниатюра *(mee-nee-ah-tyoo-rah)* miniature
минут *(mee-noot)* minutes

минуте *(mee-noot-yeh)* .... minutes
мира *(mee-rah)* .... peace
миссия *(mees-see-yah)* .... mission
митинг *(mee-teeng)* .... meeting
мне *(men-yeh)* .... to me
мне нужно *(men-yeh)(noozh-nah)* .... I need
много *(mnoh-gah)* .... a lot, many
модель *(mah-dyel)* .... model
мой *(moy)* .... my
Молдова *(mahl-doh-vah)* .... Moldova
молдованин *(mahl-dah-vah-neen)* .... Moldavian
молодая баранина *(mah-lah-dah-yah)(bah-rah-nee-nah)* ... lamb
молодой *(mah-lah-doy)* .... young
молоко *(mah-lah-koh)* .... milk, dairy
молока *(mah-lah-kah)* .... milk
момент *(mah-myent)* .... moment
мороженое *(mah-roh-zhen-ah-yeh)* .... ice cream
Москва *(mahsk-vah)* .... Moscow
Москву *(mahsk-voo)* .... Moscow
Москвы *(mahsk-vih)* .... Moscow
мотор *(mah-tor)* .... motor
мотоцикл *(mah-tah-tsee-kul)* .... motorcycle
мочь *(mohch)* .... to be able to, can
я могу *(yah)(mah-goo)* .... I can
можете *(mohzh-yet-yeh)* .... (you) can, are able to
мужчина *(moozh-chee-nah)* .... man
мужская одежда *(moozh-skah-yah)(ah-dyezh-dah)* men's clothing
мужская обувь *(moozh-skah-yah)(oh-boov)* ..... men's footware
мужские головные уборы *(moozh-skee-yeh)(gah-lahv-nih-yeh)* *(oo-bohr-ih)* .... men's hats
мужской *(moozh-skoy)* .... men's (restroom)
муза *(moo-zah)* .... muse
музей *(moo-zay)* .... museum
музея *(moo-zyeh-yah)* .... museum
музыка *(moo-zih-kah)* .... music
музыкальные товары *(moo-zih-kahl-nih-yeh)(tah-var-ih)* .... musical articles
мусульманин *(moo-sool-mah-neen)* .... Moslem man
мусульманка *(moo-sool-mahn-kah)* .... Moslem woman
мы *(mwee)* .... we
мы хотим купить *(mwee)(hah-teem)(koo-peet)* we would like to buy
мыло *(mwee-lah)* .... soap
мясо *(myah-sah)* .... meat
мясо-гриль *(myah-sah-greel)* .... grilled
мясной магазин *(myahs-noy)(mah-gah-zeen)* .... butcher shop

Н

на *(nah)* .... on, into
на углу *(nah)(oo-gloo)* .... on corner
набережная (наб.) *(nah-byair-yesh-nah-yah)* ...... embankment
наверху *(nah-vyair-hoo)* .... upstairs
над *(nahd)* .... over
название *(nahz-vah-nee-yeh)* .... name
названия *(nahz-vah-nee-yah)* .... names
налево *(nah-lyev-ah)* .... to the left
нам нужно *(nahm)(noozh-nah)* .... we need
напитки *(nah-peet-kee)* .... beverages
напишите *(nah-pee-sheet-yeh)* .... write out
направо *(nah-prah-vah)* .... to the right
нас зовут *(nahs)(zah-voot)* .... our name is
находите *(nah-hoh-deet-yet)* .... (you) find
нация *(naht-see-yah)* .... nation
начинается *(nah-chee-nah-yet-syah)* .... begins
не *(nyeh)* .... not, no
не надо *(nyeh)(nah-dah)* .... (it is) not right
неделя *(nee-dyel-yah)* .... week
недели *(nee-dyel-ee)* .... week
нейлон *(nay-lohn)* .... nylon
немецкий *(nee-myet-skee)* .... German
несерьёзный *(nyeh-syair-yohz-nee)* .... not serious
нет *(nyet)* .... no, not
Нижний Новгород *(neezh-nee)(nohv-gah-rahd)* Nizhny Novgorod
никель *(neek-yehl)* .... nickel
но *(noh)* .... but
Новгород *(nohv-gah-rahd)* .... Novgorod
новых *(noh-vik)* .... new
новые *(noh-vih-yeh)* .... new
новым *(noh-vim)* .... new
нож *(nohzh)* .... knife
ноль *(nohl)* .... zero
номер *(nohm-yair)* .... number (room), hotel room
Норвегия *(nar-vyeh-gee-yah)* .... Norway
норма *(nor-mah)* .... norm, standard
нормальная *(nar-mahl-nah-yah)* .... normal
нос *(nohs)* .... nose
носильщик *(nah-seel-shcheek)* .... porter
носки *(nah-skee)* .... socks
ночь *(nohch)* .... night
ночная рубашка *(nahch-nah-yah)(roo-bahsh-kah)* .... nightshirt
ноябрь *(nah-yah-bair)* .... November
нужно *(noozh-nah)* .... need
мне нужно *(men-yeh)(noozh-nah)* .... I need

О

обгон запрещён *(ahb-gohn)(zah-presh-chyohn)* .... no passing
обед *(ah-byed)* .... meal, mid-day meal, dinner
объезд *(ahb-yezd)* .... detour
овощи *(oh-vahsh-chee)* .... vegetables, greengrocer
одежда *(ah-dyezh-dah)* .... clothes
одежды *(ah-dyezh-dih)* .... clothes
Одесса *(ah-des-sah)* .... Odessa
одеяло *(ah-dee-yah-lah)* .... blanket
одеялом *(ah-dee-yah-lahm)* .... blanket
один *(ah-deen)* .... one
одиннадцать *(ah-deen-nud-tset)* .... eleven
одну минуту *(ahd-noo)(mee-noo-too)* .... just a minute
окно *(ahk-noh)* .... window
октябрь *(ahk-tyah-bair)* .... October
оленина *(ahl-yeh-nee-nah)* .... venison
олимпиада *(ah-leem-pee-ah-dah)* .... Olympics
он *(ohn)* .... he
она *(ah-nah)* .... she
они *(ah-nee)* .... they
опера *(oh-pyair-ah)* .... opera
оплатить *(ah-plah-teet)* .... to pay
оранжевый *(ah-rahn-zheh-vwee)* .... orange (color)
органист *(ar-gah-neest)* .... organist
оркестр *(ar-kyes-tair)* .... orchestra
осенью *(oh-syen-yoo)* .... in autumn
остановка *(ahs-tah-nohv-kah)* .... stop
остановка автобуса *(ahs-tah-nohv-kah)(ahv-toh-boo-sah)* .... bus stop
остановка трамвая *(ahs-tah-nohv-kah)(trahm-vah-yah)* .... trolley stop
от себя *(aht)(syeb-yah)* .... push (doors)
отварное *(aht-var-noh-yeh)* .... boiled
ответы *(aht-vyet-ih)* .... answers
отель *(ah-tyel)* .... hotel
отец *(aht-yets)* .... father
отца *(aht-tsah)* .... father
открывается *(aht-krih-vah-yet-syah)* .... opens
открыта *(aht-krih-tah)* .... open
открытка *(aht-krit-kah)* .... postcard
открытки *(aht-krit-kee)* .... postcards
открытку *(aht-krit-koo)* .... postcard
открыток *(aht-krih-tahk)* .... postcards
отправление *(aht-prahv-lyen-ee-yeh)* .... departures
отправления *(aht-prahv-lyen-ee-yah)* .... departures
отходить *(aht-hah-deet)* .... to depart (vehicles)
офицер *(ah-feet-syair)* .... officer
официальный *(ah-feet-see-ahl-nee)* .... official
официант *(ah-feet-see-ahnt)* .... waiter
официантка *(ah-feet-see-ahnt-kah)* .... waitress
очень *(oh-chen)* .... very
очки *(ahch-kee)* .... eyeglasses

П

павильон *(pah-veel-yohn)* .... pavilion
пакет *(pah-kyet)* .... package
Пакистан *(pah-kee-stahn)* .... Pakistan
пальто *(pahl-toh)* .... overcoat
парад *(pah-rahd)* .... parade
парикмахерская *(pah-reek-mahl-yairs-kah-yah)* .... hairdresser
парк *(park)* .... park
парламент *(par-lah-myent)* .... parliament
партия *(par-tee-yah)* .... party
паспорт *(pahs-part)* .... passport
пассажир *(pahs-sah-zheer)* .... passenger
Пасха *(pahs-hkah)* .... Easter
перед *(pyeh-red)* .... in front of

перец *(pyeh-rets)* ... pepper
перчатки *(pyair-chaht-kee)* ... gloves
Петербург *(pyeh-tyair-boorg)* ... St. Petersburg
пиво *(pee-vah)* ... beer
пиджак *(peed-zhahk)* ... jacket, blazer
пижама *(pee-zhah-mah)* ... pajamas
пирог *(pee-rohg)* ... cake, pie, pastry
пирожки *(pee-rahzh-kee)* ... pastries, small cakes
пирожные *(pee-rohzh-nee-yeh)* ... pastries, small cakes
писать *(pee-saht)* ... to write
письмо *(pees-moh)* ... letter
пить *(peet)* ... to drink
платить *(plah-teet)* ... to pay
платить за *(plah-teet)(zah)* ... to pay for
платок *(plah-tohk)* ... handkerchief, shawl
платформа *(plaht-for-mah)* ... platform
платье *(plaht-yeh)* ... skirt
плащ *(plahshch)* ... raincoat
плита *(plee-tah)* ... stove
птица *(pteet-sah)* ... poultry
плохо *(ploh-hah)* ... bad
плохая погода *(plah-hah-yah)(pah-go-dah)* ... bad weather
площадь (пл.) *(plahsh-chahd)* ... square
по *(poh)* ... on
повторять *(pahv-tar-yaht)* ... to repeat
повторите *(pahv-tah-reet-yeh)* ... repeat!
поговорить *(pah-gah-vah-reet)* ... to speak
погода *(pah-go-dah)* ... weather
погоды *(pah-go-dih)* ... weather
под *(pohd)* ... under
подвал *(pahd-vahl)* ... basement
подушка *(pah-doosh-kah)* ... pillow
поезд *(poh-yezd)* ... train
поезда *(poh-yez-dah)* ... trains
поездка *(pah-yezd-kah)* ... trip, journey
поехать *(pah-yek-haht)* ... to go
пожалуйста *(pah-zhahl-oos-tah)* ... please, you're welcome
пожар *(pah-zhar)* ... fire
позвонить *(pah-zvah-neet)* ... to phone, to call
поздравления *(pahz-drahv-lyen-ee-yah)* ... congratulations
позже *(pohzh-yeh)* ... later
позиция *(pah-zeet-see-yah)* ... position
показывать *(pah-kah-zih-vaht)* ... to show
покупать *(pah-koo-paht)* ... to buy
полиция *(pah-leet-see-yah)* ... police
половина *(pah-lah-vee-nah)* ... half
полотенца *(pah-lah-tyent-sah)* ... towels
Польша *(pohl-shah)* ... Poland
понедельник *(pah-nee-dyel-neek)* ... Monday
понимать *(pah-nee-maht)* ... to understand
по-английски *(pah-ahn-glee-skee)* ... in English
по-русски *(pah-roos-skee)* ... in Russian
порт *(port)* ... port
портрет *(part-ryet)* ... portrait
послать *(pah-slaht)* ... to send
постельное бельё *(pah-styel-nah-yeh)(byel-yoh)* ... bedding
посылать *(pah-sih-laht)* ... to send
посылка *(pah-sil-kah)* ... package
посылки *(pah-sil-kee)* ... packages
посылку *(pah-sil-koo)* ... package
потом *(pah-tohm)* ... then
почему *(pah-chee-moo)* ... why
почта *(poach-tah)* ... mail, post office
почту *(poach-too)* ... mail, post office
почты *(poach-tih)* ... post office
почтовый ящик *(pahch-toh-vee)(yahsh-chik)* ... mailbox
пояса *(pah-yah-sah)* ... belts
православная *(prah-vah-slahv-nah-yah)* ... Orthodox woman
православный *(prah-vah-slahv-nee)* ... Orthodox man
прачечная *(prahch-yech-nah-yah)* ... laundry
прибытие *(pree-bit-ee-yeh)* ... arrival
прибытия *(pree-bit-ee-yah)* ... arrivals
пригородов *(pree-gah-rah-dahv)* ... suburbs
пригородные *(pree-gah-rahd-nee-yeh)* ... suburban
приезжать *(pree-yez-zhaht)* ... to arrive
примеры *(pree-myair-ih)* ... examples
принадлежности туалета *(pree-nahd-lehzh-nah-stee)(too-ahl-yet-ah)* ... toiletries
приходить *(pree-hah-deet)* ... to arrive (vehicles)
придёт *(pree-dyoht)* ... arrives (a vehicle)
прилетите *(pree-lee-teet-yeh)* ... (you) arrive by plane
приятного аппетита! *(pree-yaht-nah-vah)(ah-peh-tee-tah)* ... enjoy your meal, good appetite
правильное *(prah-veel-nah-yeh)* ... correct
программа *(prah-grahm-mah)* ... program
прогресс *(prahg-ryes)* ... progress
продавать *(prah-dah-vaht)* ... to sell
продмаг *(prahd-mahg)* ... food store
продукт *(prah-dookt)* ... product
проект *(prah-yekt)* ... project
пройдёте *(prah-ee-dyoht-yeh)* ... go!
проспект (пр.) *(prah-spekt)* ... avenue, boulevard
профессия *(prah-fyes-see-yah)* ... profession
профессор *(prah-fyes-sar)* ... professor
процент *(praht-syent)* ... percent
прочитать *(prah-chee-taht)* ... to read
прямо *(pryah-mah)* ... straight ahead
птица *(pteet-sah)* ... poultry
путешественник *(poot-yeh-shest-vyen-neek)* ... traveler
путешествовать *(poot-yeh-shest-vah-vaht)* ... to travel
путь *(poot)* ... line, route
пятница *(pyaht-neet-sah)* ... Friday
пять *(pyaht)* ... five
пятнадцать *(pyaht-nahd-tset)* ... fifteen
пятьдесят *(peed-dyes-yaht)* ... fifty

Р

радио *(rah-dee-oh)* ... radio
разговор по телефону *(rahz-gah-vor)(pah)(teh-leh-foh-noo)* ... telephone conversation
размер *(rahz-myair)* ... size
ракета *(rah-kyet-ah)* ... rocket
ранг *(rahng)* ... rank
рапорт *(rah-port)* ... report
расписание *(rah-spee-sah-nee-yeh)* ... schedule, timetable
расчёска *(rahs-chohs-kah)* ... comb
револьвер *(ryeh-vahl-vyair)* ... revolver
революция *(ryeh-vahl-yoot-see-yah)* ... revolution
регистрация *(ryeh-geest-raht-see-yah)* ... registration
рекорд *(ryeh-kord)* ... record
религия *(ree-lee-gee-yah)* ... religion
религии *(ree-lee-gee-ee)* ... religions
ресторан *(res-tah-rahn)* ... restaurant
ресторане *(res-tah-rahn-yeh)* ... restaurant
Рига *(ree-gah)* ... Riga
родители *(rah-dee-tee-lee)* ... parents
родственники *(rohd-stveen-nee-kee)* ... relatives
розовый *(roh-zah-vwee)* ... pink
Россия *(rahs-see-yah)* ... Russia
Россию *(rahs-see-yoo)* ... Russia
России *(rahs-see-ee)* ... Russia
российского *(rahs-see-skah-vah)* ... Russian
рубашка *(roo-bahsh-kah)* ... shirt
рубль *(roo-bil)* ... ruble
рублей *(roo-blay)* ... rubles
русский *(roos-skee)* ... Russian
по-русски *(pah-roos-skee)* ... in Russian
русские *(roos-skee-yeh)* ... Russian
русское *(roos-skah-yeh)* ... Russian
ручка *(rooch-kah)* ... pen
рыба *(rih-bah)* ... fish
рыбу *(rih-boo)* ... fish
рыбный рынок *(rib-nee)(rin-ahk)* ... fish market
рынок *(rin-ahk)* ... market
рынке *(rin-kyeh)* ... market
рядом с *(ryah-dahm)(suh)* ... next to

С

с *(suh)* ... with
сад *(sahd)* ... garden
салат *(sah-laht)* ... salad
салфетка *(sahl-fyet-kah)* ... napkin
самовар *(sah-mah-var)* ... samovar
самолёт *(sah-mahl-yoht)* ... airplane
самолёте *(sah-mahl-yoht-yeh)* ... airplane
сандалии *(sahn-dahl-ee-ee)* ... sandals
Санкт-Петербург *(sahnkt-pyeh-tyair-boorg)* ... St. Petersburg
сапоги *(sah-pah-gee)* ... boots
свинина *(svee-nee-nah)* ... pork
свитер *(svee-tyair)* ... sweater

свободно *(svah-bohd-nah)* free, available
сделать *(suh-dyeh-laht)* to do
сдача *(sdah-chah)* change
сдачу *(sdah-choo)* change
север *(syev-yair)* north
Северная Америка *(syev-yair-nah-yah)(ah-myeh-ree-kah)* North America
Северная Дакота *(syev-yair-nah-yah)(dah-koh-tah)* North Dakota
Северная Каролина *(syev-yair-nah-yah)(kah-rah-lee-nah)* North Carolina
Северная Корея *(syev-yair-nah-yah)(kah-reh-yah)* North Korea
сегодня *(see-vohd-nyah)* today
сезон *(syeh-zone)* season
секретарь *(syek-ryair-tar)* secretary
секунда *(see-koon-dah)* second
семинар *(syem-ee-nar)* seminar
семь *(syem)* seven
семнадцать *(sim-nahd-tset)* seventeen
семьдесят *(syem-dyes-yet)* seventy
семья *(syem-yah)* family
сентябрь *(syen-tyah-bair)* September
серый *(syeh-ree)* gray
сестра *(see-strah)* sister
сигара *(see-gah-rah)* cigar
сигарета *(see-gah-ryet-ah)* cigarette
сидит *(see-deet)* it fits
симфония *(seem-foh-nee-yah)* symphony
синий *(see-nee)* blue
сколько *(skohl-kah)* how much
сколько времени? *(skohl-kah)(vreh-mee-nee)* what time is it?
сколько это стоит? *(skohl-kah)(et-tah)(stoy-eet)* how much does this cost?
скорая помощь *(skoh-rah-yah)(poh-mashch)* emergency medical help
сладкие блюда *(slahd-kee-yeh)(bloo-dah)* sweets
слово *(sloh-vah)* word
слов *(slohv)* words
слова *(slah-vah)* words
словарь *(slah-var)* dictionary
словаре *(slah-var-yeh)* dictionary
служба газа *(sloozh-bah)(gah-zah)* heating gas service
Смоленск *(smahl-yensk)* Smolensk
снег *(snyeg)* snow
собака *(sah-bah-kah)* dog
собаку *(sah-bah-koo)* dog
Собор Василия Блаженного *(sah-bohr)(vah-see-lee-yah)(blah-zhen-nah-vah)* St. Basil's Cathedral
советский *(sah-vyet-skee)* Soviet
Советский Союз *(sah-vyet-skee)(say-yooz)* Soviet Union
сок *(sohk)* juice
соль *(sole)* salt
сорок *(so-rahk)* forty
сосиски *(sah-see-skee)* sausages
сот *(soht)* one hundred
соус *(soh-oos)* sauce
спальня *(spahl-nyah)* bedroom
спальне *(spahl-nyeh)* bedroom
спальню *(spahl-nyoo)* bedroom
спальный вагон *(spahl-nee)(vah-gohn)* sleeping wagon
спасибо *(spah-see-bah)* thank you
спать *(spaht)* to sleep
спиртные напитки *(speert-nih-yeh)(nah-peet-kee)* alcoholic beverages
спокойной ночи *(spah-koy-nay)(noh-chee)* good night
спортивные товары *(spar-teev-nih-yeh)(tah-var-ih)* sporting goods
справочное бюро *(sprah-vahch-nah-yeh)(byoo-roh)* information bureau
среда *(sree-dah)* Wednesday
стадион *(stah-dee-ohn)* stadium
стакан *(stah-kahn)* glass
станция *(stahnt-see-yah)* station
станция метро *(stahnt-see-ah)(myeh-troh)* metro station
старый *(stah-ree)* old
старейший *(star-yeh-shee)* oldest
старт *(start)* start
стирать *(stee-raht)* to wash, to clean (clothes)
стоит *(stoy-eet)* costs
сто *(stoh)* one hundred
стол *(stohl)* table
столовая *(stah-loh-vah-yah)* cafeteria, dining room
стоп *(stohp)* stop
стоянка *(stah-yahn-kah)* parking lot, taxi stand
стоянка запрещена *(stoh-yahn-kah)(zah-presh-chen-ah)* no parking
страница *(strah-neet-sah)* page
страниц *(strah-neets)* pages
странице *(strah-neet-seh)* page
студент *(stoo-dyent)* student
стул *(stool)* chair
суббота *(soo-boh-tah)* Saturday
сувениры *(soo-veh-neer-ih)* souvenirs
сумка *(soom-kah)* purse, handbag
сумму *(soom-moo)* sum
суп *(soop)* soup
Счастливого пути! *(schahst-lee-vah-vah)(poo-tee)* Have a good trip!
счёт *(shyoht)* bill
счета *(shyeh-tah)* bills
счёте *(shyoht-yeh)* bill
США *(seh-sheh-ah)* the United States
сын *(sin)* son
сына *(sin-ah)* son
сыр *(seer)* cheese

Т

табак *(tah-bahk)* tobacco
Таджикистан *(tahd-zheek-ee-stahn)* Tajikistan
таджик *(tahd-zheek)* Tajik
такси *(tahk-see)* taxi
там *(tahm)* there
таможня *(tah-mohzh-nyah)* customs
тапочки *(tah-poach-kee)* slippers
тарелка *(tar-yel-kah)* plate
Ташкент *(tahsh-kyent)* Tashkent
театр *(tee-ah-ter)* theater
Театр Кирова *(tee-ah-ter)(kee-rah-vah)* Kirov Theater
телевизор *(teh-leh-vee-zar)* TV set
телеграмма *(teh-leh-grahm-mah)* telegram
телеграмму *(teh-leh-grahm-moo)* telegram
телескоп *(teh-leh-skope)* telescope
телефон *(teh-leh-fohn)* telephone
телефон-автомат *(teh-leh-fohn-ahv-tah-maht)* public telephone
телефонист *(teh-leh-fahn-eest)* operator
телефонная книга *(teh-leh-fohn-nah-yah)(kuh-nee-gah)* telephone book
телятина *(tyel-yah-tee-nah)* veal
температура *(tem-pee-rah-too-rah)* temperature
температура замерзания *(tem-pee-rah-too-rah)(zah-myair-zah-nee-yah)* freezing point
теннис *(tyen-nees)* tennis
теперь *(tyep-yair)* now
терять *(tyair-yaht)* to lose
тёмные очки *(tyohm-nih-yeh)(ahch-kee)* sunglasses
тётя *(tyoh-tyah)* aunt
тогда *(tahg-dah)* then
тоже *(toh-zheh)* also
товары для кухни *(tah-vah-rih)(dil-yah)(koohk-nee)* kitchen wares
томат *(tah-maht)* tomato
тост *(tohst)* toast
трамвай *(trahm-vy)* streetcar, trolley
три *(tree)* three
тридцать *(treed-tset)* thirty
тринадцать *(tree-nahd-tset)* thirteen
триста *(tree-stah)* three hundred
трусы *(troo-sih)* underpants
туалет *(too-ahl-yet)* toilet
туалетные *(too-ahl-yet-nih-yeh)* toiletries
туда и обратно *(too-dah)(ee)(ahb-raht-nah)* roundtrip, there and back
турист *(too-reest)* tourist
Туркменистан *(toork-men-ee-stahn)* Turkmenistan
туркмен *(toork-myen)* Turkmenian
туфли *(too-flee)* shoes
тушёное *(toosh-yoh-nah-yeh)* stewed
тысяча *(tih-syah-chah)* one thousand
тысячи *(tih-syah-chee)* one thousand
тысяч *(tih-syahch)* one thousand

У

у вас есть *(oo)(vahs)(yest)* you have
у вас есть? *(oo)(vahs)(yest)* do you have
у меня есть *(oo)(men-yah)(yest)* I have

у него есть *(oo)(nyeh-voh)(yest)* .... he has
у неё есть *(oo)(nyeh-yoh)(yest)* .... she has
у нас есть *(oo)(nahs)(yest)* .... we have
у них есть *(oo)(neehk)(yest)* .... they have
уезжать *(oo-yez-zhaht)* .... to leave
Узбекистан *(ooz-bek-ee-stahn)* .... Uzbekistan
узбек *(ooz-bek)* .... Uzbek
угол *(oog-ahl)* .... corner
углу *(oo-gloo)* .... corner
удачи *(oo-dah-chee)* .... good luck
ужин *(oo-zheen)* .... evening meal
укладывать *(oo-klah-dih-vaht)* .... to pack
Украина *(oo-krah-ee-nah)* .... Ukraine
украинец *(oo-krah-ee-nyets)* .... Ukrainian
улетает *(oo-lee-tah-yet)* .... (it) flies away
улица (ул.) *(oo-leet-sah)* .... street
умывальник *(oo-mih-vahl-neek)* .... washstand
универмаг *(oo-nee-vyair-mahg)* .... department store
универсальный магазин *(oo-nee-vyair-sahl-nee)(mah-gah-zeen)* .... department store
университет *(oo-nee-vyair-see-tyet)* .... university
уступите дорогу *(oo-stoo-peet-yeh)(dah-roh-goo)* yield right of way
утро *(oo-trah)* .... morning
утра *(oo-trah)* .... morning
утром *(oo-trahm)* .... morning
уходить *(oo-hah-deet)* .... to leave (on foot)

Ф

факс *(fahks)* .... fax, facsimile
фарфор *(far-for)* .... china
Фаренгейт *(fah-ren-gate)* .... Fahrenheit
фаршированный *(far-shee-roh-vah-nee)* .... stuffed
февраль *(fyev-rahl)* .... February
фильм *(feelm)* .... film
фотоаппарат *(foh-tah-ahp-pah-raht)* .... camera
фотограф *(fah-toh-grahf)* .... photographer
фотоплёнка *(foh-tah-plyohn-kah)* .... film
фототовары *(foh-tah-tah-vah-rih)* .... camera supplies
Франция *(frahn-tsee-yah)* .... France
по-французски *(pah-frahn-tsoo-skee)* .... in French
фри *(free)* .... fried
фрукт *(frookt)* .... fruit
футбол *(foot-bohl)* .... soccer, football

Х

химчистка *(heem-cheest-kah)* .... dry cleaner's
хлеб *(hlyeb)* .... bread
ходит *(hoh-deet)* .... goes
холодильник *(hah-lah-deel-neek)* .... refrigerator
холодная *(hah-lohd-nah-yah)* .... cold
холодно *(hoh-lahd-nah)* .... cold
хорошая *(hah-roh-shah-yah)* .... good
хорошая погода *(hah-roh-shah-yah)(pah-go-dah)* . good weather
хорошо сидит *(hah-rah-shoh)(see-deet)* .... it fits well
хотим *(hah-teem)* .... (we) would like
хотите *(hah-teet-yeh)* .... (you) would like
хочу *(hah-choo)* .... (I) would like
я хочу есть *(yah)(hah-choo)(yest)* .... I am hungry
я хочу купить *(yah)(hah-choo)(koo-peet)* .... I would like to buy
я хочу пить *(yah)(hah-choo)(peet)* .... I am thirsty
хрусталь *(hkroos-tahl)* .... crystal

Ц

царь *(tsar)* .... czar, tsar
цвет *(tsvet)* .... color
цвета *(tsvet-ah)* .... colors
цветок *(tsvet-ohk)* .... flower
цветы *(tsvet-ih)* .... flowers
Цельсий *(tsel-see)* .... Celsius
цена *(tsyen-ah)* .... price
цене *(tsyen-yeh)* .... price
цены *(tsyen-ih)* .... prices
центр *(tsen-ter)* .... city center
центра *(tsen-trah)* .... center
церквей *(tsair-kvay)* .... churches
цирк *(tseerk)* .... circus

Ч

чай *(chy)* .... tea
чая *(chah-yah)* .... tea
час *(chahs)* .... o'clock, hour
который час? *(kah-toh-ree)(chahs)* .... what time is it?
часов *(chah-sohv)* .... o'clock
часто *(chah-stah)* .... often
часы *(chah-sih)* .... clock, watch, watchmaker
часах *(chah-sahk)* .... clocks, watches
чашка *(chahsh-kah)* .... cup
чашки *(chahsh-kee)* .... cups
чашку *(chahsh-koo)* .... cup
чемодан *(cheh-mah-dahn)* .... suitcase
четверть *(chet-virt)* .... a quarter (toward)
без четверти *(byez)(chet-virt-ee)* .... a quarter from
четверг *(chet-vyairg)* .... Thursday
четыре *(cheh-tir-ee)* .... four
четырнадцать *(cheh-tir-nud-tset)* .... fourteen
чёрный *(chyor-nee)* .... black
Чили *(chee-lee)* .... Chile
числа *(chee-slah)* .... numbers
число *(chee-sloh)* .... number
читать *(chee-taht)* .... to read
что *(shtoh)* .... what, that
чулки *(chool-kee)* .... stockings

Ш

шарф *(sharf)* .... scarf
Швеция *(shvet-see-yah)* .... Sweden
шесть *(shest)* .... six
шестнадцать *(shest-nahd-tset)* .... sixteen
шестьдесят *(shest-dyes-yaht)* .... sixty
шкатулка *(shkah-tool-kah)* .... lacquer box
шкаф *(shkahf)* .... wardrobe, cupboard
школа *(shkohl-ah)* .... school
школе *(shkohl-yeh)* .... school
шляпа *(shlyah-pah)* .... hat
шорты *(shohr-tih)* .... shorts
шоссе *(shahs-syeh)* .... main road
штат *(shtaht)* .... state
шторм *(shtorm)* .... storm

Э

экватор *(ek-vah-tar)* .... equator
экзамен *(ek-zah-myen)* .... exam
экономика *(ek-ah-noh-mee-kah)* .... economics
экспресс *(ek-spres)* .... express
электроприборы *(el-ek-troh-pree-bohr-ih)* ...... electrical goods
электрички *(el-ek-treech-kee)* .... suburban trains
эра *(air-ah)* .... era
эскалатор *(es-kah-lah-tor)* .... escalator
Эстония *(es-toh-nee-yah)* .... Estonia
эстонец *(es-toh-nyets)* .... Estonian
этаж *(eh-tahzh)* .... floor (of building)
это/этой/эту *(et-tah)/(et-toy)/(et-too)* .... that, this
это всё *(et-tah)(vsyoh)* .... that's all
эти/этими *(et-tee)/(et-tee-mee)* .... these
этого *(et-tah-vah)* .... that

Ю

ювелирные изделия *(yoo-vee-leer-nee)(eez-dyeh-lee-yah)* jewelry
юбка *(yoob-kah)* .... skirt
юг *(yoog)* .... south
Южная Америка *(yoozh-nah-yah)(ah-myeh-ree-kah)* .... South America
Южная Африка *(yoozh-nah-yah)(ah-free-kah)* ..... South Africa
Южная Дакота *(yoozh-nah-yah)(dah-koh-tah)* .... South Dakota
Южная Каролина *(yoozh-nah-yah)(kah-rah-lee-nah)* .... South Carolina
юрта *(yoor-tah)* .... yurt

Я

я *(yah)* I
я хочу есть *(yah)(hah-choo)(yest)* .... I am hungry
я хочу пить *(yah)(hah-choo)(peet)* .... I am thirsty
яблоко *(yah-blah-kah)* .... apple
яблок *(yah-blahk)* .... apples
язык *(yah-zik)* .... language, tongue
яйца *(yight-sah)* .... eggs
январь *(yahn-var)* .... January
январе *(yahn-var-yeh)* .... January
Япония *(yah-pohn-ee-yah)* .... Japan
яхта *(yahk-tah)* .... yacht

25 Beverage and Menu Guides

This beverage guide is intended to explain the variety of beverages available to you while **в России**. It is by no means complete. Some of the experimenting has been left up to you, but this should get you started.

ГОРЯЧИЕ НАПИТКИ (hot drinks)

кофе .... coffee
кофе с молоком .... coffee with milk
чёрный кофе .... black coffee
кофе по-восточному ..... Turkish coffee
какао .... cocoa

чай с лимоном .... tea with lemon
чай с вареньем .... tea with jam
чай с молоком .... tea with milk
чай с мёдом .... tea with honey

Чай was traditionally made in a **самовар.** A very strong tea was made in a teapot which was kept warm on top of the samovar. A small portion of the tea was poured into a cup and diluted with hot water from the samovar.

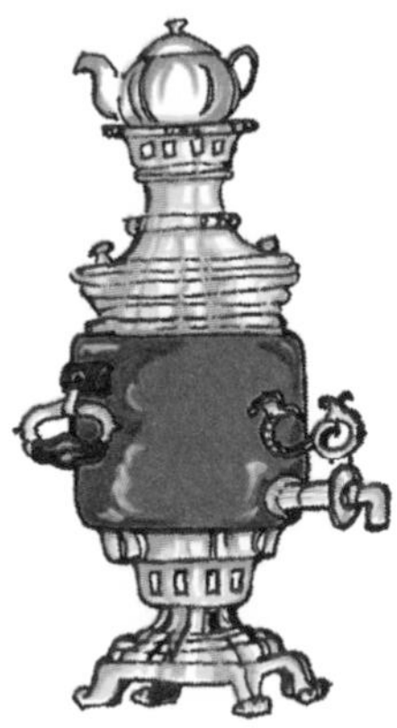

ФРУКТОВЫЙ СОК (fruit juice)

Don't miss a chance to sample Russian fruit juices. They are delicious. You'll find juice bars in the larger grocery stores.

апельсиновый сок .... orange juice
яблочный сок .... apple juice
виноградный сок .... grape juice
клюквенный морс .... cranberry juice
сливовый сок .... prune juice
абрикосовый сок .... apricot juice
персиковый сок .... peach juice
томатный сок .... tomato juice

ХОЛОДНЫЕ НАПИТКИ (cold drinks)

молоко .... milk
фруктовый коктейль ..... milkshake
кефир .... sour-milk drink
ряженка .... thick, sour milk
кисель .... sour-fruit drink
лимонад .... lemonade
"Байкал" .... cola drink
минеральная вода .... mineral water
квас .... kvass

ПИВО (beer)

If you are visiting during the summer, you'll want to visit the streetside beer stalls.

светлое пиво .... light beer
тёмное пиво .... dark beer

ВИНО (wine)

красное вино .... red wine
белое вино .... white wine
розовое вино .... rosé wine
вермут .... vermouth
портвейн .... port
херес .... sherry
шампанское .... champagne

СПИРТНЫЕ НАПИТКИ (alcohol)

Both **спиртные напитки** and **вино** can be purchased by the bottle or by weight. A shot is 50 grams and a glass of wine is approximately 150 grams.

водка .... vodka
виски .... whisky
джин .... gin
ром .... rum
аперитив .... aperitif
ликёр .... liqueur
коньяк .... cognac
лёд .... ice
со льдом .... with ice

CUT ALONG DOTTED LINE, FOLD AND TAKE WITH YOU

Десерт (dessert)

мороженое	ice cream
ванильное мороженое	vanilla ice cream
шоколадное мороженое	chocolate ice cream
кисель	jello-style dessert
компот	compote
крем	cream
взбитые сливки	whipped cream
рисовый пудинг	rice pudding
шоколадный соус	chocolate sauce
торт	torte, cake
кекс	muffin, spongecake
пирог, печенье	pie, cake, tart
пряники	pastries, honeycake
пирожные	cake

Фрукты (fruit)

апельсин	orange
арбуз	watermelon
банан	banana
виноград	grapes
вишня	cherries
грейпфрут	grapefruit
груша	pear
дыня	melon
клубника	strawberries
лимон	lemon
малина	raspberries
персик	peach
яблоко	apple
ягоды	berries

Птица и дичь (poultry and game)

курица/цыплёнок	chicken
гусь	goose
утка	duck
индейка	turkey
куропатка	partridge
вальдшнеп	woodcock
перепел	quail
кролик	rabbit
оленина	venison

FOLD HERE

Овощи (vegetables)

баклажаны	eggplant
горох	peas
грибы	mushrooms
капуста	cabbage
красная капуста	red cabbage
цветная капуста	cauliflower
картофель	potatoes
кукуруза	corn
лук	onions
морковь	carrots
перец	pepper/green pepper
перец горький	pimentos
помидоры	tomatoes
редиска	radishes
репа	turnips
свёкла	beets
шпинат	spinach

(pree-yaht-nah-vah) *(ah-peh-tee-tah)*

Приятного аппетита!

FOLD HERE

Меню

menu

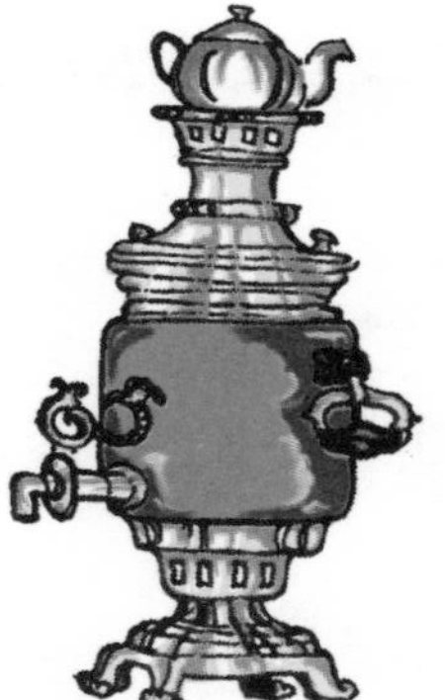

Завтрак? Обед? Ужин?

отварное	boiled
жареное	roasted, fried
тушёное	stewed
запечённое	baked
фаршированный	stuffed
на вертеле	grilled on a rotisserie
паровой	steamed

Что мне нужно? (what do I need?)

масло	butter
сахар	sugar
варенье	jam
мёд	honey
соль	salt
перец	pepper
уксус	vinegar
растительное масло	oil
оливкое масло	olive oil
горчица	mustard
соус	sauce, gravy
сыр	cheese
вода	water
лёд	ice
майонез	mayonnaise
сметана	sour cream
кефир	kefir, soured milk
творог	farmer's cheese
йогурт	yogurt

Закуски (appetizers)

икра	caviar
красная икра	red caviar
чёрная икра	black caviar
сардины	sardines
сельдь	herring
креветки	shrimp
балык	smoked sturgeon
сосиски	sausages
колбаса	cold cuts
паштет	pâté
форшмак	potato-and-meat hash
бутерброды открытые	open-faced sandwiches
бутерброды закрытые	sandwiches

Хлеб (bread and dough dishes)

чёрный хлеб	black/rye bread
ржаной хлеб	black/rye bread
белый хлеб	white/wheat bread
пшеничный хлеб	white/wheat bread
булочки	rolls
блины	pancakes, blinis
пельмени	stuffed dumplings
каша	hot cereal
манная	farina
пирожки	small meat or cabbage pies
кулебяка	breaded fish or meat loaf
рис	rice
пирог	pie filled with meat or vegetables
нон	flatbread
самса	baked, stuffed puff pastry
лагман	long, stout noodles
манты	steamed dumplings

Яйца (eggs)

яйца вкрутую	hard-boiled eggs
яйца всмятку	soft-boiled eggs
яичница	fried eggs
взбитая яичница	scrambled eggs
фаршированные яйца	stuffed eggs
яйца с икрой	eggs with caviar

FOLD HERE

Суп (soup)

борщ	borsch
шурпа	broth with vegetables
щи	cabbage or sauerkraut soup
уха	fish soup
лапша	noodle soup
молочная лапша	milk soup with noodles
суп грибной	mushroom soup
суп овощной	vegetable soup
харчо	Georgian mutton and rice soup
шурпа	Uzbek mutton, bean and tomato soup
суп картофельный	potato soup
суп гороховый	pea soup
солянка	spicy, thick soup
бульон	bouillon
бульон с яйцом	bouillon with an egg
бульон с фрикадельками	bouillon with meatballs

Рыба (fish dishes)

треска	cod
камбала	flounder
карп	carp
лосось	salmon
кета	Siberian salmon
щука	pike
раки	crayfish
краб	crab
окунь	perch
судак	pike perch
палтус	halibut
форель	trout
осетрина	sturgeon

FOLD HERE

Мясо (meat dishes)

баранина	mutton
ветчина	ham
говядина	beef
свинина	pork
телятина	veal
бараньи котлеты	lamb chops
ветчина жареная	fried ham
колбаса жареная	fried sausages
телятина жареная	roast veal
ростбиф	roast beef
поджарка	roast pork
бефстроганов	beef stroganoff
бифштекс	beefsteak
рагу	stew
рулет	meatloaf
гуляш	goulash
котлеты	chopped beef
шашлык	shashlik, kebabs
долма	stuffed grape leaves
голубцы мясные	stuffed cabbage
язык	tongue
печёнка	liver
бекон	bacon
битки/биточки	meatballs
купаты	spicy pork sausage
плов	pilaf

Салат (salad)

салат из фруктов	fruit salad
салат из огурцов	cucumber salad
салат из помидоров	tomato salad
салат из фасоли	bean salad
салат из редиса	radish salad
салат картофельный	potato salad
салат из белых грибов	white-mushroom salad
салат "столичный"	meat-and-vegetable salad
винегрет	beets and other vegetables

(yah)
я

(ohn)
он

(ah-nah)
она

(mwee)
мы

(vwee)
вы

(ah-nee)
они

(zah-kah-zih-vaht)
заказывать

(yah) *(zah-kah-zih-vah-yoo)*
я заказываю

(pah-koo-paht)
покупать

(yah) *(pah-koo-pah-yoo)*
я покупаю

(ee-zoo-chaht)
изучать

(yah) *(ee-zoo-chah-yoo)*
я изучаю

(pahv-tar-yaht)
повторять

(yah) *(pahv-tar-yah-yoo)*
я повторяю

(pah-nee-maht)
понимать

(yah) *(pah-nee-mah-yoo)*
я понимаю

(gah-vah-reet)
говорить

(yah) *(gah-vah-ryoo)*
я говорю

he	I
we	she
they	you
to buy I buy	to order/reserve I order/I reserve
to repeat I repeat	to learn I learn
to speak/say I speak/I say	to understand I understand

(yek-haht) **ехать** *(yah) (yeh-doo)* **я еду**	*(pree-yez-zhaht)* **приезжать** *(yah) (pree-yez-zhy-yoo)* **я приезжаю**
(vee-dyet) **видеть** *(yah) (vee-zhoo)* **я вижу**	*(zheet)* **жить** *(yah) (zhee-voo)* **я живу**
(zhdaht) **ждать** *(yah) (zhdoo)* **я жду**	*(ees-kaht)* **искать** *(yah) (eesh-choo)* **я ищу**
(yest) **есть** *(yah) (yem)* **я ем**	*(peet)* **пить** *(yah) (pyoo)* **я пью**
(yah) (hah-choo) **я хочу . . .**	*(men-yeh) (noozh-nah)* **мне нужно . . .**
(men-yah) (zah-voot) **меня зовут . . .**	*(oo) (men-yah) (yest)* **у меня есть . . .**

to arrive I arrive	to go (by vehicle) I go (by vehicle)
to live/reside I live/I reside	to see I see
to look for I look for	to wait for I wait for
to drink I drink	to eat I eat
I need . . .	I would like . . .
I have . . .	my name is . . .

(prah-dah-vaht) **продавать** *(yah) (prah-dah-yoo)* **я продаю**	*(pah-sih-laht)* **посылать** *(yah) (pah-sih-lah-yoo)* **я посылаю**
(spaht) **спать** *(yah) (splyoo)* **я сплю**	*(zvah-neet)* **звонить** *(yah) (zvah-nyoo)* **я звоню**
(die-tee) (men-yeh) **дайте мне . . .**	*(pee-saht)* **писать** *(yah) (pee-shoo)* **я пишу**
(pah-kah-zih-vaht) **показывать** *(yah) (pah-kah-zih-vah-yoo)* **я показываю**	*(zah-plah-teet) (zah)* **заплатить за** *(yah) (zah-plah-choo) (zah)* **я заплачу за**
(znaht) **знать** *(yah) (znah-yoo)* **я знаю**	*(mohch)* **мочь** *(yah) (mah-goo)* **я могу**
(chee-taht) **читать** *(yah) (chee-tah-yoo)* **я читаю**	*(poot-yeh-shest-vah-vaht)* **путешествовать** *(yah) (poot-yeh-shest-voo-yoo)* **я путешествую**

to send

I send

to sell

I sell

to phone

I phone

to sleep

I sleep

to write

I write

give me . . .

to pay for

I pay for

to show

I show

to be able to/can

I am able to/I can

to know (fact)

I know (fact)

to travel

I travel

to read

I read

(lee-tyet) **лететь** *(yah) (lee-choo)* **я лечу**	*(oo-yez-zhaht)* **уезжать** *(yah) (oo-yez-zhah-yoo)* **я уезжаю**
(dyeh-laht) **делать** *(yah) (dyeh-lah-yoo)* **я делаю**	*(dyeh-laht) (pyair-yeh-sahd-koo)* **делать пересадку** *(yah) (dyeh-lah-yoo) (pyair-yeh-sahd-koo)* **я делаю пересадку**
(oo-klah-dih-vaht) **укладывать** *(yah) (oo-klah-dih-vah-yoo)* **я укладываю**	*(pree-hah-deet)* **приходить** *(poh-yezd) (pree-hoh-deet) (vuh)* **Поезд приходит в . . .**
(aht-hah-deet) **отходить** *(poh-yezd) (aht-hoh-deet) (vuh)* **Поезд отходит в . . .**	*(oo-hah-deet)* **уходить** *(yah) (oo-hah-zhoo)* **я ухожу**
(yek-haht) (nah) (mah-shee-nyeh) **ехать на машине** *(yah) (yeh-doo) (nah) (mah-shee-nyeh)* **я еду на машине**	*(stee-raht)* **стирать** *(yah) (stee-rah-yoo)* **я стираю**
(tyair-yaht) **терять** *(yah) (tyair-yah-yoo)* **я теряю**	*(zah-nee-maht)* **занимать** *(zah-nee-mah-yet)* **занимает**

to leave I leave	to fly I fly
to transfer I transfer	to make I make
to arrive (trains, etc.) the train arrives at . . .	to pack I pack
to leave (on foot) I leave	to depart (trains, etc.) the train departs at ...
to wash/clean (clothes) I wash/ I clean (clothes)	to drive I drive
to occupy/take up it occupies/it takes up	to lose I lose

(kahk) (dee-lah) **Как дела?**	*(dah) (svee-dahn-yah)* **До свидания!**
(pah-zhahl-oos-tah) **пожалуйста**	*(eez-vee-neet-yeh)* **извините**
(spah-see-bah) **спасибо**	*(see-vohd-nyah)* **сегодня**
(zahv-trah) **завтра**	*(vchee-rah)* **вчера**
(skohl-kah) (et-tah) (stoy-eet) **Сколько это стоит?**	*(oo) (vahs) (yest)* **У вас есть . . .?**
(aht-krih-tah) (zah-krih-tah) **открыто - закрыто**	*(bahl-shoy) (mah-lyen-kee)* **большой - маленький**

good bye!	How are things/ How are you?
excuse me	please/you're welcome
today	thank-you
yesterday	tomorrow
do you have . . .?	How much does this cost?
big - small	open - closed

(zdah-rohv) *(bohl-yen)* **здоров - болен**	*(hah-rah-shoh)* *(ploh-hah)* **хорошо - плохо**
(gor-yah-chah-yah) *(hah-lohd-nah-yah)* **горячая - холодная**	*(kah-roht-kah-yah)* *(dleen-nah-yah)* **короткая - длинная**
(vwee-soh-kah-yah) *(mah-lyen-kah-yah)* **высокая - маленькая**	*(nahd)* *(pohd)* **над - под**
(nah-lyev-ah) *(nah-prah-vah)* **налево - направо**	*(myed-lyen-nah)* *(bis-trah)* **медленно - быстро**
(stah-ree) *(mah-lah-doy)* **старый - молодой**	*(dah-rah-gah-yah)* *(dyeh-shyoh-vah-yah)* **дорогая - дешёвая**
(bah-gaht) *(byed-yen)* **богат - беден**	*(mnoh-gah)* *(mah-lah)* **много - мало**

good - bad

healthy - sick

short - long

hot - cold

above - below

tall/high - small

slow - fast

to the left - to the right

expensive - inexpensive

old - young

a lot - a little

rich - poor

Learn another language ... in just 10 minutes a day®

More than 2,000,000 people around the world have learned a language the *10 minutes a day®* way and had fun doing it!

Turn this page to read about the new *Language Map™* Series!

You can e-mail us at: info@ bilingualbooks.org

To order call

1-800-488-5068
1-206-284-4211

or

Complete the order form and mail it with payment to:

Bilingual Books, Inc.
1719 West Nickerson
Seattle, WA 98119
USA

ORDER FORM

Cut out this form and send with payment to:
Bilingual Books, Inc. • 1719 West Nickerson Street
Seattle, WA 98119 USA

***10 minutes a day®* Series**			
Title	Qty.	Price	Total
Chinese		US $17.95	
French		US $17.95	
German		US $17.95	
Hebrew		US $17.95	
Inglés		US $17.95	
Italian		US $17.95	
Japanese		US $17.95	
Norwegian		US $17.95	
Portuguese		US $17.95	
Russian		US $19.95	
Spanish		US $17.95	
***Language Map™* Series**			
Title	Qty.	Price	Total
French		US $7.95	
German		US $7.95	
Inglés		US $7.95	
Italian		US $7.95	
Norwegian		US $7.95	
Portuguese		US $7.95	
Spanish		US $7.95	
		Subtotal	$
		* Shipping - Books	+
		* Shipping - Language Maps™	+
		WA residents add tax	+
		TOTAL ORDER	$

*** SHIPPING PRICES**
(all prices in US dollars)
In the United States add $5 for the first book and $2 for the first Language Map™. For each additional item add $1.

On foreign orders add $9 for the first book and $5 for each additional book for airmail shipment. Add $4 for the first Language Map™ and $2 for each additional Language Map™.

Please Check:

☐ Bill my credit card account ☐ Visa ☐ MC
No. ____________________
Exp. date ____________________
Signature ____________________

☐ My check for $ ____________ is enclosed.
Name ____________________
Address ____________________
City ____________ State ____ Zip ________
Telephone No. (______) ____________________

Now that you've finished...

You've done it!

You've completed all the Steps, stuck your labels, flashed your cards, clipped your menu and pocketed your Pal™. Do you realize how far you've come and how much you've learned? You've accomplished what it could take years to achieve in a traditional language class.

You can now confidently

- ask questions,
- understand directions,
- make reservations,
- order food and
- shop anywhere.

And you can do it all in a foreign language! You can now go anywhere — from a large cosmopolitan restaurant to a small, out-of-the-way village where no one speaks English. Your experiences will be much more enjoyable and worry-free now that you speak the language and know something of the culture.

Yes, learning a foreign language can be fun. And no, not everyone abroad speaks English.

Kris Kershul

Kristine Kershul